21st Century Europe

General Editor: Helen Wallace

Drawing upon the latest research, this major series of concise thematically-organized texts provides state-of-the-art overviews of the key aspects of contemporary Europe from the Atlantic to the Urals for a broad student and serious general readership. Written by leading authorities in a lively and accessible style without assuming prior knowledge, each title is designed to synthesize and contribute to current knowledge and debate in its respective field.

PUBLISHED

Andrew Cottey: *Security in 21st Century Europe*
Christopher Lord and Erika Harris: *Democracy in the New Europe*
Colin Hay and Daniel Wincott: *The Political Economy of European Welfare Capitalism*

FORTHCOMING

Tom Casier and Sophie Vanhoonacker: *Europe and the World*
Klaus Goetz: *Governing 21st Century Europe*
Ben Rosamond: *Globalization and the European Union*
Anna Triandfyllidou: *What is Europe?*
Vivien Schmidt: *Political Economy of 21st Century Europe*

IN PREPARATION

Citizenship and Identity in 21st Century Europe
Society and Social Change in 21st Century Europe

21st Century Europe
Series Standing Order
ISBN 9780333960424 hardback
ISBN 9780333960431 paperback
(outside North America only)

You can receive future titles in this series as they are published. To place a standing order please contact your bookseller or, in the case of difficulty, write to us at the address below with your name and address, the title of the series and the ISBN quoted above.
Customer Services Department, Macmillan Distribution Ltd
Houndmills, Basingstoke, Hampshire RG21 6XS, England

The Political Economy of European Welfare Capitalism

Colin Hay
and
Daniel Wincott

palgrave
macmillan

First published 2012 by
PALGRAVE MACMILLAN

Palgrave Macmillan in the UK is an imprint of Macmillan Publishers Limited,
registered in England, company number 785998, of Houndmills, Basingstoke,
Hampshire RG21 6XS.

Palgrave Macmillan in the US is a division of St Martin's Press LLC,
175 Fifth Avenue, New York, NY 10010.

Palgrave Macmillan is the global academic imprint of the above companies
and has companies and representatives throughout the world.

Palgrave® and Macmillan® are registered trademarks in the United States,
the United Kingdom, Europe and other countries

ISBN 978–1–4039–0223–8   hardback
ISBN 978–1–4039–0224–5   paperback

This book is printed on paper suitable for recycling and made from fully
managed and sustained forest sources. Logging, pulping and manufacturing
processes are expected to conform to the environmental regulations of the
country of origin.

A catalogue record for this book is available from the British Library.

A catalog record for this book is available from the Library of Congress.

10 9   8   7   6   5   4   3   2   1
21 20 19 18 17 16 15 14 13 12

Printed in China

To Ailsa and Ian, Ceire and Calum

Contents

List of Illustrative Material

Tables

Figures

Boxes

Foreword

This volume addresses one of the most testing issues of our times, namely the sustainability of the European welfare state – in its many variants. Colin Hay and Daniel Wincott build their analysis firmly on political economy foundations. They carefully and cogently lay out the several paths through which European countries have achieved their welfare states, identifying both similarities and many important differences. West European countries were able in the period following the Second World War to invest in the welfare of their citizens through increasingly elaborate public policy measures and with increasingly expensive public budgets. Economic growth provided the means and politicians across the spectrum of those in government were willing to use these means to produce a European version of welfare capitalism. Yet that version was always multi-faceted and differentiated, a reflection of different societal and political cultures in individual countries. The story was of course different in central and eastern Europe, in which state socialism had generated a different approach to welfare, leaving a complex legacy as these countries turned to liberal market economies. Hay and Wincott challenge many of the conventional wisdoms about these patterns of evolution across the continent. They also contest the view that neoliberalism came to trump other political economy approaches in the late twentieth century.

Many commentators expected that membership of the European Union and transversal pressures would lead to alignment on a shared version of European welfare capitalism. As the phenomenon of globalisation took root, many commentators also expected that European countries facing similar external challenges from lower-labour-cost countries and similar domestic pressures, not least the demographics, would tend to converge on a shared readjustment of their welfare models. Hay and Wincott vigorously contest these expectations. They argue, to the contrary, that the differences among European countries remain striking and stubborn and that the so-called European 'social model' is something of a mirage. Current fiscal and recessionary pressures raise huge questions for the sustainability of European welfare capitalism, but those pressures have quite different characteristics and consequences country by country. Hay and Wincott expect those pressures to meet persistently differentiated responses in individual coun-

tries. This volume provides a thoughtful, well-evidenced and challenging analysis of the diverse experiences of the welfare states of Europe.

HELEN WALLACE

Acknowledgements

Books invariably take far longer to write than would ever seem possible at the moment of their inception – and this one has certainly proved no exception. It was first contemplated, at a very different time for European welfare capitalism, over a decade ago. Yet it is only really in the last couple of years that we have worked in any concerted way to put down on paper the ideas that now form the text we here share with you. But those ideas have been developing and crystallising for at least a decade. That evolution reflects both the parallel development of our thinking on the paths and trajectories of European welfare capitalism as it does our reflections on the current dynamics, unleashed by the global financial crisis, that is still in the process of reconfiguring them.

Over the last ten years we have accumulated more than our fair share of debts, both intellectual and personal, to those without whom this book would, in some cases, never have been started, in others never completed. To prevent the possibility of any more fine-grained assignment of responsibility and culpability we merely list (alphabetically) the cast of potential suspects. They are (or, at least, include – we are bound to have omitted someone): Kenneth Armstrong, Mark Blyth, Kenneth Dyson, Sue Evans, Florence Faucher, Andrew Gamble, Peter Hall, Jonathan Hopkin, Chris Howell, Jo Hunt, Charlie Jeffery, Helen Mackenzie, Dave Marsh, Andy Martin, Anand Menon, Mick Moran, Craig Parsons, Tony Payne, Jiri Priban, Ben Rosamond, George Ross, Vivien Schmidt, Len Seabrooke, Stijn Smismans, Andy Smith, Nicola Smith, Elspeth Stewart, Gerry Stoker, Grahame Thompson, Helen Thompson and Matthew Watson.

In addition we would like particularly to single out Helen Wallace, our most supportive and sympathetic of series editors and, of course, the legendarily inexhaustible Steven Kennedy, without whom this book would neither have been started nor completed. We are also immensely grateful to two anonymous readers whose perceptive and insightful comments led to a number of significant changes in the form and substance of the argument at key points in the text. None, of course, can be held responsible for the text itself.

Given the at times rather bleak prognosis for European welfare capitalism that this book presents, especially for the Anglo-liberal welfare regimes in which they reside, it seems poignantly appropriate to dedicate this volume to our children: Ailsa and Ian, Ceire and Calum. We can only hope that throughout their lives, when they have need of it, they are able to draw upon an inclusive and generous welfare state that is less liberal, less miserly and less residual that our prognosis leads us to fear.

COLIN HAY
DANIEL WINCOTT

Introduction

The welfare state is deeply embedded and institutionally entrenched. Yet it is at the same time under constant and seemingly ever growing pressure to justify its very existence. The consequences of the credit crunch, the global finance crisis and the ensuing period of low or no growth in which we are still mired have sharpened this paradox, posing with renewed force the question of the viability and sustainability of the welfare state in Europe. That question – our core concern in this volume – is, we contend, an urgent priority for social and political analysts as well as for politicians and policy-makers more generally. We believe that making sense of it requires a fundamental rethinking of the conventional wisdom about the political economy of European welfare capitalism. This is as true, we argue, for the social systems of southern, eastern and east–central Europe as it is for the much-studied welfare states of northern and western Europe. We argue, in effect, for the development of a new political economy of European welfare capitalism – a political economy grounded in the analysis of the past yet sensitive to the contingency of current trends, a political economy which shows the continued centrality of the welfare state to Europe's social, political and, above all, economic futures.

Conventionally, the story of the rise of the welfare state spans a relatively short period of history. This extraordinarily influential, surprisingly conserved, and highly stylised narrative will undoubtedly be familiar. It runs something like this. The thirty years or so following the Second World War marks the 'golden age' of European welfare. This was a benign period of relatively rapid economic growth, when nation states were largely able to control their domestic economic fortunes. In these relatively comfortable circumstances states could afford to divert a large, growing and previously unthinkable share of their taxation revenues to the luxury of social security and welfare provision. From diverse origins, then, all (western) European states developed comprehensive and generous welfare states. But the economic crisis of the 1970s provided a reality check for welfare state largesse, re-imposing a

1

harsh trade-off between social equity and economic efficiency. The welfare state was exposed as a drain on competitiveness and economic performance. While (western) European states may initially have diverged, as some adjusted to these new harsh realities more rapidly than others, by the 1990s the pressures of globalisation and European integration had imposed on all the rigours of disciplinary neoliberalism. Across Europe a new convergence mandated an economically liberal and ever more residual form of social provision, a process since reinforced by the consequences of the global financial crisis and the crisis of European debt that it has prompted. For despite ostensibly revealing the flaws and contradictions of financial liberalisation and the inherent instability of deregulated global financial markets, the real impact of the global financial crisis and the crisis of debt to which it has led has been to ratchet up the fiscal pressure on the state. This in turn has triggered a further massive wave of retrenchment that is set to destroy anything but the most liberal and market-conforming of welfare states, condemning Europe to continent-wide welfare residualism in a new age of public austerity.

In the chapters that follow we interrogate and challenge each aspect of this conventional narrative. We begin by tracing the history of the welfare state before the so-called golden age (1945–mid-1970s). In chapter one, we look back to the origins of modern social policy in the nineteenth century, developing in the process a significant revision of the prevailing orthodoxy. In this we seek to uncover, draw attention to, and incorporate into a revised account of the origins of European welfare the early development of social insurance in east–central Europe under the Habsburg Empire. Setting the welfare state in this longer historical perspective helps better to account for the pervasive sense that it has become deeply entrenched: European states are now enmeshed in the economic and social life of their citizens to a degree that would have been unimaginable a century and a half ago. The analysis also interrogates the 'golden age' itself. If European welfare states ever enjoyed such an epoch comparative analysis suggests that it generally began later than 1945. And (many) welfare states continued to grow and develop, certainly in aggregate terms, after the mid-1970s. Removing 'golden age' blinkers may reveal significant and distinctive social policy developments after this period (later – in Chapter 6 – we suggest 1985 as Europe's turning point from welfare expansion to retrenchment). Our longer historical perspective also helps to draw out the complex and dynamic relationship between social policies and economic structures that justifies our central focus on the political economy of welfare capitalism itself. Yet it also leads us to reassess and in part to challenge much conventional wisdom. For, while differences between Bismarckian and Beveridgean forms of welfare states have a long history, it was really only towards the end of the so-called golden age that the distinctive 'varieties' of European welfare capitalism might credibly be said to have emerged. Yet it is such a 'varietal' perspective that continues to provide the core focus of welfare state analysis today.

In Chapter 2 we turn our attention directly to the question of welfare state variation and diversity. This we do by engaging with Esping-Andersen's seminal analysis of *The Three Worlds of Welfare Capitalism* (1990), as well as the large and often sophisticated critical literature that it has spawned. We develop, in the spirit of much of that literature, a series of pointed if nonetheless sympathetic criticisms of Esping-Andersen's core concepts and their empirical application – including the idea of welfare state regime-types and its conflation with regime-clusters, his operationalisation of the notion of 'decommodification' (the idea of the welfare as an antidote to market inequality) and his conceptualisation of three 'dimensions' of welfare state stratification. Nevertheless, in developing alternative empirical operationalisations of welfare state variation we find, like Esping-Andersen, considerable evidence that welfare capitalism generates distinct 'clusters' of states. Indeed, while the evidence is complex, we also uncover some preliminary indications that the distinctiveness of (some of) these clusters may have increased in recent years – as hinted at by our critique of the 'golden age' thesis. These alternative operationalisations also allow us to include in our analysis a wider range of cases – especially those from the south and east of Europe.

The conventional wisdom depicts the welfare state as facing profound – and arguably increasing – pressures. In Chapter 3 we consider the status of the most widely invoked of these source of pressure in Europe – globalisation. We find that the conventional globalisation narrative remains amazingly influential, providing a background set of assumptions that are rarely scrutinised and yet which provide much of the context in which the political economy of European welfare capitalism is seen to unfold. Moreover, we find that this conventional narrative is based on a series of premises about both the character and extent of economic interdependence, which are not only false empirically, but which have already been demonstrated as such in a substantial body of the existing literature. As we show, that impression is only reinforced by the most recent empirical evidence. The globalisation thesis, certainly in the form in which it still tends to appear in the political economy of European welfare, presents a largely inaccurate account of the changing nature of Europe's internal and external economic interdependence. Too often globalisation is invoked simply as a synonym for economic openness. When defined more precisely, we find that, rather than globalisation *per se*, Europe's experience in recent decades is primarily one of *regionalisation*. This, we suggest, is likely to have had rather different – and more differentiated – implications for the welfare state. In other words, substituting regional economic integration for globalisation makes a considerable difference to our expectations about the viability and sustainability of the welfare state in Europe. But, in a recurrent theme of the volume more generally, we argue that the extent and nature of the difference varies from case to case. There is, in other words, no universal or general relationship between economic interdependence and European welfare trajectories. Such effects cannot, as is so often the case, be derived from the drawing of deductive inferences from stylised theoretical models.

Yet even were globalisation and the economic imperatives of market competition to take the form conventionally described, we are not convinced that the welfare state is accurately depicted as a simple drain on economic performance and competitiveness – nor as any obvious barrier to economic efficiency. Some of the most generous of Europe's welfare states are also widely heralded as having its most efficient and successful economies – and their comparative economic performance since the global financial crisis has been impressive. Chapter 4 offers a detailed, critical and, we hope, forensic analysis and interrogation of the influential view that state welfare provision necessarily undercuts economic efficiency. We find that the relationship between the welfare state, economic efficiency and competitiveness is more complex than is typically assumed, but that many policies and services associated with the welfare state offer positive support for and, in effect underpin, strong economic performance. The relationship between the welfare state and competitiveness is also rather more contingent on the character of both elements than is usually recognised. While some forms of economic production and welfare provision dovetail effectively, those countries that concentrate on cost-based competition and perhaps also on financial services tend to experience a greater tension between social protection and economic competitiveness. Both the complexity of the relationship between the welfare state and the economy and the distinctive configurations it can take strongly support our view of the profound interdependence of the economic, the social and the political, our conceptualisation of this in terms of *welfare capitalism* and our more general argument for the need for a new political economy of European welfare capitalism better able to capture such interdependence (see also Hay 2010).

If the argument of Chapter 3 is that *regionalisation* captures the recent trajectory of economic integration rather better than the popular concept of *globalisation*, in Chapter 5 we address the process of European integration more directly. In so doing we interrogate the implications of the integration process itself for welfare capitalism in Europe. Here, the conventional wisdom suggests that the European Union has been a crucial site for the imposition of a disciplinary neoliberalism, thereby undermining Europe's welfare states. The reality we find is rather different. On the one hand, Europe's much discussed 'social dimension' or 'social model' has typically proved rather more limited and elusive than might have been anticipated. In particular, we argue that the European Union largely failed to offer positive guidance and support to the development of social policy for its most recent member states. Yet, on the other hand, it would be wrong to characterise this neglect of social policy as the effective targeting of the welfare state for a neoliberal assault. For example, while economic and monetary union (EMU) is often identified as a key element of the conservative economic constitution imposing disciplinary neoliberalism on Europe, our reconstruction of the political history of the process of integration – and, indeed, many current trends – suggests that the neoliberals have lost out at least as much as they have won during the design and, especially, the implementation of EMU.

Were the welfare state a simple drain on economic performance and were some combination of globalisation and European integration to have increased massively the economic pressures on Europe's welfare states, we would expect to witness a process of convergence with European welfare capitalisms moving towards a common economically liberal and residual approach to social provision. In Chapter 6 we turn our attention directly to the question of convergence. Marshalling a range of evidence we find little to support a general argument of this kind. In fact, our analysis might even suggest that Europe's varieties of welfare capitalism are clustering more closely than they had in the past and are perhaps becoming increasingly distinctive. Our conclusions here are intriguing and serve, once again, to challenge existing and enduring orthodoxies. In terms of both aggregate measures of welfare effort and more differentiated measures of welfare generosity, we find strong and consistent evidence of *convergence* amongst European welfare regimes in the period until 1985 and just as strong evidence of *divergence* in the period since 1985. This is in almost direct conflict with the expectations of the globalisation thesis and it is not much more easily reconciled with the influential 'varieties of capitalism' perspective (Hall and Soskice 2001a). Yet it is, we suggest, both intuitively plausible and credibly explicable, especially when it is noted that 1985 is the point at which, in terms of the generosity of welfare benefits, European welfare states move from expansion to retrenchment. In other words, we find convergence, which we largely attribute to 'catch up' effects, in the period of welfare state expansion, but retrenchment seems to cause divergence, perhaps due to the more enthusiastic conversion to neoliberalism among the less generous welfare regimes. Thus, whilst almost all European welfare states have partaken in some way in the process of retrenchment, such retrenchment has been implemented at different paces to produce, to date at least, divergent not convergent outcomes. Our earlier argument was that clear varieties of welfare capitalism emerged late in Europe (towards the end of the orthodox golden age); this analysis suggests that retrenchment further *increased* the distinctiveness of these welfare regime clusters.

This account brings us to the most contemporary, as well as potentially the most controversial aspect of our analysis. We have sought to set European welfare capitalism in a long-term historical perspective and to identify both the character and the robustness of the varieties in and through which it has developed. But we are also interested in the pressures that it now faces, especially in the context set by the legacy of the global financial crisis. Often heralded as a 'debt crisis' and even as a 'crisis of European welfare' these events have a peculiar character. For, unlike previous global 'crises', recent events do not seem to be associated with the rise to ascendency of any major new ideas – no radical new solutions seem to have emerged from any part of the political spectrum. Our final chapter considers the implications of this, the most recent and arguably the most acute set of 'hard times' for European welfare capitalism. All European states face economic uncertainty, risk a long period of low – and perhaps even negative – economic growth and further rounds of retrenchment in public spending. But, we argue, different European welfare states face quite different prospects – prospects that may serve to reinforce some of the trends identified in the previous chapter. Emphasising the interplay between different patterns and models of economic growth, we argue that the future for those – already typically least generous – welfare states is much bleaker than elsewhere. For these economies, the 'first-wave' economies as we term them, the crisis was largely internal. Here growth in the pre-crisis years had become reliant on elements of what we term the 'Anglo-liberal' growth model. This was predicated on house price inflation and high and rising levels of personal – and, also typically – state indebtedness. It was a phenomenon present in a number of liberal, southern European and east–central European cases (in a variety of different forms). Here the prospects both for the return of growth and for the welfare state in a context of austerity look bleak indeed. Yet beyond the 'first-wave' economies things do not look quite so bad. In general terms, the depth of the recessions these economies have faced was not so pronounced – though clearly there are exceptions, most notably a number of southern European eurozone members with especially high levels of public debt going into the crisis. But, in general, the 'second-' and 'third-wave' economies were exposed to the crisis not principally through the frailty of their own growth models, but through a series of contagion effects radiating outwards from the implosion of the Anglo-liberal growth model elsewhere. These revealed, in effect, how parasitic such economies had become on the demand generated by Anglo-liberal growth. This is perhaps the principal problem they face going forward – sustaining an export-led growth strategy in the absence of the contribution of Anglo-liberal consumer debt to world consumption. Most significantly, though, austerity is far less entrenched politically in these economies and it is rather more credible to think that they will be capable of rebalancing their public finances, albeit slowly, without a drastic reduction in the size of their public sectors.

If that is indeed correct, then it generates a tentative prediction – of continued welfare regime divergence in Europe in the years ahead. Retrenchment and austerity, it would seem, are now very much the order of the day. But retrenchment implemented at different paces in different regimes through the differential imposition of austerity is likely to continue to produce divergent not convergent outcomes. The future of European welfare capitalism is then likely to remain one of variation, diversity and considerable flux.

Chapter 1

European Welfare Capitalism in Good Times and Bad

In 2005 the prospects for the global economy seemed bright. Over the previous decade and a half, banks and financial institutions had made increasingly large profits from a fiendishly complex system of credit, debt and risk – and the continued growth of the world's leading economies seemed guaranteed. But by 2008 financial markets were in turmoil and the international banking system itself seemed to be on the brink of collapse. Indeed, already in 2007 it was clear that a bubble in the US housing market had burst and that this was likely to have global ramifications. The expansion of 'sub-prime' mortgage lending had helped to inflate house prices, and these loans had become tightly woven into a complex fabric of financial instruments and deals. This fabric unravelled in 2008, with the value of key financial assets collapsing at precisely the same time as the liabilities of financial institutions grew. But, unable to calculate the extent of their losses, they sought to limit (and, failing that, to disguise) their exposure. The strategies they adopted to do so dramatically worsened the overall problem. The mutual trust essential for the operation of these markets evaporated, as the very viability of the global banking system came into question for the first time since the 1930s. The usually smooth transactions that make up the profitable routines of the sector slowed down and seized up. To prevent the ruin of banks and other financial institutions deemed 'too big to fail' – and consequently the possibility of the annihilation of the entire banking system – governments across the western world intervened on a massive scale supplying liquidity to ease the workings of the financial machine.

Such a series of events was always going to have major consequences for the development of the welfare state, in Europe as elsewhere, though the full implications may take decades to work themselves through. We are, in effect, in the midst of a critical juncture in the fortunes of the European and global economy, with profound implications for European welfare trajectories in the years and decades ahead.

What is clear is that the 'global financial crisis', which started in 2007–08, has prompted large-scale re-evaluation of public debt, public spending and the social commitments of states. In this respect it might be seen as the latest in a series of major crises – that is periods of global war or economic turmoil – each widely regarded as a prime cause of significant change in the political economy of welfare capitalism (Gourevitch 1978, 1986; Hay 1996a, 1999b; Ikenberry 2001; Blyth 2002; Widmaier *et al.* 2007; Chwieroth 2010). The transformative impact of crisis-episodes has bulked large in the general history of the welfare state. The standard, if somewhat stylised, narrative has its golden age commencing in 1945 – a reaction to the Great Depression and the Second World War – and is brought to an end by the economic turmoil of the 1970s. Although the link is not as tightly drawn in the literature, the emergence of 'modern social policy' – usually seen to date from Bismarck's social reforms of the 1880s – (Esping-Andersen 1999: 34) might equally be linked to the economic 'crisis' of the 1870s.

The events set in train by 2007–08 certainly invite comparisons with these earlier episodes and their associated transformations of European welfare capitalism. Yet such comparisons aren't as easily drawn or as self-evident as they might at first seem. Andrew Gamble, for instance, is hardly alone in suggesting that the '2007–2008 financial crisis … [is] an event in the international political economy … [that] ranks with the major shocks that occurred in the Great Depression and the 1970s stagflation' (2009b: 461). Yet, this latest crisis is also for him a somewhat strange, even paradoxical phenomenon. For, writing in 2009, he detected little sense that this major shock to the international political economy had yet generated, or was in the process of generating, significant new political projects for change from any part of the political spectrum (for a similar and more recent appraisal, see Hay 2011a). As this perhaps suggests, the latest crisis needs to be placed in a rather wider historical and comparative context if its implications for the future of welfare capitalism in Europe are to be assessed properly. That is our task in this introductory chapter. We offer an overview of the historical development of the welfare state in Europe considering the relationship between crises and change. In so doing we develop a perspective on the history of the welfare state since the closing decades of the nineteenth century that is revisionist both analytically and substantively. We include in this re-evaluation those periods conventionally seen to mark European welfare capitalism's golden age and those in turn seen to herald its demise. In the process we call into question both the stylised characterisation of the welfare state's rise and demise and the standard 'crisis-driven' model of transformation with which it is typically associated. Our aim is to provide both a baseline and a point of departure for the much-needed assessment of the viability and sustainability of European welfare capitalism in undoubtedly hard times that we aim to provide in this volume more generally. In the final chapter we draw together the implications of this to provide an assessment of the likely trajectory of European welfare capitalism in a decade of austerity and retrenchment and the factors most likely to influence that trajectory. But it is to the history and pre-history of European welfare capitalism that we must turn first.

The 'golden age'

During the dark days of the early 1940s Archbishop Temple sought to give new purpose to the British war effort: as well as defeating the Nazi 'power state', the fight, he suggested, was for an alternative 'welfare state' (1941). But Temple was no mere rhetorician. He also published a remarkably detailed and, as it happens, prescient set of social policy proposals (1941–2). For within twelve months a country facing the most real and existential of threats was offered the prospect of building a new kind of social security in a government report on *Social Insurance and Allied Services* (1942). The principal author of that report – William Beveridge – became forever linked with the 'universalistic' model of the welfare state with which it came to be associated, an association that has proven globally influential (perhaps reflecting the impact of the Beveridge Report on Governments exiled in London in the 1940s). Yet we do need to be cautious about the 'universalism' implied here. Beveridge's vision was one that was universalist only in that it was not built around occupational groups. For despite being ostensibly intended for the 'whole' national population, it was far from universalist in its treatment of men and women (see also Hay 1996b: 35–7; Riley 1983; Summerfield 1988). But in the context of 1940s Britain his report was still a very radical document – and widely understood at such at the time. *Social Insurance and Allied Services* was an immediate bestseller with 257,000 copies of the full report and 373,000 abridged versions sold by February 1944 (Assheton 1994). The Penguin special edition of Temple's *Christianity and Social Order* (1942) also sold an impressive 140,000 volumes (Kynaston 2007: 55).

If Beveridge provided the plan, between 1945 and 1948 Clement Attlee's post-war Labour government is widely thought to have built the legislative foundations for the world's 'first coherent and systematic architecture of a universalistic welfare state' (Ferrera 2005: 64). It is also worth noting that this legislation was passed during a period when British public debt was at a uniquely high level – exceeding 180 per cent of GDP by the end of the Second World War and peaking at almost 250 per cent before the end of the decade. By contrast, in November 2010 debt at 58 per cent of GDP was widely viewed as an unsustainable burden that mandated major cuts in public provision.

Like Beveridge's plan, the legislation passed by Attlee's Labour government influenced policy-makers in other countries, furnishing much of the language and many of the concepts through which social policies are still understood today. Partly because of this, the social legislation enacted under Attlee after 1945 'appeared to mark the dawn of a new era' (Gough 1979: x), the age of the welfare state. Thus, in an early (and still highly influential) analysis, the eminent social historian Asa Briggs argued that the 'the phrase "welfare state" ... was first used to describe Labour Britain after 1945 ... from Britain it made its way around the world' (Briggs 1961: 221). That 1945 marked the start of its golden age has become a commonplace of welfare state analysis (for instance, Hall 1986; Gough 1979; Offe 1984; Marglin and Schor 1990; Pierson 1998; Taylor-Gooby 2002; Wincott 2011b, forthcoming). Indeed, not simply an artefact of British history, the golden age is widely understood to be a key feature of western European history – and that of the western world more generally.

If it is widely held to have begun in 1945, the golden age is also generally agreed to have come to an end in the mid-1970s (for instance Gourevitch 1986; Marglin and Schor 1990; Pierson 1994). The end of the Bretton Woods system governing international currency exchange together with two oil 'crises' provoked by OPEC imposing sharp price rises, is generally seen as inaugurating a period of economic turmoil marked by 'stagflation' – a perplexing mixture of economic stagnation and simultaneously rising inflation and unemployment. Widely characterised as a period of economic crisis, social pressures of various kinds emerged during the 1970s. Though the evidential basis for the claim is in fact extraordinarily thin (see for instance Hay 2007a: 97–113), the dominant understanding of this time is that of a revolution of rising social expectations, with the demands on the state growing sharply at precisely the point that it could no longer afford to satisfy even historic demands. Government became seen as increasingly 'overloaded', society as essentially 'ungovernable' (Buchanen and Wagner 1977, 1978; Crozier, Huntingdon and Watanuki 1975; King 1975).

By the end of the 1970s, then, the welfare state was facing an intellectual and political backlash. Keynesian economics was excoriated for its failure to make sense of stagflation, while the welfare state was increasingly depicted as both dragging down economic efficiency and wearing away the moral fabric of society. Politically, Britain was once again in the vanguard, with the election of a Conservative government, led by a viscerally anti-welfare prime minister, Margaret Thatcher, in 1979. Thatcher's election began a period of nearly two decades in power for the Conservative right in the UK, but it was not the only sign that times might have changed for the welfare state. Thatcher's triumph was closely followed by the electoral success in the USA of her ideological soulmate, Ronald Reagan. But beyond the Anglo-Saxon countries, the late 1970s and early 1980s saw the expulsion from office of the German Social Democrats, as the *Wende* brought the Christian democratic right back into government, while even in the Nordic welfare state heartland, anti-tax parties enjoyed new-found electoral success.

Overall, then, a standard historiography of the welfare state has developed, centred on the idea of a golden age lasting from 1945 until the mid-1970s. This idea is widely assumed by commentators and analysts to apply generally across the western world. But for all its pervasiveness, the golden age thesis is also typically rather vague and amorphous: its core assumptions are rarely explicitly stated and seldom if ever defended or even exposed to sustained analysis.

The attraction of the framework is enhanced by the way it dovetails with widespread assumptions about the relationship between crises – especially wars and episodes of economic turmoil – and the turning of social, political and economic epochs. The dawning of the welfare state is often understood as a basic transformation of the state – 'an explicit redefinition of what the state is all about' (Esping-Andersen 1999: 34). Yet equally the golden age can be seen as 'a rather abnormal period' – a benign interlude, even – after which the advanced capitalist world reverted to type as the anomalous 'long boom' which had allowed the welfare states to develop ran its (for some, inevitable) course (Gough 1979: x).

As we have suggested, the golden age of the welfare state is a somewhat general, abstract, stylised and comfortable narrative. It is perhaps about time that we question how well this framework actually fits the historical experience of particular states. The conventional periodisation points to 1945 and the mid-1970s as general turning points in the development of the welfare state. Were they? It also implies that there was something homogenous about states' experience between these dates that distinguished it from other periods. Was there? The following sections will place the history of the golden age welfare state in a longer historical perspective. We start with the pre-war period before turning to the years after the 'crisis' of the mid-to-late 1970s, concluding by examining the three post-war decades for evidence of 'within period' heterogeneity. Yet before doing so, we consider the cases to which the golden age narrative has never applied – those of central and eastern Europe.

Welfare state development in central and eastern Europe after 1945

Developed from an extrapolation of trends in western Europe and used to characterise the wealthy liberal democracies more generally, the golden age framework was never intended to – and clearly does not – apply to the (then) Soviet bloc states of central and eastern Europe. If we are to correct the distortions such a framework might generate for an analysis of European welfare capitalism today, it is first important, then, that we address this, its most glaring, omission.

As Bob Deacon has suggested, after 1945, a 'broadly coherent and, in general terms, similar system of welfare policy and provision' did develop 'across the whole of the USSR and Eastern Europe' (2000: 147). The system was based on a government monopoly over the allocation of resources, with welfare provision an integral part of the broader economic and political system. Employment was key, for access to social security and health care benefits was generally organised through the workplace. This, in turn, was made possible by the dual status of employment as both required and, for the most part, guaranteed. Technically, the previously independent social insurance systems were brought under state budgetary and administrative processes after 1945, and some formal features of the earlier systems endured (Wagener 2002: 155). The inherited schemes had a broadly 'Bismarckian' character in east–central Europe – or more precisely, as we shall see, they were a legacy of late nineteenth-century Habsburg social reform under Eduard von Taaffe. State control over allocation also meant that basic necessities, including housing, food and transport were heavily subsidised in the decades before 1989. Broadly adequate provision was made for health care and education. This was typically free, at least formally. Yet informal systems of bribes and patronage undoubtedly allowed some to access more generous provision, with the hidden privileges of the elite 'nomenklatura' including superior access to 'social' services of various kinds.

Women were mobilised into formal employment more fully and earlier in the Soviet bloc than in western Europe. In some countries – notably the German Democratic Republic and Hungary – a distinctive gender contract included provision of childcare grants, and rights for women to resume previous employment after having a child as well as rights of access to abortion – some of which were restricted after 1989. Yet the gendered division of domestic labour remained highly patriarchal (Pascall and Manning 2000: 241). Moreover, national and other minorities did not always enjoy full access to social provision. This was particularly true for Roma people across central and eastern Europe – not least because they often lived 'outside the rigid work-eligibility requirements of the system' (Deacon 2000: 148). More generally, of course, in the absence of the civil society organisations of liberal democratic regimes, social provision had little capacity to respond to pressures and demands from below. This was very much a top-down and centralised welfare state; but it was nonetheless reasonably comprehensive for its time (Deacon 2000; Wagener 2002).

The demise of the Soviet system after 1989 had a direct and dire impact on this mode of highly centralised welfare provision. The basis of the system – state control of the economy – simply collapsed. At least initially, most states sought to sustain something like the inherited level of social provision, although some central European states attempted to separate social insurance out as a distinct set of practices and policies, (re)constructing a broadly Bismarckian system (Wagener 2002; Nelson 2010: 370). Indeed, post-communist 'constitutional charters' generally included 'catalogues of so-called "positive", socio-economic rights', arguably 'much more inspired by post-Second World War European (continental) constitutionalism' following 'the German, French, and Italian ... prototypes' (Sadurski 2002: 227, 224). However, key foundations of this system – including subsidised prices and guaranteed employment – could no longer be sustained. At the same time, needs and demands for social provision skyrocketed. The scale of economic reversal was monumental, but also highly variable – over the five years before 1993 real income declined by 54 per cent in Russia and the Slavic republics, but by only 25 per cent in central Europe (Deacon 2000). We will consider the fate of state welfare provision in central and eastern Europe below, focusing on the intense pressure on state budgets from the mid-1990s.

Was 1945 a turning point?

While the idea of the golden age of the welfare state is almost invariably dated to the period between 1945 and the mid-1970s, related analyses focused on the rise and fall of Keynesian economic ideas and the associated construction of 'embedded liberalism' generally start somewhat earlier (Ruggie 1982). Indeed, such developments are typically cast as responses to the Great Depression of the 1930s rather than to the war itself (Blyth 2002). Here it is not Britain, but the USA and Sweden that are typically presented as exemplary. Developed between 1933 and 1936, Roosevelt's New Deal remained the most significant moment of social innovation in the US before the 1960s; similarly, Albin Hansson and the Swedish social democrats promoted the idea of the 'People's Home' from the late 1920s and the Saltsjöbaden Agreement of 1938 supplied key ingredients what tends now to be seen as a 'historic compromise' (Hicks 1999). If important gaps remained within the US social policy framework and its economic aspects offered less ambitious interventions than did those in Sweden at the time, reforms in both counties affirmed the potential compatibility of welfare and capitalism (C. Pierson 1998: 114–19; Swenson 2002). While today the US and Sweden are generally regarded as sitting at opposite ends of the political economy spectrum of advanced capitalist democracies (Blyth 2002), their reforms during the 1930s can be seen as 'parallel efforts to rewrite the relationship between citizen and state' (Esping-Andersen 1999: 34).

By contrast, the reaction to the Great Depression in Britain was muted and modest in terms of changes to economic as well as social policies. Here, in terms of policy innovation, 'the creative impulse of the welfare state progressed little from the 1910s to the 1940s' (Parry 1986: 159), although underlying policy and ideational changes during the interwar period arguably made the post-war welfare state transformation possible. More than marking the *start* of a novel period, then, perhaps the post-war welfare state designed by Beveridge and legislated under Attlee is better seen as a 'rationalization' of pre-existing provision (C. Pierson 1998: 120). And, when set in comparative context, the British social reforms of the 1940s represent a catching up with innovations already made in countries like the US and Sweden during the 1930s. If so, perhaps the 1930s and 1940s are better seen *together* as a distinct *phase* of social reform across the western world. This analysis has an intriguing corollary: the central role played by the electoral triumph of parties of the (social democratic) left. For it suggests the significance of 'a kind of Golden Age of social democracy' spanning the period 'from Hansson's 1932 assumption of government [in Sweden] to Attlee's 1951 replacement by Winston Churchill [in the UK]' (Hicks 1999: 109).

Concepts and language

Even for Britain, then, the golden age idea is somewhat idealised and its place within the narrative arguably somewhat anachronistic. This, we suggest, is reflected in widespread myths and inaccuracies attached to the history of the concepts and language used to describe the welfare state. As we have seen, distinguished social historian Asa Briggs saw the origins of the welfare state phrase as British, intimately connected with the social legislation of the Attlee government (1961: 221), while many commentators treat Archbishop Temple's wartime interventions as a key source of the idea. Yet in Germany the concept of the *Wohlfahrtsstaat* can be traced back at least as far as the 1860s, when it was used largely in the context of academic and intellectual debate (Petersen and Petersen 2011).

To be fair, Temple did use the 'welfare state' term – first doing so in writing as early as 1928 (probably the first example of its published use in Britain); and he was undoubtedly a strong supporter of the extension of social provision. Moreover, that his positive reference to the welfare state was made at more or less the same time as Beveridge's influential report on *Social Security and Allied Services* has certainly fed the myth that the 1940s witnessed an 'explicit redefinition' – to use Esping-Andersen's phrase (1999: 34) – of the British state *as* a welfare state. Yet that does not make it right. For recent scholarship has shown that Temple's conception of the welfare state in fact belonged to the realm of international relations rather than social policy (Edgerton 2006; Petersen and Petersen 2011). Temple saw the First World War as a struggle between the German 'power-state' on the one hand and the British 'welfare-state' on the other. In contrast to the power state, the welfare state was 'the organ of community, maintaining its solidarity by law designed to safeguard the interests of the community' (cited in Petersen and Petersen 2011: 14). The same contrast – both between countries and types of state – gained a sharper edge after the Nazis gained control of Germany during the 1930s, when it was deployed by the leading international relations idealist, Alfred Zimmern (inaugural holder of both the Woodrow Wilson Chair of International Politics at the (then) University College of Wales and the Montague Burton Chair of International Relations at Oxford University). This concept of the welfare state seems primarily to have referred to a state governed by the rule of law, one based on responsibility rather than force (Edgerton 2006, 56, 59–60, Petersen and Petersen 2011: 14, 17). It does, however, also seemed to have carried at least an implicit (if vague) notion of state largesse, at least for the critics of idealism in international relations theory. Thus, Zimmern was castigated by E. H. Carr, in the latter's famous 'realist' manifesto, for his failure to recognise that the 'soft' characteristics of the welfare states – defined as their ability to 'afford butter' – would endure only while they 'already enjoy ... a preponderance of power' (Carr 1939: 110). In any event, the concept did *not* refer to the domestic provision of social security. Tellingly, despite deploying the concept in another book published at about the same time, Temple did not use the phrase 'welfare state' in his proposals for social policy reform (Petersen and Petersen 2011: 15).

Furthermore, post-war British welfare institutions were not typically described in the language of the welfare state as they were being created during the 1940s. If the post-1945 Labour government had seen itself as redefining Britain as a welfare state, we would expect to see evidence of this project in parliamentary debates. Yet the use of the phrase in parliament during the 1940s was confined to the very end of the decade, after the major social legislation had all been passed. With the exception of a single reference in the context of a discussion of Burma in 1947, the first parliamentary use of the term in that decade was as late as April 1949 – when critics used the term to attack the Labour record (Eccles 1949; Hinchingbrooke 1949). The phrase was then used more than fifty times in the remainder of the year, as the Conservatives continued their assault, while Labour MPs increasingly came to adopt the phrase as a positive way of encapsulating what they saw as their achievements.

The anachronistic backward projection of the concept of the 'welfare state' into history is also evident in more recent academic studies of social policy. A key example is the characterisation of T. H. Marshall's seminal essay on *Citizenship and Social Class* (1963 [1950]). This work is routinely described as providing the theoretical foundation for the welfare state (for example, by Esping-Andersen 1990). Yet Marshall refers not once to the 'the welfare state' in the entire essay. Indeed, key social policy scholars remained reluctant to use the term until well into the 1960s, and even when they did it was often with a note of scepticism. Thus Titmuss sought to unveil 'The "Welfare State" Myth' (1963: 219) while Wedderburn noted that 'just as the trend has been towards accepting "the welfare state" as an "essential" feature of capitalist society, so there has been a trend towards a narrowing of the content of the concept itself' (1965: 128). Marshall described the phrase as a dangerous generalisation, 'cunningly expressed in tabloid form', that had passed 'into the language of common speech as [a] familiar truth' (1961: 284). Moreover, almost as soon as he had begun to use the concept in print his argument took on a strikingly nostalgic tone. 'The thing to which we had first given the name of "Welfare State" passed away' he argued; its 'institutions, practices, procedures and expertise are still with us, but they are operating in a different setting and without the original consensus which welded them into a social system with a distinctive spirit of its own' (1963: 287).

Social reform before 1930

If the concept of the welfare state itself significantly post-dates the emergence of the institutions and policies with which it has tended to be associated, then it also true that many of those policies in fact pre-date 1945. In fact many major social policy innovations occurred before the Great Depression. Thus, five major European states (or empires) – Sweden, Denmark, the UK, Germany and Austria – are identified by Hicks as 'early welfare consolidators' because they had, by 1930, established 'binding *and* extensive and funded programmes' in 'at least three of ... four' of the 'principal extant types of social insurance' (that is, pensions, as well as accident, sickness and unemployment insurance). Moreover, viewed comparatively, new welfare programmes were adopted at a much faster rate during the 1910s than they were in the 1920s (Hicks 1999: 74, 68, 81).

While the emergence of western European welfare states has been the focus of extensive analysis, developments in central and eastern Europe have been much neglected. Here, it was only after the First World War that distinct states in more-or-less national form emerged: most of this territory had previously been governed under the Habsburg and Ottoman Empires. As independent states after 1918, Bulgaria and Romania, Hungary, Czechoslovakia and Poland, all pursued social reforms, in such areas as pensions and health, along generally corporatist lines, with social solidarity tightly linked to professional or occupational groups (Cerami 2005: 10; 2007: 5). On their declaration of independence in 1918, new health policies were introduced in the Czech lands. The signal social reforms among these states occurred six years later, also in Czechoslovakia, under President Masaryk. The 1924 reforms included health insurance for employees. This covered about one-third of the population: while reforms were introduced in other countries in this region, generally they did not provide coverage on this scale, with social insurance in Poland, for instance, covering only about 7 per cent of the population (Cerami 2007: 5).

Liberal reform in the early twentieth century

Elsewhere in Europe, welfare reform was more advanced and more inclusive. The Weimar Republic engaged in extensive social reform and innovation during the 1920s, developing what was known as the *Sozialstaat* or the *sozialer Rechtsstaat*. Yet, as the Weimar regime weakened, these policies came under attack. When von Papen became Chancellor in 1932 he immediately condemned such policies as undermining German strength. He labelled them as a morally enfeebling *Wohlfahrtsstaat* (or welfare state), in what may have been the first major political use of the term. Equally, however, the *Wohlfahrtsstaat* was not simply a term of abuse. As in Britain nearly two decades later, supporters of these policies adopted the label as a positive description of their aims (Petersen and Petersen 2011). Yet the similarities with Britain of course end at this point. For even when democratic social policy was re-instated after the Nazi period, it developed under the banner of the *Sozialsstaat*, not the *Wohlfahrtsstaat*.

Liberal-led reforms were mainly concentrated slightly earlier, closer to the start of the twentieth century. Here the UK is generally taken as an exemplar. The first wave of state-wide social reform was that undertaken by the British Liberal government elected in 1906. The pace of reform accelerated after 1908, when Asquith became prime minister, with the introduction of old-age pensions in the same year and the beginnings of national health and unemployment insurance in 1911. Indeed 'in terms of social policy', John Saville has argued, 'the Labour Government [1945–50] showed much less originality and initiative and was more in the stream of tradition than were the Liberals before 1914' (1957/8: 17). Although led by the Liberals, Hicks argues that these reforms are best seen as the archetype of a 'Lib-Lab model' of social reform, which he extends to cover Sweden, Denmark and Italy (1999: 64, 62, 63).

Nineteenth-century conservatism

But it is, in fact, the 'corporatist' approach to social insurance pioneered by German Chancellor Otto von Bismarck during the late nineteenth century that is generally credited as the original source of modern social policy on a state-wide – or more accurately, pan-imperial – scale (Esping-Andersen 1999: 34). Like Beveridge, Bismarck has left a powerful legacy in social policy analysis – his name becoming synonymous with the occupationally linked and segmented contributory social insurance systems. Rather than using state policy to control employers and the work process, the new approach to social insurance adopted during the 1880s sought to safeguard 'wage workers against poverty when they were unable to work because of disability, illness or old age' (Grandner 1996: 79).

By meeting some of the social needs of the working class, Bismarck's strategy was to head off demands for political equality and mass suffrage. Moreover, those covered by social insurance gained a stake in the existing system and the creation of a highly segmented, occupationally-based scheme of social insurance, drew distinctions among different fractions of the working class. In a sense, then, 'the growing organizational strength of an emerging industrial working class' led Bismarck 'consciously' to use 'state power to develop social policy' as a means to temper the perceived 'threat to the existing social order' posed by working-class mobilisation (Esping-Andersen and Korpi 1984: 8). Yet although the *Wohlfahrtsstaat* was an established concept in German academic debate at the time, Petersen and Petersen find no examples of the use of the term 'in political discussions of Bismarck's reforms' (2011: 9).

Eduard von Taaffe pursued a broadly similar 'corporatist' approach in the Habsburg Empire from the 1880s. Taaffe's social insurance system may have been may have been less radical than that of Bismarck, with the regulation of the workplace and the terms of employment remaining key – a reflection perhaps of the stronger influence of Catholicism in the Habsburg Empire (Grandner 1996: 79). Nevertheless, the insurance element was also prominent in Taaffe's social reforms. It is also worth noting the strong territorial dimension to the Habsburg system of social insurance in the late nineteenth century. As Grandner has noted, the organisation of accident insurance along 'territorial lines, not on the basis of industrial branches ... strongly distinguished' this system 'from the German model'. In a concession to conservative federalists, the Habsburg 'Crownlands' – viewed as economic as well as historic unities – were used as 'the administrative basis for accident insurance' (1996: 99). Even so, the central state retained considerable influence of the territorial *Unfallversicherungsanstalten* (accident insurance institutions), not least by nominating one-third of their executive boards. This aspect of the legacy left to the newly independent central European states of the interwar period by the Taaffe social reforms bears emphasis: the broadly corporatist model of social insurance had a territorial foundation in the Crownlands.

In summary, then, social policy development began in central Europe during the 1880s with conservative efforts to pre-empt growing working class mobilisation. A second phase of reform, concentrated in the UK, Sweden and Denmark, occurred in the early years of the twentieth century. These later reforms had more of a progressive character. They were generally led by Liberals and usually influenced and often supported by Social Democratic or Labour parties. Equally, however, these 'progressive' reformers were themselves often heavily influenced by the innovative social insurance schemes devised by Bismarck – they were, for example, used by Lloyd George as a model in the design of British national insurance legislation in 1910–11 (Hennessy 1992: 121). The first explicitly social democratic reform effort to achieve major success in Europe took place in Sweden during the 1930s. As it had a significant influence on social aspirations and ideas in Europe, the US New Deal must also be mentioned here.

This brief review raises two questions that are significant for our broader analysis here. First, how, in general terms, should these changes be explained? In particular, what role do 'crises' play? Second, given the widespread view that 1945 marks a decisive break in the history of social policy – the date at which the 'golden age' of the welfare state began – what, if anything, changed after the Second World War? It is to these twin issues that we now turn directly.

What role for crises in early social reform?

As we have seen, the literature on crisis generally emphasises major economic downturns and wars. While Bismarck's tenure as Imperial Chancellor followed on from victory in the Franco–Prussian War, and the 1870s were marked by episodes of financial panic and a sharp economic recession, war and economic crisis do not generally feature strongly in the standard accounts of his social reforms during the next decade. Instead, his anti-socialism is usually placed at the front and centre of explanations for his decision to develop social insurance. The early years of the twentieth century were not marked by a general economic crisis. The First World War put an end to the developing processes of social reform from the 1900s and 1910s, particularly in Britain. Here, however, the experience of the Boer War had a clear impact on social reform processes – albeit in a 'top-down' manner, with reforms driven by elite and expert concerns about the 'feeble masses' and the threat they might pose to Imperial efficiency and security (Semmel 1960). But although the climate of elite opinion was certainly altered by the experience of this war, it is much more difficult to argue that it changed popular attitudes or patterns of social mobilisation.

By contrast, the major crises of the 1930s and 1940s – the Great Depression and the Second World War – are widely seen to have had a direct and dramatic impact on social reform largely through their influence on *mass* public attitudes (albeit in a geographically uneven manner). Here, though, it is important to note an interesting difference between the standard analysis of welfare history – which identifies 1945 as the start of the golden age – and influential accounts that depict the 1930s as a decade of 'deep seated institutional change' (Blyth 2002; see also Gourevitch 1986). As the end of the Second World War, 1945 offers itself as an obvious choice as a turning point. Perhaps it does mark the moment at which 'social policy ceased to be "imposed from above"' and became instead 'the *object* of the concerns and worries of the traditional elite' (Esping-Andersen and Korpi 1984: 180) – the point at which the welfare state emerged as 'a unique historical construction, an explicit redefinition of what the state is all about' (Esping-Andersen 1999: 34). Yet this is by no means the only credible view. An alternative analysis suggests that, from the perspective of social policy, the 1930s and 1940s might be better understood as a single period during which the previous fifty or sixty years of gradual reform were consolidated, increasingly under the influence of social democrats (Hicks 1999). We will return to the question of what is distinctive about the welfare state – what distinguishes it from 'whatever menu of social benefits a state happens to offer' (Esping-Andersen 1999: 34) – below, when we focus on the issue of change within the period conventionally regarded as its golden age. For now, we simply wish to raise the possibility that, even in Britain, the 1940s might be seen more as the rounding off and consolidation of an earlier episode of reform, rather than as representing the dawning of the golden age itself.

'Within period' change

We have argued that it may be more accurate to see the 1940s as the culmination of two decades of social democratic reform than as the start of a new 'golden age'. Perhaps the most compelling evidence for this view is the record of social policy development during the next decade: the 1950s. Across western Europe, average growth in social spending as a proportion of GDP grew by less than 1 per cent between 1950 and 1959. That said, there were some significant developments during the 1950s. After the post-war chaos of the 1940s, sustained growth in Germany allowed for consolidation of welfare provision. Towards the end of the decade major pensions reforms were the subject of intensive political debate in Sweden. Although rapid economic growth often allowed for significant growth in real expenditure, the fate of the welfare state during the 1950s nevertheless stands in sharp contrast to the 1940s and, as we shall see, the 1960s (C. Pierson 1998: 132–3).

For Britain, arguably the archetype for the 1945-mid-1970s golden age illusion, the 1950s stand out sharply, not least for political reasons. For all that history has judged it a ringing success, Attlee's Labour administration was unceremoniously expelled from office in 1951. And, whilst their basic acceptance of the welfare state is a dominant theme in much commentary on the Conservative governments of the 1950s, the new guardians of the welfare state in Britain clearly lacked enthusiasm for the new social policy regime they inherited (C. Pierson 1998). Perhaps their attention was distracted from welfare issues by the seemingly more pressing economic agenda and/or by the policy innovations from which they took more evident delight, such as the de-nationalising of the steel industry. Yet whatever the reason, the limited development of welfare policy during the 1950s makes it more plausible to characterise the 1940s as the culmination of an earlier phase of social reform, rather than the start of a distinctive new era in itself.

The 1960s and 1970s

The limited development of social policy during the 1950s stands in sharp contrast to its rapid expansion from the early 1960s. Across the wealthy democracies, the proportion of GDP spent on social policy rose from 12.3 per cent in 1960 to 21.9 per cent in 1975, by which date Belgium, Denmark, France, Germany, the Netherlands and Sweden all committed more than a quarter of their GDP on welfare expenditure (C. Pierson 1998: 133). In fact, on the basis of careful empirical analysis, some influential welfare experts have argued that the welfare state's golden age only really began in earnest in the early 1960s (Flora 1986: xii). Indeed, some go so far as to see the period from 1960-1975 as a distinctive phase of 'major expansion' (C. Pierson 1998: 31).

Alongside a rapid growth in transfer-oriented social policies (predominantly linked to the employment-based risks of the male breadwinner – accident, sickness and unemployment) on which comparative welfare analysis has traditionally focused, another major transformation also took place in the 1960s: an expansion in the importance of social services (primarily focused on the non-working age population). In his seminal analysis of this change, Alber (1995) links the development of such programmes to new socio-demographic patterns rooted in population ageing and shifting gender roles and family forms. While Alber's empirical evidence focuses on the position of older people, studies of childcare policy (Morgan 2001; Wincott 2011a) corroborate his general argument and again identify the 1960s as a key period of significant change.

What are the implications of identifying the years after 1960 as a distinctive period of social policy change for the general conceptualisation of the welfare state? If the welfare state is understood as an historically distinctive institutional form or complex – a definitional standard that cannot be satisfied just by the mere presence of social policy commitments – then perhaps it was brought into being by the expansion of the 1960s, rather than the earlier reforms of the 1930s and 1940s? Analytical fragments from influential welfare state scholars hint at precisely such an interpretation. So, for Esping-Andersen, the 1950s and 1960s were 'surely not an epoch of mature welfare states and generous social rights'. He goes on to assert that most countries 'had yet to achieve anything close to universal coverage, benefit adequacy, or the levels of employment protection *that today are taken for granted*' (1999: 1, emphasis added). This is a remarkable statement – particularly if we recall his definition of 'social citizenship' as 'the core idea of a welfare state' (Esping-Andersen 1990: 21). It suggests that the welfare state came into existence fully only after the expansion that began in the 1960s. Moreover, close historical analysis of Germany and France, suggests that expansive changes to these 'Bismarckian' welfare states during the 1970s, resulted in the creation of state-wide social solidarity 'by the back door' (Baldwin 1992). This vision of the 1960s and 1970s as the period during which the welfare state moved towards completion stands in stark contrast to the standard golden age analysis.

The question of crisis

Not everyone would regard the 1960s and early 1970s as a period of 'normal politics'. Major societal change – and social upheaval –

undoubtedly occurred during these years. As well as a growing emphasis on civil rights and equality – initially emanating from the struggles
of African Americans and early feminist demands for dramatic changes
in gender roles in the US and in Europe – these years also witnessed the
large-scale student revolts across the western world that are forever
associated with 1968. Equally, this was hardly an era of peace – the war
in Vietnam had a major impact on political mobilisation and social
consciousness in the western world. However, in neither political economy nor state theory are these years generally identified as a period of
crisis. Instead, the social upheaval of the 1960s and 1970s is generally
seen as a product of twenty years of peace, prosperity and democracy
(see, for example, Streeck and Thelen 2005: 3). As we have already
seen, this was a period of significant – even transformative – change in
welfare policy, arguably inaugurating the 'real' golden age of the
welfare state. If so, this poses a challenge to standard, crisis-based political models of change.

Ending the 'golden age'? The 'crisis' of the 1970s and its legacy

The 'Great Depression' can be linked fairly clearly to the stockmarket
crash of 1929. By contrast, it is less obvious that the 'crisis' of the 1970s
can be linked back to any single event. This difficulty is reflected in a
lack of consensus about when the welfare state's golden age finally
came to an end. Gourevitch identifies the start of the crisis in 1971
(1986: 29), whereas some welfare state analysts see the golden age
continuing as late as 1975 (C. Pierson 1998). Yet whilst clear about his
preferred starting date, Gourevitch is strikingly reticent about the triggering event(s) for the crisis. A possible candidate is US President
Nixon's decision to arrest the dollar's convertibility into gold that year.
The 'Nixon Shock' was, in effect a unilateral termination of the
'Bretton Woods' system of international currency arrangements. As oil
was priced in dollars Nixon's decision to float the dollar, and the subsequent deprecation of the currency, reduced the revenues of oil producing states. With political hostility towards US support for Israel also
hardening their attitudes, oil-producing countries agreed a rapid rise in
oil prices (of some 70 per cent), matched by supply restrictions, and an
outright embargo of sales to the US. If these were its triggering events,
the 'crisis' of the 1970s is also often linked to the combination of stagnation and inflation that seemed to baffle mainstream economists

(most notably the Keynesians) at the time. Thus, Gamble (2009a) describes the difficulties of the period as the 'stagflation' crisis.

Just as with the Great Depression, countries responded to the trials and tribulations of the 1970s in strikingly different ways. Such is the variation in European politics and policy during the 1970s and 1980s that more weight may need to be placed on domestic and political factors than an analysis focused on the 'international economic crisis' might suggest. Only in 1966 did the social democrats became a party of government in Germany; the party's first post-war Chancellor was elected three years later – shortly before the Nixon Shock. From 1969 to 1972, the social democrats were in a sufficiently strong position within the governing coalition to hold both the finance and the economics ministries. Although they remained the dominant party in the governing coalition until 1982, two major factors reined in any Keynesian ambitions they may have had. The pressures of coalition government meant that in 1972 they had to relinquish the economics ministry to the liberal Free Democrats; in addition, from the early 1970s the *Bundesbank* began to assert its autonomy in monetary policy by counteracting expansionary moves in fiscal policy with a monetary tightening.

The wait for reform-oriented socialists to achieve electoral office was even longer in France. Yet when they did eventually gain power – in 1981 – the French Socialists initially embarked on a programme for the basic transformation of the economy and society, including nationalisation on a large scale. However, after a brief phase of radicalism, the French Socialist governments reined back, and replaced this approach with one focused on European integration (Hall 1986; Loriaux 1991). Nevertheless, the French experience (the 'Mitterrand Experiment') shows that the stagflation of the 1970s did not necessarily lead to the electoral ascendancy of the right.

In electoral terms, social democrats seem to have suffered more where they had enjoyed a longer tenure in office. The Nordic countries witnessed a strengthening of right-wing political forces during the 1970s. The Danish Progress Party was formed in 1972. It became the second largest party in parliament after running an anti-tax campaign in the 1973 general election. In 1976, the Swedish social democrats lost power for the first time in decades. The centre-right retained power in the 1979 election, and it was six years before the social democrats returned to government. Nevertheless, even during this interlude, the centre-right did little to unravel the Swedish welfare model. Accordingly, whatever electoral reversals they suffered in the 1970s, the social democratic quality of Nordic social policy was maintained through the 1970s and in it was consolidated in the 1980s. In fact, Esping-Andersen suggests that the distinctive character of these regimes only emerged from the 1970s (a view we endorse in later chapters). As he puts it, earlier Britain and Scandinavia would almost certainly have been 'put in the same cluster of universal, flat-rate benefits, national health care and ... full employment'. Yet by the 1970s British 'social democratization' had stalled, whilst it was in precisely this period that 'the essence of the social democratic regimes in Scandinavia' emerged (1999: 87).

This comparison with Scandinavia suggests that there was at least one state – Britain – for which the 1970s did mark a decisive moment in social policy history. Here, Margaret Thatcher – a key symbolic leader for the anti-welfare state New Right – became prime minister after the Conservative electoral victory of 1979. Yet even before Thatcherism the British welfare state was in retreat, with the significant earlier retrenchment of public spending and the humiliating turn to the International Monetary Fund for a loan under a Labour administration. Still, close analysts of welfare retrenchment argue that, even in Britain, where the conditions were particularly propitious for the New Right, welfare retrenchment was only limited in its success (Pierson 1994). Rather than a fully fledged dismantling of the British welfare state, the overall impact of retrenchment in the 1970s and 1980s might be better seen as stunting its potential for further growth, reinforcing Esping-Andersen's conception of its 'stalled' development (1999: 87).

Overall, mainstream analysts do not paint a clear picture of the fate of the welfare state in western Europe since the 1970s. On the one hand, analysts generally describe the welfare state as facing enormous pressures, an era of 'permanent austerity' (P. Pierson 1998). On the other hand, the same analysts see the welfare state as having remarkable capacities to endure these pressures. Such remarkable resilience might be thought to yield rather dull outcomes. For, despite the challenges to which it has been exposed, in this account the welfare state is generally depicted as an 'immoveable object' (P. Pierson 1998). By the late 1990s, partly under the influence of 'third way' ideas, some analysts did suggest a slightly more dynamic and, indeed, optimistic view of the future of welfare. Rather than simply enduring, new welfare policies began to develop in response to the new social risks thrown up by economic and social change (Bonoli 2005). But even in such a conception, the welfare state was largely seen to have entered something of a 'silver age'. Equally, 'activation' has become a byword of social reform in many countries, bringing with it potentially much stricter work obligations, re-employment strategies and 'responsibilization' programmes. The impact of these changes may not be seen in the generosity of benefit levels as such, but in ever more exacting eligibility criteria (Cox 2004). This is a theme to which we return in Chapters 4 and 6 in more empirical detail.

Central and eastern Europe after 1989

The immediate pressures of economic collapse and regime change in central and eastern Europe after 1989 were huge. Even so, many countries sought to maintain their social provision or – particularly in central Europe – to consolidate and entrench this provision through significant social reforms. In its first year (and before the 'velvet divorce') the Czechoslovak Republic worked out a system of social security benefits that went on to provide a 'relatively solid foundation' for the successor Czech Republic. In the immediate post-Communist period Hungary, Poland, Estonia and Slovenia also (re)introduced or strengthened significant elements of 'Bismarckian' (or better 'Taaffean') social insurance (Cerami 2007). By contrast, as late as a decade after the fall of the Berlin Wall, such states as Bulgaria, Romania and Ukraine were 'still attempting to conserve state and workplace benefits in the face of declining resources' (see Deacon 2000: 151). However, by the mid-1990s the transitions states were in the depths of a major economic depression – and budgetary pressure had grown substantially even in the relatively prosperous states of central Europe. In this context, most states developed more radical social reforms. For example, the new socialist government in Hungary passed an *Act on Economic Stabilization* in 1995, which proposed significant cutbacks in social provision (Sajó 1996). Most transition states engaged in significant retrenchment – particularly with respect to (residual) social assistance – which has generally been hit even harder than (contributory) unemployment insurance (Nelson 2010: 372). As a result, retrenchment may have enhanced the 'Bismarckian' character of most central European states: among the transition states, Hungary and the Baltic republics are 'possible exceptions' to this claim, as the relative emphasis of social assistance seems to have grown (Nelson 2010: 370).

During the 1990s, the transition states received some financial support and a large amount of policy advice both from the institutions associated with the Washington Consensus – the IMF and the World

Bank – and from the European Union. All this advice emphasised the importance of market liberalisation and privatisation, together with the rule of law and the protection of minority rights. Yet social policy was not a high priority – despite some differences of emphasis in the advice emanating from Brussels and Washington. The attempt to implant a Washington Consensus model – based on free markets and the rule of law – was not wholly successful. Rather than following the market-supporting doctrines and interpretive methods associated with the US Supreme Court, senior judges in central Europe sometimes turned out to be robust defenders of (inherited) social and economic rights. Thus, for example, the Hungarian Constitutonal Court declared many provisions of the 1995 social reform package invalid (Sajó 1996). It seems that advocates of the Washington Consensus had not anticipated that central European judges would follow a Germanic tradition of legal interpretation, rather than their much favoured US model (Robertson 2007).

Europe after the 'golden age'

Overall, then, the political and policy consequences of the 'crisis' of the 1970s have played out very differently in various western European states – in relation to both their timing and (partly as a consequence) their immediate substance. There is little evidence of agreement over when the crisis of the 1970s came to an end. Indeed, writing in the 1980s, Gourevitch (1986) regarded it as still ongoing. While analysts broadly agree that the mid-1970s marked the end of the golden age of the welfare state, analysts also assert that while is has faced a prolonged period of economic pressure – perhaps even permanent austerity – the welfare state has, nonetheless, endured. This interpretation differs both from state theorists, who decisively consign the welfare state to history, and from 'the Great Moderation' notion shared by conventional economists. Let us briefly review some of these major themes.

State theory after 'stagflation'

The state has been conceptualised in various different ways for the period since the 1970s. Some of these characterisations – such as the 'post-Fordist state', the 'competition state' or the 'Schumpeterian post-national workfare regime' (SPWR) (Jessop 2000, 2002) – are explicitly constructed so as to describe a contrast with the state's character in an earlier period. Others have attempted to encapsulate the character of the state during these years more positively, substantively and concisely: like Jessop, though, they all focus on the role of the state in promoting competition or economic efficiency (compare Majone's vision of the 'regulatory state' (1996) with Cerny's notion of the 'competition state' (1997b). Moreover, the developments on which these various proposals focus overlap at least to some degree. For example, all agree that states continue to engage in social policies of one sort or another, while nonetheless suggesting that the new regime can no longer be characterised as a welfare state. Precisely when and how these new state regimes emerged from the chaos of the 1970s is, however, generally left unclear.

The 'Great Moderation'

In contrast to state theorists, orthodox economists take a different view again. Arguably this dovetails better with Gourevitch's conception of international economic crisis (1986). Rather than focusing on when the 'hard times' that began in the 1970s came to an end, in the early years of the twenty-first century, mainstream economists began to argue that we had entered a period of relative economic calm: a time of low volatility in such key economic variables as output growth and inflation. The period became known as the 'Great Moderation', and is usually dated to the mid-1980s (for convenience, say, 1987 – a date which makes an interesting comparison with Gourevitch's (1986) view of the long crisis of the 1970s). Scratch the surface of this orthodox economic consensus, though, and considerable differences in interpretation remain. Economists disagree over whether the Great Moderation emerged due to structural change, effective macro-economic policies, good luck, or some combination of all of these factors (discussed in Bernanke 2004). Nevertheless, most mainstream economists came to accept the broad argument about the new stability, as well as its periodisation. And for all that some analysts attributed the 'Moderation' to luck, leading academic economists and policymakers expressed deep confidence in their ability to make effective policies and, specifically, to avoid economic calamity (Lucas 2003; Bernanke 2003).

Neoliberalism?

Perhaps 'neoliberalism' is the closest thing we have to such an agreed overarching characterisation. But even here there are substantial differences in interpretation. Neoliberalism generally refers to a process (of renewed or further liberalisation) rather than to a more specific state-form. The notion of the 'neoliberal state' has not gained much analytical grip: even where the concept has been canvassed (Harvey 2005: 64) it is depicted as the inherently unstable partner to the process of neoliberalisation. In other words, while the 'crisis' of the 1970s seemed to undermine Keynesian economic strategies (at least in many states) and to allow both anti-welfare state and pro-market economy arguments to be articulated forcefully, it is not clear that it was decisive in generating a shared general understanding of the nature of the era it inaugurated – at least not one that matched the 'welfare statist' view of the western world over the preceding decades. The same is true of central and eastern Europe, despite the fact that much of the transition 'advice' such states were offered was broadly neoliberal in character. While social provision was typically cut back across central and eastern Europe in the period 1995–2005, many of these social policy regimes have maintained an essentially Bismarckian character. Moreover, while the economic growth recorded in central Europe during the latter stages of this decade did rely on neoliberal financial strategies, in many countries, the resulting growth models were already beginning to break down before the global financial crisis itself.

Conclusion

In this chapter we have sought to provide an analysis of the overall trajectory of the welfare state in western Europe from the late nineteenth century until the early years of the twenty-first century, while also addressing developments in central and eastern Europe. Our purpose has been to situate the challenges posed to the welfare state by our current economic crisis into a long-term perspective. While in no way wishing to claim that major wars and economic crises have no significant impact on the political economy of the state, our analysis here has shown that reducing the overall trajectory of European welfare state history to a set of responses to material crises is not sustainable. There is no simple equivalence between episodes of reform and major crises. We have also seen that there is no clear and common agreement about the nature of the state nor the condition of social policy during the period since the mid-1970s. Taken together, these arguments give us a mandate to re-examine the political economy of the welfare state over recent decades. This is, in fact, an urgent necessity as we seek to make sense of the prospects for social policy after 2008.

There is a widespread – if largely implicit – acceptance among commentators that the 1945-mid-1970s period was the golden age of the welfare state – or at least that the welfare state was a key defining feature of the age (alongside perhaps Keynesianism). It seems that no real agreement has been achieved about how the decades since the 1970s – the post-golden age period – should be characterised. It may be that the characterisation of the *earlier* period is best seen as a product of the crisis-process itself. That is, defining the golden age of the welfare state as a phenomenon of the 1945-mid-1970s period was part of the process of motivating neoliberal and other reforms. This argument certainly fits with our evidence that the idea of the welfare state was, in effect, projected back onto the history of social reform during the 1940s (rather than being the authentic language contemporary actors used to promote those reforms). If the ability to characterise the earlier period is indeed a crucial part of defining the path out of a 'crisis', then contesting the nature of the period from the late-1970s to 2007 becomes an urgent political task.

In this chapter our analysis has focused on the *common* history of the welfare state across Europe, but European states have also differed substantially over matters such as the timing, sequence and substance of their social policy development. The next chapter deals with variations across the European welfare states, addressing the huge literature on different types, clusters and regimes.

Chapter 2

Varieties of European Welfare Capitalism

Introduction

Set in any long-term historical perspective, it is clear that the roles and responsibilities of western European states have been transformed with the development in each of welfare states in the century or so after 1880. While particular countries took the lead during specific historical periods, states came to share a common broad developmental trajectory in this overall historical process that encompassed 'an explicit redefinition of what the state is all about' (Esping-Andersen 1999: 34). In such a contest it is hardly surprising that the concept of *convergence* has become such a leitmotif of welfare state research (Wilensky and Lebeaux 1958; Wilensky 1975, 1976), whether seen as the product of more or less functional adaptation to common pressures or as a product of diffusion of ideas and ideals between countries.

But exactly what do these countries share? Despite, or perhaps because, it is widely used in public discourse, political debate and academic analysis, attempts at a precise definition of the welfare state are surprising rare (see Esping-Andersen 1990: 18, Veit-Wilson 2000 and Wincott 2001a for discussions of this issue). If the concept can be elusive, the institutions and policies denoted by the welfare state are also diverse and complex with the term referring to a vast array public policies and bureaucratic procedures – an often eclectic set of activities and commitments undertaken by the state. The mix of specific policy instruments associated with the welfare state is equally diverse, varying between social policy domains, across states and over time.

To illustrate the point, the development of 'Bismarckian' and 'Beveridgean' welfare systems can appear as a fundamental bifurcation between European states. Different initial institutional designs set countries on distinct trajectories that ultimately generated quite different forms of state welfare provision: the former rooted in occupationally fractured, status-preserving, 'corporatist' systems, while the latter provide 'universal' flat-rate benefits. As this suggests, different countries have followed distinct historical paths to welfare statehood. In recent decades growing recognition of this conceptual and historical complexity has led to an increasing acknowledgement of, and emphasis on, welfare state diversity (Esping-Andersen 1990; Swank 2002; Hay 2004b; Sapir 2006). It is this focus on institutional distinctiveness that continues to characterise current debates.

Worlds of welfare capitalism

Since its publication in 1990, Esping-Andersen's genre-defining analysis of welfare regime diversity, *The Three Worlds of Welfare Capitalism* (1990), has become the standard approach in welfare state analysis. It, and the literature it has spawned, differentiates between at least three (often more) different 'worlds' of welfare capitalism (see also Titmuss 1974). The conventional wisdom in this broadly institutionalist, analytical tradition is that welfare states come in 'types' around which groups of countries 'cluster'. It is hard to overstate the influence of this analysis, both in academic and policy debates. A vast specialist literature has developed through the sympathetic yet critical engagement with the *Three Worlds* framework (for some illustrative examples see Lewis 1992; Leibfried 1992; Castles and Mitchell 1993; Orloff 1993; Jones 1993; Kloosterman 1994; van Kersbergen 1995; Ferrera 1996; Rhodes 1997; Goodin *et al.* 1999; Becker 2000; Pierson 2001; Swank 2002; Sapir 2006; Fenger 2007). The idea of regime-types has also filtered from academic analysis into policy debate and public discussion (for example, Sapir 2006 was originally prepared as a background report for a presentation to the 2005 ECOFIN meeting in Manchester, see also Pearce and Paxton 2005). As it has become the touchstone of welfare state analysis, engagement with the *Three Worlds* framework is a theme that runs throughout this chapter.

The persuasive power of Esping-Andersen's analysis derives, in large part, from the clarity with which he proclaimed the existence of three distinct types of welfare state – **liberal, conservative-corporatist** and **social democratic**. Each is associated with a specific exemplary form of welfare provision (respectively means-testing, occupationally or sector-specific social insurance, and universalism). The presumption is that 'real world' or 'actually existing' welfare states conform to, or cluster closely around, these types. Indeed, we might be forgiven for thinking of them as 'worlds apart'.

Three worlds?

The first of these worlds, that of the 'liberal welfare state', is charac- terised by Esping-Andersen as one in which 'means tested assistance, modest universal transfers, or modest social-insurance plans predom- inate' and the 'progress of social reforms has been severely circum- scribed by traditional, liberal work-ethic norms' (1990: 26). Within such regimes, the state may actively encourage the market by subsidis- ing private welfare schemes – thereby aggravating the dualism between state-welfare recipients and the majority who use 'private' systems. This 'liberal' group is often equated with a model linked to cultural, linguistic or economic features of Anglo-Saxon states (a labeling term used, for example, by Sapir 2006). Esping-Andersen identified the US, Canada and Australia as archetypical examples of this regime-type (1990: 27). However, neither of the states usually identified as the European exemplars of Anglo-Saxon liberalism – the UK and Ireland – had strong liberal welfare regime characteristics in Esping-Andersen's (1990: 74) seminal analysis (see Table 2.4 below). As this suggests, welfare states do not always conform to their antici- pated type. Thus, despite his apparent espousal of a conception of welfare diversity in terms of clearly distinct worlds of welfare Esping- Andersen also insists that there are no 'single pure cases' of a welfare regime-type (1990: 28).

In the second world, that of the 'conservative-corporatist' regime- type, the state stands 'perfectly ready to displace the market'. Accordingly, 'private insurance and occupational fringe benefits play a truly marginal role.' In this largely state-initiated 'corporatist' social insurance system, the 'preservation of status differentials' is key, and hence the 'redistributive impact' of social policy is 'negligible'. These regimes 'are also typically shaped by the church and hence strongly committed to the preservation of traditional family-hood'. Non-work- ing wives are invariably excluded from social insurance. Although his empirical analysis focuses on social insurance and transfers rather than social services, Esping-Andersen notes that day care and families serv- ices are 'conspicuously underdeveloped' within this 'regime-type clus- ter', mentioning Austria, France, Germany and Italy as examples (1990: 27). Other analysts have associated this group with a continen- tal European or Bismarckian model (see Sapir 2006), the latter also being signalled by Esping-Andersen's conception of corporatist welfare statism.

In the third, final 'and clearly smallest' social democratic 'regime *cluster*', policy does not 'tolerate a dualism between state and market', or 'working class and middle class' (Esping-Andersen 1990: 27, emphasis added). Here the welfare state promotes 'an equality of the highest standards', not of 'minimum needs as was pursued elsewhere'. Services and benefits were 'upgraded to levels commensurate with even the most discriminating tastes of the new middle classes' and workers were guaranteed 'full participation in the quality of rights enjoyed by the better off' (1990: 27). Despite describing the social democratic regime in much more detail than the other two, Esping-Andersen does not provide an explicit list of 'archetypical' social democratic welfare states in this part of his analysis. Yet it is the Nordic countries that provide the obvious model for it. Indeed other analysts often describe it as a Scandinavian or Nordic model (Hay 2004b; Sapir *et al.* 2003, 2006).

The issue of whether or not this regime-type has developed anywhere much beyond its Scandinavian heartland is less easily resolved. The position of the Netherlands is particularly significant in this respect. The Dutch case is, as we shall see below, the only non-Nordic 'welfare' state in which Esping-Andersen detects strong elements of 'socialist' provision (1990: 74). It has been taken to exemplify 'social democracy' in other influential 'worlds of welfare' studies (see Goodin *et al.* 1999) and, perversely, sometimes even described as exhibiting a 'Nordic' social model (Sapir 2005, 2006). Yet the fit is by no means absolute. For whilst Esping-Andersen depicts a fundamental commitment to guaranteed full-employment as a defining feature of the social democratic 'regime-type' (1990: 28), the Netherlands had one of Europe's worst records of unemployment during the 1980s. Moreover, historically the Dutch welfare state was both generous and passive (transfer-oriented), displaying a mix of Christian democratic and social democratic characteristics (van Kersbergen and Becker 1988; see also Cox 1993; Becker 2000). Latterly, of course, the Netherlands has lost its reputation for passivity in social provision, and has typically come to be seen as offering a 'miraculous' model of jobs growth and welfare reform (Cox 2001). But the distinctive historical characteristics of the Dutch case have led some to question either the three worlds framework or its place within it (Kloosterman 1994). Alternatively, Christian democracy may provide a distinctive normative foundation on which a very generous welfare state might be based, with implications across continental western Europe (van Kersbergen 1995) – an issue to which we will return below.

Conceptualising welfare state diversity

As the accent has moved from convergence and common development to difference and variation, a number of different labels and associated concepts have come to be used to describe the (diverse) character of welfare states. As well as 'worlds of welfare', 'regimes', 'types' and 'clusters', these also include 'social models', 'families of nations', 'welfare (state) regimes', 'social policy regimes', 'regime-types' and 'regime-clusters'. Substantive differences between (groups of) welfare states are also described in various different ways: using major political movements and/or ideologies (liberalism, conservatism, social democracy, radical) as labels, or in terms of geographical and/or cultural/linguistic categories (continental European; southern Europe or Mediterranean; Anglo-Saxon or sometimes Anglo-liberal; eastern European, or east–central European, Baltic; Nordic, Scandinavian). Welfare states are also sometimes conceived as having different 'dimensions' (here, typically, liberal, conservative and social democratic).

These different labels are often used concurrently and interchangeably, without much consideration of what they might mean (and sometimes with peculiar results such as the categorisation of the Netherlands – and Austria too – as 'Nordic' social models in Sapir 2006). As a result, the character of the diversity they describe may have escaped scrutiny. Three aspects require particular attention: (i) the relationship between those characteristics that define the welfare state as such and those that identify variation between welfare states; (ii) the various ways (both conceptual and empirical) by which welfare states might be classified or grouped together; and (iii) the value of the analysis of welfare state variation in terms of distinct 'dimensions'. Esping-Andersen's extraordinarily rich and influential work is a key source for all three aspects: the definition of the welfare state, the classification of welfare states into types; and the dimensions of welfare state variation. Yet although seminal, it turns out that this analysis across these three aspects contains significant conceptual ambivalence and ambiguity.

For the most part, discussion of welfare worlds, types, models, regimes and clusters proceeds as if no significant analytical distinctions are made that underpin the choice of a particular terminology. We disagree: although we do recognise that the relevant distinctions may be fine, we also think that they are significant. The first three descriptors – worlds, types and models – all suggest that the wholesale differences exist between different forms of welfare state or, as we prefer, varieties of welfare capitalism. So, the idea of distinct 'worlds' of welfare suggests that the differences between (groups of) countries swamp whatever they share as welfare states. While the latter two terms – regime and cluster – though perfectly consistent with the identification of wholesale differences of this kind, do not presume or require them *a priori*.

Discussion of welfare (state) regime-*types* (Esping-Andersen 1990) and social *models* (Sapir 2006) also places stress on differences. Reference to 'types' may imply stronger differences still, because it suggests the drawing of categorical distinctions. Both certainly imply that conceptual distinctions can be made between forms of welfare state. Similarly, use of the terms 'models' or 'types' suggests that key defining features can be abstracted from a mass of empirical detail – an impression reinforced by Esping-Andersen's assertion that no pure-types exist (1990: 28). We might, therefore, legitimately expect logical clarity about the defining features of each type or model.

By contrast, the idea of a regime plays a number of different roles in welfare state analysis. As a consequence of covering a range of positions, it may embody (and perhaps also disguise) conceptual ambiguities. We have already seen that it is often linked to the idea of types, but it is also used in other ways. Crucially, it signals the ways in which social policies interconnect with other aspects of the capitalist political economy – especially the labour market. As Esping-Andersen puts it, to to talk of a regime 'is to denote the fact that in the relation between state and economy a complex of legal and organizational features are systematically interwoven'. More broadly, this reflects his contention that the welfare state is 'a principal institution in the construction of different models of post-war capitalism' (1990: 2, 5). In this usage, the idea of a regime shares features with the concept of an economic growth 'model' (such as the debt-fuelled 'Anglo-liberal growth model' that we detect at the heart of the global financial crisis discussed in Chapter 7). This conception of the inherent interconnectedness of the economy, on the one hand, and public and social policies, on the other, remains crucially important – indeed, it forms a core premise of the analysis we present in this volume. It is well expressed by Esping-Andersen in the language of welfare capitalism, a language we deploy here and in what follows.

The idea of a regime can also refer to something practical: the application of a form of welfare capitalism, the way that it works out on the ground, as it were. Acknowledgement of this practical aspect might be seen to introduce a measure of flexibility into the concept, a recognition that even within one of the three worlds, variations are likely to exist between 'actually existing' welfare regimes. Moreover, and in keeping with this, the regime idea is often used in analyses of how 'actually existing' welfare states group or cluster.

While most analysts seem to assess welfare state variation in terms of conceptually distinct models or types, the notion of (welfare/state/ regime) 'clusters' suggests a primary emphasis on the observation of empirical differences, perhaps conceived as dimensions of variation rather than as distinct categories (see Hicks and Kenworthy 2003; Salais 2003; Scruggs and Allan 2008; Scruggs and Pontusson 2008). If states are properly placed in distinct categories, the idea of clustering tends to become less significant. Of course, empirical data *might* show that states fall into clear groups such as we might associate with categorically distinct types. Such an empirical observation would amount to a powerful research finding. Thus, tight clusters of states in one dimension – say, high, medium and low scores on an index of decommodification – might suggest a typological structure. Esping-Andersen's (1990) analysis gives a strong impression of having achieved a result of precisely this kind. However, on close reading, it becomes clear that he actually treats the terms regime-types and regime-clusters as synonymous (see, for example, 1990: 26–7). In this respect he seems to commit a category error. Rather than demonstrating and reporting an empirical phenomenon, he simply presumes that conceptual and empirical aspects of welfare regimes vary together.

In general, however, the idea of clusters is more open. Its use is premised on the identification of dimensions of variation along which welfare states might be arrayed rather than logically distinct and discrete categories into which individual welfare states might fall or be placed. Analysts favouring this approach generally use principal components or cluster analysis techniques to analyse a set of variables or dimensions of variation, investigating inductively *whether or not* countries cluster into observable groups. Put slightly differently, such analyses focus on the *possibility* that countries may cluster, rather than presuming that they do. Such an approach is more open to the possibility that any groups identified might vary over time in terms of closeness and membership (that they may converge or diverge over time, losing or acquiring members in the process). It is in this spirit that we will explore the (changing) ways in which welfare regimes cluster in Chapter 6.

In short, the increasing diversity in the terminology used to discuss types of welfare state suggests that the concepts underlying welfare regime and social model analysis require closer scrutiny than they have typically received. Because it involves significant adaptation of the framework, by multiplying the number and variety of distinctions between worlds, models or regimes, the widespread adoption of the idea that welfare states come in types may, paradoxically call the underlying concept into question. For rather than a small set of 'types' we may be rather better thinking of diversity in terms of variation along one or more dimensions of welfare policy and provision.

The welfare state: dimensions and definitions

Surprisingly little attention has been paid to the quality or qualities that define a welfare state as such (discussed in Veit-Wilson 2000; Wincott 2001a). In general, clusters of welfare states are defined primarily according to the form taken by their institutions and policies. These combine in ways that are linked to the three regime-types, each associated with a distinctive form of welfare state stratification, and are sometimes described as welfare state 'dimensions' (Esping-Andersen 1990: 69). So, within the 'three worlds' framework, liberal welfare regimes are associated with the prevalence of residual, means-tested benefits, and a high relative share of private insurance or spending in pensions and health care, while conservative regimes offer multiple, occupationally specific social insurance schemes and provide privileged pensions for civil servants. Finally, social democratic regimes emphasise 'universal' coverage across a wide institutional range of possible social policies (Titmuss 1974) and a small differential between standard benefits and the maximum level available (Esping-Andersen 1990: 77–8). Each world of welfare is presented as a highly distinctive configuration of welfare institutions, in turn composed of policies that differ both in their range and underlying form, not least in terms of the rules governing how they provide benefits and services (such as universal, work-related and means-tested benefits).

In practice, however, Esping-Andersen (1990) operationalises the concepts used to identify regime-types as *three* welfare state *dimensions* on the basis of their 'stratification' effects. Each is constructed through the allocation of scores to different features of each welfare state (specifically corporatism, étatism, means testing in poor relief, the percentage of private provision in first, pensions and, second, health care, universalism and benefit equality). So, liberalism, conservatism

and socialism emerge as 'regime attributes' based on 'degrees' of variation across seven aspects of welfare provision (1990: 74, 70–1, 69).
This indicates a certain degree of ambivalence verging on conceptual
confusion about the relationship between analytically distinct worlds
of welfare and these *dimensions* of variation (along which actually
existing welfare regimes might be arrayed).

Other scholars have critically dissected and further developed
Esping-Andersen's analysis of welfare state dimensions. First, in recent
years serious questions have been raised about the empirical validity of
the indicators developed and used in the *Three Worlds* analysis, specifically in relation to measures of decommodification and stratification
(Scruggs and Allan 2006, 2008). Yet in the literature to which this has
given rise, many aspects of the original conceptual framework are
retained as new indices of decommodification (or welfare benefit
generosity) and of welfare state liberalism, conservatism and socialism
have been developed. However, replication analyses based on these
new indicators tend to be critical of the impression given by Esping-
Andersen of 'tight clustering'. Indeed, this is invariably dismissed as
'too neat' and almost 'too good to be true' (Scruggs and Allan 2008:
661, 2006; Scruggs and Pontusson 2008). Second, there is a growing
body of empirical work using statistical methods to determine the
existence and strength of possible welfare state clusters (Fenger 2007;
Draxler and Van Vliet 2010) and/or dimensions (Hicks and
Kenworthy 2003; Scruggs and Pontusson 2008). Whether or not this
generates results consistent with the idea of categorically distinct
'types' of welfare state, such studies typically identify a set of empirically grounded regime-clusters. These, we suggest, are likely to prove
useful heuristically in the analysis of welfare state continuity and
change.

While welfare state analysis has tended to focus primarily on institutions and policies, issues of similarity and difference in welfare regimes
also raise questions about how one might characterise regimes in terms
of the normative values they reflect and exhibit. Moreover, these
normative matters are related to how the welfare state is defined in the
first place – what qualities must a state have to qualify as a welfare
state? On the one hand, a single norm could be used to define the
welfare state; on the other, different welfare states could be seen to
reflect (and promote) distinct values or bundles of values. Perhaps
surprisingly given the general emphasis on institutional and policy
diversity, it is the former approach that remains more common and
influential within the existing literature. The thrust of most relevant

theory is, then, towards the identification of a single, elegant defining principle for *the* welfare state of this kind. So, for example, Esping-Andersen defines the welfare state in terms of social citizenship, which he then further specifies with respect to the concept of 'decommodification' (meaning that 'citizens can freely, and without potential loss of job, income, or general welfare, opt out of work when they themselves consider it necessary' (1990: 23)). This approach has been highly influential, with indices of decommodification widely used as scales against which to measure a country's degree of welfare statehood.

Others have extended this conceptualisation of social citizenship further. So, for example, those concerned with the position of women in western societies, stress the importance of access to paid employment (Orloff 1993). Full and equal citizenship for women may first require their *commodification*, at least in the sense of having access to paid work. Women also need to be able to form autonomous households. As this suggests, such additional 'dimensions' of social citizenship should be accorded an equal standing with decommodification (Orloff 1993; see also Esping-Andersen 1999 on 'defamilialization'). Making a social reality of citizenship across these dimensions would mean that all women and men would have alternatives – the option to work, to leave a particular job, or to change their domestic situation – which would change power relations even for those who choose not to take up such options. Empirical measures of certain aspects of this approach have been included in some recent analyses (Hicks and Kenworthy 2003; Scruggs and Pontusson 2008).

Social citizenship is often associated with egalitarianism (see, for example, Goodin *et al.* 1999: 30, 46). Ultimately, however, social citizenship analysis seems to be rooted in a different value – that of independence or autonomy. Thus, for Esping-Andersen decommmodification should 'emancipate individuals from market dependence' (1990: 22), while Orloff (1993) is also concerned with emancipation from the bonds of domestic dependence. If the purpose of the welfare state is to emancipate citizens from market and domestic dependence, then autonomy appears as its foundational normative value. Crucially, however, in this form it is not so much an autonomy *from* the state, but rather one *achieved through* the state, or at least one in which the state is a key partner (Orloff 1993; also see Goodin 1985 on 'self reliance'). The state's role in promoting self-reliance (or autonomy) by weakening bonds of social dependence (Goodin 1985) could create a kind of statist individualism (Trägårdh 1997) rooted in individuals' direct and indirect dependence on the state.

Extremely exacting standards are set for the attainment of welfare statehood within this social citizenship framework (Esping-Andersen 1990; Orloff 1993). This creates something of a problem – for arguably few if any states have ever met such standards. That this is so might be seen to render welfare statehood largely irrelevant to the analysis of differences in 'actually existing' social policy regimes or worlds of welfare capitalism. Yet if the defining features of a welfare state could be re-cast as dimensions of variation, they might still prove useful in the analysis of these differences. In practice Esping-Andersen's (1990) analysis comes close to doing something analogous in that it operationalises decommodification as a variable for empirical purposes. Yet, crucially, he does not treat decommodification as a 'dimension' (equivalent, say, to liberalism, conservatism or social democracy). Across regime-types all welfare states are defined or assessed against this singular concept (Esping-Andersen 1990: 21). This is ultimately difficult to reconcile with one that also draws categorical distinctions between different types of welfare state. The mix of categorical regime type distinctions and/or dimensions with a singular defining principle for welfare statehood seems to us conceptually unstable.

Yet to complicate things further, not all analysts agree that a single normative principle (such as decommodification) can be used to define the welfare state. Such sceptics point to the substantial differences exhibited between worlds of welfare, using this to challenge as implausible the assumption that the essence of the welfare state can be boiled down to a single norm. Might not the diversity of social policies and welfare outcomes flow from differences in underlying organisational or normative principles or objectives? For instance, might not Christian democratic welfare regimes reflect distinctly Christian democratic welfare principles – perhaps emphasising social stability and self-realisation (van Kersbergen 1995)? More generally, and continuing in this vein, we could argue that 'the welfare state is not one thing' (Goodin *et al*. 1999: 4), but instead welfarism has a range of objectives and implicates a variety of moral principles. These might include:

- promoting economic efficiency;
- reducing poverty;
- promoting social equality;
- promoting social integration and avoiding social exclusion;
- promoting social stability; and
- promoting autonomy (Goodin *et al*. 1999: 23, 22, elaborated in 24–36; cf. Commission on Social Justice 1994: 8).

Individual states place the accent on these objectives and values in different ways to generate distinctive combinations of features, even if in the end these are seen as differences of emphasis (Goodin *et al.* 1999: 23, 36). Nevertheless, these value differences are strong enough for the various 'styles of welfare state' to 'represent proto-types as much as ideal types'; they are, that is, 'intellectual constructions on the basis of which welfare regimes have been self-consciously modelled' (Goodin *et al.* 1999: 4). Goodin and his colleagues go on to trace the characteristic value sets (or proto-typical moral principles) associated with the conservative, liberal and social democratic regimes, developing in the process a stylised model of each.

The 'corporatist' (otherwise 'conservative' or 'Christian demo-cratic') welfare regime is perhaps the most interesting and distinctive in terms of its fundamental values (see generally Goodin *et al.* 1999: 51–5). Here the core norm relates to social cohesion or integration – not of a diffuse solidaristic or fraternal kind, but 'best captured in the notion of "my station and its duties"' (Goodin *et al.* 1999: 52, citing Bradley 1867). Unlike both liberalism and social democracy, here individual fulfilment or self-realisation does not flow from autonomy, but rather from playing a particular, substantive role within society. Security and stability are the ultimate goals of the conservative welfare state.

Predictably, the dominant value for the 'liberal' regime is *liberty* (sometimes rendered as freedom or autonomy – see, generally, Goodin *et al.* 1999: 40–5). Liberals have traditionally been primarily concerned with freedom from interference (especially that of the state).

By contrast, social equality is the prime value for the social demo-cratic regime, for which the elimination of poverty is a minimum precondition (see generally Goodin *et al.* 1999: 45–51). This type of welfare regime aims at taking key social goods out of the market realm (literally by 'decommodifying' them). It emphasises redistribution (by means of provision of costly social services and benefits to all, while financing these from redistributive taxation). Alternatively these welfare states promote self-reliance (or autonomy) by weakening bonds of *social* dependence (Goodin 1985; Trägårdh 1997). It is tempt-ing to treat liberal and social democratic welfare states – both often rooted in Beveridge-style systems – as pursuing two distinct versions of autonomy. On the other hand, the conservative or Christian demo-cratic regimes pursue a different, status-oriented, conception of self-actualisation.

Equally, however, Goodin *et al.* argue that, in general terms, 'a broad consensus across all welfare regimes' exists over values that underpin the welfare state, the 'list of desiderata' or 'the terms in which capitalist welfare regimes of all stripes legitimize themselves to their publics'. They detect, moreover, a 'broad consensus ... across a broad range of commentators' on these values' (1999: 23). For all the emphasis placed on differences of objective and normative orientation, ultimately Goodin and colleagues come to a conclusion that integrates them all into a strict hierarchy of welfare state effectiveness: whatever criterion you chose, they claim, social democratic welfare states achieve it better than conservative-corporatist ones, while liberal welfare states perform least well of all.

Overall, then, welfare state analysis appears to be trapped between singularity and plurality. On the one hand, there tends to be an acceptance of a common feature shared by all western democracies that drives them to welfarism. On the other, welfare states seem to come in very different forms. More significantly, perhaps, the question of what is shared by welfare states in general and what is distinctive about particular regimes can be considered and understood in relation either to institutions or to underlying values or norms. We continue this chapter by focusing on diversity, considering the various 'worlds', regime-type clusters or social models into which welfare states have been classified.

Varieties of welfare capitalism

Thus far we have seen that *The Three Worlds of Welfare Capitalism* (1990) turned the idea that the welfare state might come in different institutional types into a conventional wisdom. Although he did not provide a definitive list of which states fell into each category, Esping-Andersen offered seemingly clear and sharp distinctions between liberal, conservative/corporatist and social democratic/socialist 'regimes', 'types' or 'clusters' (1990: 26–9; an approach echoed and developed in Goodin *et al.* 1999). While his definition of the welfare state regime was more encompassing and his argument placed stronger emphasis on politics, Esping-Andersen's three-fold categorisation closely echoed the distinctions between 'residual welfare', 'industrial achievement-performance' and 'institutional redistributive' models of social policy developed much earlier by Richard Titmuss (1974: 30–1; see also Esping-Andersen and Korpi 1984). That the clear distinctions he offered between different types of regime appeared to reflect the pattern of empirical differences between welfare states *and* echo the three major political ideologies that dominated post-war Europe added to the considerable allure of Esping-Andersen's framework. But that, if anything, has only exposed it to greater critical scrutiny.

Three worlds ... or four?

The Three Worlds of Welfare Capitalism prompted an immediate response, much of it arguing for the addition of a further type, model or regime. The Netherlands is not the only example of a country that does not fit easily into the framework Esping-Andersen provides. Indeed, in some cases, the critique of the framework hinges on an analysis of a single confounding or 'deviant' case. In some other instances, the difficulty may amount to rather more than fitting a particular state into pre-existing clusters. Instead, the distinctiveness of a whole group of states is identified and the case made that Esping-Andersen's schema risks mis-characterising them. In this latter vein, many commentators have proposed a fourth welfare regime-type, but no agreement exists about its key constitutive features, nor even which states fall into it. Often, the identification and labelling of the 'fourth world' is primarily geographic – distinctive welfare regimes associated with particular regions of the world (such as southern Europe or eastern Europe) – rather than being based on a conceptually grounded specification of key features of the welfare state. Although initially identified inductively through qualitative description, it is also possible to determine how far these (and other) regimes exist empirically, through analysis of variables relevant to welfare statehood. For this reason, we delay our discussion of these regimes until after we have considered dimensions of welfare state variation. For now we limit ourselves to noting that the map of comparative social policy generated by these debates is complex, with much of the attractive parsimony and clarity of Esping-Andersen's original formulation lost.

Perhaps the best developed 'four worlds' alternative to the liberal, conservative, social democratic triptych is one that compares overall levels of social expenditure with the extent of (in)equality in social benefits – effectively turning each of these *variables* into 'high' and 'low' *categories* – to generate four distinct types (Castles and Mitchell 1993, see Table 2.1 below). This framework retains the liberal and conservative categories, but identifies a third type in terms of 'non-right hegemony' rather than social democracy *per se* and a fourth 'radical' regime. This last category mostly distinguishes among Esping-Andersen's 'liberal' regimes, differentiating them on the basis of rela-

TABLE 2.1   *Castles' and Mitchell's categorisation of welfare regimes*

Two-dimensional welfare regime categorisation		Social security and welfare transfers to households as % of GDP	
		Low	*High*
Benefit equality (guaranteed social benefit/legal maximum benefit)	*Low*	**Liberal** Canada Japan Switzerland USA	**Conservative** Austria France Germany Italy Netherlands
	High	**Radical** Australia Finland Ireland New Zealand United Kingdom	**Non-right hegemony** Belgium Denmark Norway Sweden

Source: Adapted from Castles and Mitchell (1993).

tive inequality in benefit levels. States with a stronger Labour tradition – like Australia, the UK and New Zealand – constitute the 'radical' world.

Gender, dimensions of social policy and the French case

It is, finally, important to emphasise that most analyses of welfare regime 'types' are empirically based in the structure, generosity and balance between social insurance and social assistance schemes. The typical imagined beneficiary of these schemes is a (male) standard production worker. If gender issues were brought more squarely into focus then states would be seen to vary in ways that are not consistent with standard 'worlds of welfare' clusters. Here again a single state – France – has garnered particular attention. While the social democratic and liberal states offer social and market paths towards some change in gender roles, the 'Bismarckian' states of continental Europe typically appear more traditional. Although usually classified within the conservative/Bismarckian group as far as its social insurance institutions are concerned, the traditional 'breadwinner-homemaker' domestic model has been modified significantly as a result of state policy and social provision in France – and may have moved further in this direction than any state outside of the Nordic group (Lewis 1992). Arguably this change has developed out of natalist/nationalist concerns about the French birth rate (and a consequent desire to reconcile motherhood with women's other aspirations) and has been reinforced by extensive state education and care provision for young children (the latter a legacy of conflict between the state and the Catholic church over control of education – see Morgan 2003). We will return to some of these issues when we consider different dimensions of welfare provision below.

Dimensions of welfare statehood

The main general lesson drawn from conventional comparative welfare state analysis seems to be that we can identify more or less coherent welfare regime 'types' and cluster actually existing welfare states around them. Yet closer analysis typically reveals an even more complex picture. After our analysis of the relationship between decommodification and welfare state diversity, we consider another challenge to the understanding of worlds of welfare as distinct and internally coherent. Comparing welfare provision at the *programmatic* level, rather than on a cross-country basis, allows us to consider whether particular welfare states apply specific principles (such as universalism, Bismarckian corporatism or means-tested residualism) consistently across their social provision. At one end of the conceptual spectrum – that positing wholly distinct worlds – we might expect each domain of social policy to follow country-related provision-rules. At the other, variation in provision-rules might be linked to domains, not countries within different worlds of welfare.

In what follows we consider first the programmatic analysis undertaken by Robert Salais (2003). We then return to cross-state comparisons, considering the liberal, conservative and social democratic 'dimensions' of welfare statehood initially defined by Esping-Andersen (1990). Our primary concern here is with evidence as to whether states do, in fact, cluster into three distinct regime-types on these dimensions. Recent analyses have here criticised and developed Esping-Andersen's original approach. Using principal components analysis, scholars have determined that the underlying measures of welfare from which Esping-Andersen constructed his analysis generate two dimensions not three (Hicks and Kenworthy 2003; Scruggs and Pontusson 2008).

Moreover, this result appears to be sustained even when the range of welfare state activity included is expanded to include aspects of labour market regulation as well as policies relevant to gender and family issues. These analyses undercut the idea of worlds of welfare as groups of distinct, internally coherent states. However, if we use the factors identified in them to map the position of welfare states in two-dimensional space, there is some support for the idea that loose clusters may exist.

Decommodification

For Esping-Andersen (1990), as we have seen, decommodification defines the welfare state. Used to 'flesh out' the concept of social citizenship, at root decommodification involves an emancipation of 'individuals from market dependence' (1990: 20, 22). But here we are primarily concerned with its definition and operationalisation, rather than its conceptual roots and implications. Esping-Andersen argues that decommodification 'occurs when a service is rendered as a matter of right, and when a person can maintain a livelihood without reliance on the market' (1990: 21–2). He specifies the concept more precisely in relation to sickness insurance. Here decommodification would 'require ... that individuals be guaranteed benefits equal to normal earnings, and the right to absence with minimal proof of medical impairment and for the duration that the individual deems necessary'. As he goes on to suggest, 'similar requirements would be made of pensions, maternity leave, parental leave, educational leave and unemployment insurance' (Esping-Andersen 1990: 23).

This analysis raises an immediate problem. Have any states actually satisfied – or ever come close to satisfying – such a demanding definitional criterion? Clearly not many, if any – an answer that is likely to have deep implications for how we conceptualise the welfare state. Yet what is interesting is that their failure to 'qualify' as welfare states against this criterion has hardly deterred ordinary citizens, political leaders – or even the academics that set the unmet defining criteria – from continuing to describe all western democracies as welfare states (as, for example, does Esping-Andersen; see Wincott 2001a for an analysis). In other words, we persist in describing all – or almost all – western democracies as welfare states, despite the fact that most do not fully decommodify citizens and have never done so. Decommodification is basically conceptualised as a threshold: states that cross it are transformed into welfare states. The marriage of this single conceptual threshold to a division of welfare states into three distinct 'worlds' is somewhat surprising.

But there is a way out of this morass. For decommodification can be recast from a threshold into a scale against which welfare states can be measured, with different states identified as more or less effective in this respect. This allows us to assess the degree of decommodification even of welfare programmes with no ostensible commitment to decommod-ified outcomes. Somewhat ironically it turns out that this is precisely the strategy Esping-Andersen used to operationalise decommodifica-tion empirically.

The left hand side of Table 2.2 reproduces data on the rank-order of welfare states in terms of decommodification from *The Three Worlds of Welfare Captialism* (Esping-Andersen 1990: 52). There is, of course, considerable evidence of variability in these data – even though we have no real sense of the meaning of the scale, intuitively the fact that the lowest score is less than a third of the highest one is suggestive of difference. However, the sense that countries cluster into groups that reflect 'regime-types' on their decommodification scores is more contentious. Why, for example, should the UK and Italy be placed in different clusters? What are we to make of the fact that continental European countries span the top and middle categories? Perhaps most fundamentally, how have the three clusters been defined? The gaps between them are present in and reproduced from Esping-Andersen's original table, but no rationale or justification is presented – whether for having these gaps at all or regarding between which to states each gap is placed. While a clear case can be made for significant variation across countries, the impression that countries cluster into regime-related decommodification groups is, it seems, mostly a product of the visual presentation of the data, rather than the information it contains. It is, at least, hard to resist this conclusion.

Esping-Andersen's index of decommodification raises further prob-lems. Its empirical basis was never made clear and the underlying data from which it is calculated are not publicly available. Since decommod-ification is widely used as a defining feature of the welfare state, the absence of a publicly accessible measurement of the concept (ideally in a time series) was, for a long time, a major limitation. Fortunately, recent data collection and the construction of the Comparative Welfare Entitlements Dataset (CWED) led by Lyle Scruggs has filled this gap. CWED includes a measure of Welfare Benefit Generosity (WBG), which was developed as an approximation of the concept of decom-modification. Like decommodification, this measure (also shown in

TABLE 2.2 *Esping-Andersen's decommodification scores*

Decommodification scores in *The Three Worlds of Welfare Capitalism*		Welfare Benefit Generosity for 1980 (Scruggs and Allan)	
Australia	13.0	United States	18.7
United States	13.8	Japan	20.0
New Zealand	17.1	Australia	20.1
Canada	22.0	Italy	20.5
Ireland	23.3	Ireland	21.4
United Kingdom	23.4	United Kingdom	22.9
		New Zealand	23.3
Italy	24.1	Canada	25.0
Japan	27.3	Austria	27.8
France	27.5	France	27.8
Germany	27.7	Finland	27.9
Finland	29.2	Germany	28.8
Switzerland	29.8	Netherlands	31.8
		Switzerland	32.2
Austria	31.1	Belgium	32.9
Belgium	32.4	Denmark	32.9
Netherlands	32.4	Norway	33.4
Denmark	38.1	Sweden	38.4
Norway	38.3		
Sweden	39.1		
Mean	27.2	Mean	27.0
Standard deviation	7.7	Standard deviation	5.8
Coefficient of variation	0.28	Coefficient of variation	0.21

Sources: 1980 data from Esping-Andersen (1990: 52, table 2.2) and Scruggs and Allan (2006), replication from the Comparative Welfare Entitlements Dataset.

Table 2.2) displays considerable variation and the rank order of states is also broadly recognisable. However, some states have shifted their position in the order quite substantially over time. Perhaps more significantly, the level of variability in the WBG is much compressed compared to Esping-Andersen's measure of decommodification. This weakens the idea that clear clusters of states can be sharply distinguished from one another (Scruggs and Allan 2006). Equally, however, both rankings show a core group of Nordic countries (Sweden, Norway and Denmark) in the most generous positions, with the

Netherlands, Belgium and Germany also in the more generous half of the distribution on both measures and a group of English speaking countries with the lowest scores. Switzerland's strong score in both tables comes as something of a surprise.

Provision-rules and the programmatic comparison of welfare states

Programmatic comparison is arduous. It raises technical issues where, often, 'there is no exact solution' (Salais 2003: 330). But it is of potential considerable value. Such data typically start from the International Social Security Association's (ISSA) classification of social programmes in different fields according to provision-rules – universal, work-related and/or means-tested. Combining these classifications with data from the OECD, Salais has calculated 'an approximation of social expenditure in four categories': cash transfers (by the three provision-rules) plus in-kind services (2003: 330–4). The three provision-rules or 'policy types' echo 'worlds of welfare': universalism (associated with the social democratic world), work-related (conservative-corporatism) and means-tested (liberal-residual) benefits. The calculation process is not an exact science, yet it undoubtedly offers insights into the overall pattern of social provision.

Two major lessons can be drawn from this analysis. First, work-related programmes are generally dominant. Even in so-called 'universal' welfare states, work-based provision remains a crucial element of social protection. Given the range of programmes and issues covered by the welfare state, this should not be surprising. Most universal provision comes in the form of in-kind services suggesting that universalism is not, typically oriented towards equalising incomes, but facilitates equal access to some services (though family allowances – often a universal cash benefit – are a partial exception). Means-tested benefits appear to be the most unusual (only 22 from 108 systems) and combine to account for the smallest proportion of GDP (only 1.33 per cent). Two further points (neither wholly obvious from the table) need to be emphasised. First, most 'means tested systems' are 'concentrated in Anglo-Saxon countries (Australia, Canada, the United Kingdom, Ireland and New Zealand)' (Salais 2003: 330). Second, no country uses 'the same rule for all risks, whether it be universal, work-related, or means-tested. Even the countries that most focus on a particular rule do not apply it to every risk, and often combined two, sometimes three rules for a single risk at the same time or in succession' (Salais 2003:

TABLE 2.3 'Policy-types', provision-rules and social expenditure, 1995

Type of expenditure		Rule of provision				Totals (no. of dual regimes)
		Universal (cash benefit spending)	Work-related (cash benefit spending)	Means-tested (cash benefit spending)	In-kind services	
1. Old age, disability, survivors	No. of programmes	8	26	3		37 (10)
	Expenditure as % GDP	2.09	5.94	0.83	0.76	9.62
3. Occupational injury and disease	No. of programmes	1	27	0		28 (1)
	Expenditure as % GDP	0	0.26	0	0	0.26
4. Sickness	No. of programmes	9	24	3		36 (9)
	Expenditure as % GDP	0	0.48	0.05	5.86	6.39
7. Family	No. of programmes	15	7	8		30 (3)
	Expenditure as % GDP	0.88	0.2	0.22	0.45	1.75
10. Un-employment	No. of programmes	0	24	8		32 (5)
	Expenditure as % GDP	0.13	1.26	0.23	0.56	2.29
Total	No. of programmes	33	108	22		163
	Expenditure as % GDP	3.10	8.13	1.33	7.63	20.31

Source: Calculated from Salais (2003: 331, 334: tables 12.1 and 12.2).

Notes: Calculations based on ISSA and OECD data. Row numbers based on OECD Social Expenditure Database classification of social protection. (Database covers 27 OECD countries – Poland and Hungary excluded.)

330–1). In other words, gradations of difference are present among 'actually existing' welfare models or regimes.

A second core observation is that, across welfare states, particular provision-rules or policy types predominate in certain social policy fields. So, for example, risks associated with sickness appear to be addressed overwhelmingly through in-kind services. The vast majority of spending on in-kind services is incurred in relation to sickness, where all universal provision appears to be in the form of these services. The only category of spending that exceeds in-kind services for the sick is that related to old age, disability and survivors. Here, in-kind services appear to play a much smaller role. While work-related provision dominates cash benefits (and is the largest single spending category), significant spending on pensions and related benefits is also incurred in the universal category.

To the extent that the 'worlds of welfare' concept suggests that welfare states are internally homogenous and fall into mutually distinct groups, it is misleading. No welfare state relies wholly on any one provision-rule for its social policies and countries tend to deploy similar provision-rules within particular social policy domains. Nevertheless, analysis of programme-level evidence does show that welfare states differ from one another. Broadly speaking, universal provision is more prominent in Nordic states and means testing mostly concentrated in the English-speaking countries. If the idea of wholly distinct models or types is unsustainable, in terms of their broad social policy dispositions, states may still differ and perhaps even cluster into more or less tightly defined groups.

Welfare state dimensions

Even within the genre-defining analyses of 'worlds of welfare', detailed analysis of state welfare provision shows that individual cases display features associated with more than one regime. Table 2.4 reproduces the classic categorisation and scores for liberal, conservative and socialist welfare regime features (Esping-Andersen 1990: 74). For the most part, the countries seen as archetypes are found among those that show 'strong' features of that kind of welfare policy. However, this distribution of 'regime attributes' across countries suggests a complex mosaic at least as much as it displays a clear 'grouping' or clustering into distinct regime-types. Moreover, three countries – the UK, New Zealand and Ireland – do not display strong features of any welfare state 'type'.

TABLE 2.4   *Esping-Andersen's degrees of conservatism, liberalism and socialism in welfare states*

Degree of Conservatism		Liberalism	Socialism
Strong	Austria (8)	Australia (10)	Denmark (8)
	Belgium (8)	Canada (12)	Finland (6)
	France (8)	Switzerland (12)	Netherlands (6)
	Germany (8)	United States (12)	Norway (8)
	Italy (8)		Sweden (8)
Medium	Finland (6)	Denmark (6)	Australia (4)
	Ireland (4)	France (8)	Belgium (4)
	Japan (4)	Germany (6)	Canada (4)
	Netherlands (4)	Italy (6)	Germany (4)
	Norway (4)	Netherland (8)	New Zealand (4)
		United Kingdom (6)	Switzerland (4)
			United Kingdom (4)
Weak	Australian (0)	Austria (4)	Austria (2)
	Canada (2)	Belgium (4)	France (2)
	Denmark (2)	Finland (4)	Ireland (2)
	New Zealand (2)	Ireland (2)	Italy (0)
	Sweden (0)	New Zealand (2)	Japan (2)
	Switzerland (0)	Norway (0)	United States (0)
	United Kingdom (0)	Sweden (0)	
	United States (0)		

Source: Esping-Andersen (1990, 74, table 3.3), based on data from 1980.

In addition, these scores have a rather elusive quality. For their basis remains obscure. Thus, the scale for liberalism is a third longer than those for socialism and conservatism, because three underlying elements go to make it up while the other dimensions are based on only two underlying indicators – but no convincing rationale is given for this difference. Nor is it clear why a score of 6 sees Finland classified as 'medium' in terms of conservatism, but the same score places both Finland and the Netherlands in the 'strongly socialist' category. More consistent ranking of the scores would see Finland 'promoted' to strong conservatism, which would have meant a single country showing strong characteristics of two regime-types. Finally, as with presentation of data on decommodification, to the extent that this table suggests a clear 'clustering' of states into regime-types within and across these three dimensions, it appears to be an artifact of the presentation of the table rather than emerging directly from the data themselves.

As with decommodification, the underlying data on which Esping-Andersen's dimensions of welfare state stratification are based remain somewhat obscure. Moreover, serious questions have been asked about the scoring process and coding decisions involved. Re-analysis undertaken following broadly the same underlying logic, but using newly constructed indices and publicly accessible data presents a somewhat different picture, with much less evidence of the clear clustering of states into three 'regime type' groups (Scruggs and Allan 2008). For example, both Denmark and Canada show strong features of liberalism *and* socialism. These data can also be replicated for more recent time periods, so rather than treating characteristics from around 1980 as permanently defining of a welfare regime, we can begin to consider questions of change over time. In Table 2.5, we report regime dimension scores for eighteen states in the early 1980s and early 2000s, noting those states that occupy a different position to that allocated to them by Esping-Andersen in bold. And there are some striking differences. Particularly notable are the 'Anglo-Saxon' countries, the UK and Canada especially – both of which appear in the strong socialist category at *each* time point. Similarly, Finland seems more conservative than socialist in character.

Three dimensions or two?

Further analysis strongly reinforces the idea that welfare states diversity might be better understood primarily in terms of *dimensions* rather than *types*. Principal components analysis can help to identify structural patterns within quantitative data. In this context, essentially, it provides scores that locate countries along one or more dimensions uncovered in the data. Applied to the indicators that underpin Esping-Andersen's measures of conservatism, liberalism or socialism in state welfare provision, this technique generates some very interesting results (Hicks and Kenworthy 2003; Scruggs and Pontusson 2008; see also Table 2.5). Rather than three dimensions of welfare statehood, the empirical analyses suggest that there are only two (although authors differ over their precise character).

Esping-Andersen's welfare state dimensions are narrowly focused on social insurance. Hicks and Kenworthy extend their analysis to include other aspects of the welfare state. In particular they measure labour market and family policies alongside those for social insurance. Their 'full' model also includes Esping-Andersen's decommodification index plus a measure of income security spending as a proportion of GDP:

TABLE 2.5 Degrees of conservatism, liberalism and socialism in welfare states, early 1980s and early 2000s

Degree of	Conservatism		Liberalism		Socialism	
	Early 1980s	Early 2000s	Early 1980	Early 2000s	Early 1980s	Early 2000s
Strong	Austria (8) Finland (8) France (8) Germany (8) Italy (8)	Austria (8) Finland (8) France (8)	Australia (12) Canada (12) USA (12) Denmark (10) Japan (10) Swit. (10)	Australia (12 Canada (12) USA (12) Denmark (10) Japan (10) Swit. (10)	UK (8) Canada (6) Denmark (6) Netherlands (6) Sweden (6)	Denmark (8) Ireland (8) Belgium (6) Canada (6) Norway (6) Sweden (6) UK (6)
Medium	Belgium (6) Japan (6) Norway (4) Sweden (4) USA (4)	Belgium (6) Norway (6) Italy (4) Germany (4) Japan (4) UK (4) USA (4)	Finland (8) France (8) UK (8) Germany (6) Netherlands1 (6) NZ (6)	Finland (8) NZ (8) UK (8) France (6) Germany (6) Ireland (6) Netherlands (6) Norway (6)	Australia (4) Austria (4) Belgium (4) France (4) Germany (4) Ireland (4) NZ (4) Norway (4) Switzerland (4)	Australia (4) Austria (4) Finland (4) Germany (4) Netherlands (4) NZ (4)
Weak	Denmark (2) Ireland (2) Ntl (2) UK (2) Australia (0) Canada (0) NZ (0) Switzerland (0)	Australia (2) Denmark (2) Ireland (2) Ntl (2) Sweden (2) Canada (0) NZ (0) Switzerland (0)	Austria (4) Ireland (4) Norway (4) Belgium (2) Italy (2) Sweden (2)	Austria (4) Belgium (4) Italy (4) Sweden (4)	Finland (2) Italy (2) Japan (0) USA (0)	France (2) Italy (2) Japan (2) Switzerland (2) USA (0)

Source: Calculated from Scruggs and Allan (2008: 662, table 5).

these elements are excluded from their pared-down model because they are core outputs of the welfare state (2003: 34–5). Their basic result stands for the wider models. It generates two factors, along broadly similar lines. The idea of welfare states varying along these two dimensions is attractive, perhaps reflecting differences between the Bismarckian and Beveridgean traditions or 'autonomy' and 'status' oriented approaches.

Yet enticing though it may be, because this analysis relies on Esping-Andersen's indicators (and his scoring and coding protocols), it is vulnerable to the same criticisms that have previously been levelled against *The Three Worlds* (Scruggs and Allan 2006, 2008). Re-analysis using alternative public domain data generates results that share some key features of Hicks and Kenworthy, but also differ in important respects. Scruggs and Pontusson (2008) re-analyse the 'fully' extended model of welfare regime dimensions. They also find two dimensions of welfare statehood, not three, but differ as to the character of these dimensions. The first factor varies between conservative and liberal features, with the second identifying a distinct 'egalitarian' dimension. While the relative position of various states does change, the basic 'dimensional' structure found for data from the early 1980s remains in place in the early 2000s.

Alongside analysis at the programmatic level, empirical investigation of the dimensions along which welfare states vary as a whole has serious implications for the 'worlds of welfare' idea. The notion of three internally coherent and distinctly different worlds or types is seriously compromised by this research (though Esping-Andersen, we should recall, expressed reservations himself about the existence of 'pure types' – 1990: 28). It is, however, worth considering whether empirical *clusters* of states can be detected in the two-dimensional space of conservatism-liberalism and egalitarianism. The two broadly similar dimensions are present, it appears, in both years. So, while comparisons across analyses of principal components for different time periods may lack precision, we may be able to gain a general indication of whether – and, if so, how – these clusters have changed over time.

This view of the data appears relatively familiar. It suggests that a reasonably close cluster of continental European states existed in the early 1980s. The Anglo-Saxon countries all appear in the lower, liberal half of the table, although this is probably better described as a loose grouping than a cluster of any kind. What is most striking for this period is the absence of a socialist-egalitarian cluster. Sweden stands

TABLE 2.6 *Conservative–liberal and egalitarian dimensions of welfare states, 1980 and 2002*

Country	Conservative–Liberal 1980	Country	Egalitarian 1980	Country	Conservative–Liberal 2002	Country	Egalitarian 2002
France	1.33	Sweden	2.34	France	1.92	Denmark	2.39
Belgium	1.32	UK	1.35	Austria	1.24	Sweden	1.59
Italy	1.2	Denmark	1.07	Belgium	1.05	Norway	0.97
Germany	1.05	Norway	0.46	Finland	0.82	Belgium	0.59
Austria	0.98	Belgium	0.43	Sweden	0.8	Ireland	0.53
Sweden	0.84	Canada	0.38	Italy	0.7	Canada	0.44
Finland	0.74	NZ	0.3	Germany	0.63	Finland	0.21
Norway	0.49	Netherlands	0.27	Norway	0.57	UK	0.21
Netherlands	0.1	Ireland	0.25	Netherlands	0.23	NZ	-0.19
Japan	-0.32	France	-0.24	Japan	-0.34	France	-0.2
Ireland	-0.51	Australia	-0.32	UK	-0.57	Netherlands	-0.21
Denmark	-0.66	Finland	-0.37	USA	-0.59	Germany	-0.25
UK	-0.75	Germany	-0.49	Denmark	-0.82	Australia	-0.51
USA	-0.75	Switzerland	-0.58	Ireland	-0.89	Austria	-0.89
Switzerland	-1.07	Austria	-0.67	Switzerland	-0.91	Italy	-0.91
NZ	-1.11	Italy	-0.84	NZ	-1.09	Switzerland	-0.93
Australia	-1.38	USA	-1.39	Australia	-1.16	USA	-1.39
Canada	-1.5	Japan	-1.95	Canada	-1.59	Japan	-1.43

Source: Calculated from Scruggs and Pontusson (2008).

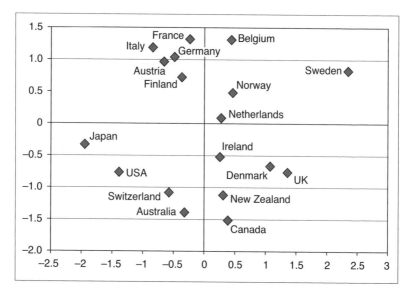

Source: Based on data from Scruggs and Pontusson (2008).

FIGURE 2.1   *Conservative–liberal (Y-axis) and egalitarian (X-axis)
dimensions of welfare statehood, early 1980s*

out as strongly egalitarian, and Finland sits in the non-egalitarian half
of the distribution. Equally, these states also differ in their placement
on the conservative-liberal dimension, with Denmark standing out as
particularly liberal, while other Nordic states appear to have surprisingly strong conservative characteristics. Overall, though, if we treat
them as bundles of characteristics rather than ontological categories,
these data do show some evidence of clustering. While challenging
conventional assumptions in some respects, the patterns revealed in
this analysis are relatively familiar in others.

Turning to the more recent period, we can make a broadly similar
argument. While the conservative cluster was most clearly defined in
the early 1980s, it seems to have become much looser by the early
2000s, largely as a result of many states becoming more liberal – a
tendency from which only France appears to stand out. On the other
hand, the majority of these states remain in the top left-hand 'conser-
vative-non-egalitarian' quadrant. All the English-speaking states
remain in the bottom 'liberal' half of the graph and the surprising

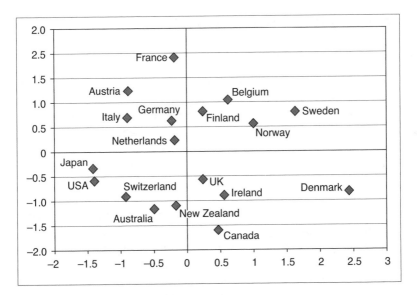

Source: Based on data from Scruggs and Pontusson (2008).

FIGURE 2.2 *Conservative–liberal (Y-axis) and egalitarian (X-axis) dimensions of welfare statehood, early 2000s*

egalitarian initial score for the UK weakened substantially (as did that for New Zealand). On the other hand, Ireland's already relatively strong egalitarianism strengthened over this period. Although it would probably still stretch the pint to call this grouping a cluster, it does seem to be tighter in the early 2000s than it had been in the 1980s. Finally, while the Nordic countries remain fairly widely dispersed (particularly on the conservative-liberal dimension), by the early 2000s they have emerged more clearly as the leading egalitarian welfare states.

We have found substantial conceptual and empirical grounds on which to criticise the conventional 'worlds of welfare' approach to social policy diversity. Yet beyond these, there does seem to be a sense in which the welfare states of western Europe – and the established wealthy democracies more generally – do differ and, to an extent, cluster into loose groups empirically. This finding does not revive any notion of clearly distinct worlds of welfare, but it may help to account for the enduring and recurring attraction of such a conception.

Three regime-clusters or more?

'Southern' and 'eastern' regimes

Although less conceptually sophisticated, perhaps the most popular way of adding a fourth 'world' is the identification of a geographically based cluster of states that seem to share some distinctive features. The question of whether distinct regimes exist in central and eastern or southern Europe is much more pertinent to our concerns here. The idea of a 'southern European' or 'Mediterranean' regime is well established academically and has had some impact on policy debates (Leibfried 1992; Ferrera 1996; Rhodes 1997; Sapir 2006). Comprising Greece, Italy, Portugal and Spain, this social 'model' tends to concentrate spending on older people – particularly for pensions – and to protect the employment status of those in work as a priority over providing unemployment insurance for those who lose their jobs (Sapir 2005, 2006).

There is less clarity about the existence of a 'type' or 'model' of welfare state shared by the former communist states. During the initial transition, social policy analysts generally regarded central and Eastern Europe as sharing a model, although some regarded this as a transitory phase (Deacon 2000).

In recent years empirical comparisons that include this wider group of southern and eastern countries with those of western Europe (and typically some North American and Antipodean states as well) have begun to appear (Fenger 2007; Draxler and Van Vliet 2010). Generally using cluster analysis, they typically identify two major clusters, each made up of a number of significant sub-clusters. The more expansive group is made up of the older welfare states and typically includes all northern and western European countries. In general, the pattern shown by these states is reasonably familiar – the usual three clusters show up clearly in Fenger's analysis (2007), but while Draxler and Van Vliet (2010) distinguish a liberal cluster, they find the Nordic and continential European countries intermixed. The former communist countries typically fall within the other cluster. Importantly, these studies do not agree on the position of southern European states as between these two major clusters. Fenger (2007) identifies southern Europe as a sub-group within the conservative regime-type, in effect an underdeveloped version of continental Bismarckianism, while Draxler and Van Vliet (2010) find southern Europe mixed in with the former communist states.

As far as central and eastern Europe is concerned, the initial tendency to treat the former communist bloc as a distinct and coherent regime type was understood to be temporary, and likely to be undone by subsequent developments (Deacon 1992), although some scholars have returned to the idea more recently (Cerami 2005). As time has passed and more detailed analyses have developed, the differences between the paths followed by various states in central and eastern Europe have been emphasised more strongly. So, Estonia, Lithuanian and Latvia appear to have followed a relatively 'residual' path and cluster fairly closely together in empirical analyses (see Fenger 2007; Draxler and Van Vliet 2010). This residualism is arguably characteristic of the successor states that emerged from the Soviet Union – Fenger (2007) describes this as a 'Former-USSR' cluster – and in the Baltic states it has also featured some nationality-based discrimination against ethnic Russians (Feldmann 2006; Fenger 2007; Bohle and Greskovits 2009; Bohle 2010).

Ideational influences from Germany together with social insurance legacies from the communist period – and even earlier – seem to have been stronger in central Europe. Fenger (2007) identifies a post-communist European cluster made up of Bulgaria, Croatia, the Czech Republic, Hungary, Poland and Slovakia (his analysis does not include Slovenia). Other analysts detect greater variability across these states. While the levels of provision always remained significantly lower than in the west, most central European states have continued to emphasise social insurance more than social assistance – although Hungary may be a partial exception here (see Nelson 2010). Even where countries took a clear neoliberal turn – as in Slovakia after 2002 – commentators do not detect a complete replacement of inherited welfare structures by a new 'neoliberal regulatory state' (Fisher, Gould and Haughton 2007). Of course, the relative economic strength of states in central and eastern Europe also makes a difference, particularly in relation to the development and sustainability of Bismarckian style provision, with the Czech Republic and Slovenia identified as relatively prosperous (Feldmann 2006). Some eastern European states – such as Romania (which Fenger 2007 describes as a developing welfare state) and perhaps Bulgaria – operate at a significantly lower level of development, in both economic and social terms.

Differences between the welfare regimes of the former communist states in central and eastern Europe raise questions about whether they form a clear cluster. More research and better data is required before we will be in a position to provide clear and robust answers to these questions. Nevertheless, existing comparative analysis indicates that in terms of their welfare effort, all these states fall below their western neighbours (Fenger 2007; Draxler and Van Vliet 2010). Intriguingly, however, Draxler and Van Vliet (2010) suggest that the states of eastern and southern Europe may form one large cluster.

Conclusion

The idea that welfare states cluster in 'types', or form distinctly different (and by implication largely self-contained) 'worlds', has proven enormously seductive. This idea has dominated academic analysis and been influential within policy debate. The attraction of a small number of conceptually appealing and ideologically distinctive welfare regime types is clear. The 'regime-types' notion remains valuable as a conceptual heuristic, or means of conceptual clarification (sharing some characteristics of an ideal type).

But the assumption or assertion that 'actually existing' welfare states cluster tightly around these conceptual types is, it appears, much more difficult to sustain. Indeed, Esping-Andersen's original framework turns out to have been much more complex than it might have appeared at first glance. As we have seen, it juxtaposed three seemingly distinct worlds of welfare, three dimensions of welfare state variation and a singular defining concept of decommodification. Scrutinising this original work on regimes (Esping-Andersen 1990), we have seen that the clusters turn out to have been an artifact of data-presentation as much as the result of forensic empirical analysis. Moreover, the (relatively inaccessible) underlying data used in this analysis and the coding decisions used to construct indicators from it have been subjected to strong criticism (Scruggs and Allan 2006, 2008).

In addition, the temptation to elaborate on the *Three Worlds* framework has proven irresistible. But this process has only complicated – and thereby muddied – the attractive clarity and parsimony of Esping-Andersen's original analysis. The underlying idea of categorising regimes into types, or of defining social models, remains very popular. It is, however, not always clear precisely which conceptual or empirical distinctions underpin the differences between these models. As a consequence, despite using the language of types and models, the original framework of conceptual categories sometimes seems to have been replaced by a pattern of almost continuous variation across numerous social models or regime-types – sometimes even of individual states.

One other important issue should be raised at this point. We have seen that the language of welfare regime-types or distinct social models has proven attractive to analysts of southern, east–central and eastern Europe. Although some important empirical analyses of these states have begun to be published (Fenger 2007; Draxler and Van Vliet 2010), these countries have not yet been fully integrated into the cutting-edge analyses that have been developed for western Europe, northern America and the Antipodes. As a consequence, we have not been able to integrate the experience of these countries as fully into this part of our analysis as we would have liked.

Recently, major efforts have been made to reconstruct the basis of the *Three Worlds* approach and to place it on a firmer empirical footing. However, attempts to replicate the original analysis using these data do not support the idea of clear and distinctly different clusters, although do show significant cross-country variation (Scruggs and Allan 2006, 2008). Moreover, these differences among countries exhibit some structure, although the variation is across two (not three) dimensions of welfare statehood. Even so, we find evidence of states *clustering* into recognisable groups within this two-dimensional space.

Putting this all together, on the one hand we have accumulated considerable evidence to show that states do not form tightly defined, internally coherent and distinctly different *types* or *worlds*. Indeed, every welfare state uses multiple provision-rules in its social policy (Salais 2003). So differences among countries may best be understood as variations along *dimensions* of welfare statehood. Yet, on the other hand empirical analysis provides a clear basis for the idea that welfare states form *clusters*. So, while we criticise the conventional wisdom that welfare states come in types, interrogation of welfare regime clusters, particularly as they change over time, remains a fruitful task of social and political analysis – and arguably an essential one in the context of policy responses to the credit crunch of the late 2000s.

Chapter 3

Globalisation, Europeanisation and the Welfare State

In this chapter we present a detailed assessment of the extent to which exogenous pressures — principally globalisation and European economic integration — might be seen to create distinct pressures for welfare reform and retrenchment in contemporary Europe. We review the theoretical arguments that posit a connection between the globalisation of trade, finance and foreign direct investment on the one hand and the need for welfare reform on the other, before examining in empirical detail the claim that European economies have been globalised and that this has served to reward (in terms of economic performance) welfare residualism. We present a similar analysis of the process of European economic integration, arguing on the basis of the empirical evidence that European integration is a rather more significant factor in the process of contemporary welfare reform in contemporary Europe than globalisation, but that neither can account for observed welfare retrenchment. This suggests the significance of a range of endogenous factors, considered in Chapter 4.

It is increasingly difficult to discuss welfare reform and the trajectories of European welfare states more generally without immediately considering the concept of globalisation. For in recent years there is quite simply no single factor that has attracted anything like the attention received by globalisation in both public and academic debate about the future of the welfare state. In much, though by no means all of this, the welfare state is cast as a somewhat outdated institutional legacy of a time and a politics now long since gone. Indeed, the persistence of public welfare institutions which betray anything of their origins is now often taken as an index of an economy's failure to embrace the new times ushered in with the advent of globalisation (for instance Tanzi and Schuknecht 2000).

As this suggests, globalisation is widely seen to pose a serious challenge to the welfare state, certainly as developed in much of Europe in the post-war years. Good economic performance in an ever more tightly integrated world economy, in such a view, is likely to correlate closely with a willingness, if not perhaps to dismantle the welfare state in its entirety, then certainly to engage in wholesale welfare reform and significant retrenchment.

The typical argument here casts the welfare state simply as a fiscal burden – an additional and unnecessary cost which businesses and citizens must bear, thereby suppressing the former's profits and willingness to invest and the latter's spending power. In the intensely competitive environment ushered in by the globalisation of markets, so the argument goes, the welfare state is a drain on competitiveness and economic performance – an increasingly anachronistic luxury of a bygone era.

It is this thesis and the assorted propositions on which it is based that we explore in this chapter. To do so we need to establish what globalisation is and why it might be seen to pose so profound a challenge to inclusive welfare states. It is to these tasks that we turn first.

Globalisation and welfare retrenchment: a question of semantics

Given the seeming certainty with which so many commentators discern the consequences of globalisation for welfare reform and the viability of the welfare state, once might expect a clearly expressed and highly conserved understanding of the term within the existing literature. Yet nothing could be further from the truth.

Globalisation is in fact a generic term for a rather disparate array of things and, where it is defined at all, it is understood in a great variety of different ways. For the most part, however, these understandings can be arrayed along a continuum. This ranges from the geographically least precise and inexacting to the geographically most restrictive and demanding. At the definitionally inexacting end of the spectrum, to point to globalisation means little more than to identify cross-border flows of goods, services, finance, migrants and so forth. By contrast, at the definitionally demanding end of the spectrum, such flows need to be increasingly planetary in their scope to be regarded as evidence of globalisation. Yet this is not the only definitional divide. It is important also to distinguish between contending understandings of globalisation in terms of whether they see globalisation as a condition or property of the world system (or of the units from which it is comprised) that has *already been achieved* or as a *still ongoing* process or tendency (which may be resisted) for the world system (or the units within it) to become more global or global*ised* over time.

The crucial point is that such definitional choices have significant implications – both for whether we see evidence of globalisation or not and, indeed, for the significance of any such observation. Clearly, if to confirm the globalisation thesis we need only show a proliferation of cross-border flows of goods, services and so forth, then evidence of globalisation abounds. But, and this is perhaps the key point, understood in this way globalisation may be rather less significant a factor than we tend to assume. Conversely, if to confirm the globalisation thesis we need to establish that such flows are in fact both increasingly *extensive* in their (planetary) scope and increasingly *intensive* in their magnitude, then evidence of globalisation is going to be rather more difficult to find – but all the more significant if, as and when we do find it (on extensity and intensity, see Held *et al.* 1999).

There is clearly plenty of room for conceptual confusion here. Authors who may well agree on the facts themselves may nonetheless disagree over the extent of globalisation simply because they impose upon the term different definitional standards. Indeed, on closer inspection what may seem at first like a dispute over the evidence itself often boils down to little more than a semantic difference of opinion (compare, for instance, Hirst and Thompson 1999, 2000 and Perraton *et al.* 1997, with O'Rourke and Williamson 1999, 2002 and Frank and Gills 1993). This makes it all the more important that we are clear from the start about what we mean by globalisation – whatever that happens to be – and fully aware of the implications of our choice for the significance of identifying evidence of globalisation.

But it is at least equally important that we are consistent. And herein lies a second problem with much of the existing literature and, indeed, the public debate on globalisation. As we shall see presently, when it comes to demonstrating that we live in a 'globalised' world, many commentators appeal explicitly or, far more likely, implicitly, to the most inexacting of definitional standards. In making the case for globalisation, they show a proliferation of cross-border flows and little more. Yet, having ostensibly demonstrated 'globalisation' in this way, they then invariably go on to infer from it a variety of highly significant effects. This they do typically by assuming the existence of a perfectly integrated single world market, for which of course they have presented no evidence whatsoever. In other words, they switch from the least to perhaps the most exacting of definitional standards at precisely the point at which they turn from evidential induction to logical deduction. The effect is to exaggerate the significance of the 'actually existing' globalisation they have demonstrated.

The full implications of this become clear if we look at those theories that suggest that globalisation and the welfare state are likely to be in significant tension with one another. For, as we shall see, what many of these share is a common analytical structure in which the effects for the welfare state (and, in particular, the taxation receipts out of which it is funded) of globalisation are derived logically from a series of stylised assumptions about both the behaviour and motives of business and the degree of integration of the world economy. It is to such theories directly that we now turn.

Globalisation against the welfare state: the 'incommensurability' thesis

The damage which globalisation is widely seen to inflict on the welfare state and, in particular, the capacity to fund the welfare state out of taxation receipts, is attributed in most models to one of two related factors. These are: (i) the increased mobility of capital under conditions of globalisation; and (ii) the drain on profits that high non-wage labour costs and levels of corporate taxation are seen to represent. It is worth considering each in turn.

Capital mobility

Somewhat ironically, the logic of the argument here is perhaps best captured by Adam Smith in his *Inquiry into the Nature and Causes of the Wealth of Nations* published in 1776. This, it might be protested, is hardly the high point of globalisation in most accounts. Yet it is remarkable quite how prescient Adam Smith is in capturing, in the following passage, the essence of the contemporary case against the welfare state.

> The . . . proprietor of stock is properly a citizen of the world, and is not necessarily attached to any particular country. He would be apt to abandon the country in which he is exposed to a vexatious inquisition, in order to be assessed a burdensome tax, and would remove his stock to some country where he could either carry on his business or enjoy his fortune at his ease. A tax that tended to drive away stock from a particular country, would so far tend to dry up every source

of revenue, both to the sovereign and to the society. Not only the profits of stock, but the rent of land and the wages of labour, would necessarily be more or less diminished by its removal. (Smith 1776 [1976]: 848–9).

In its more contemporary form, the argument goes something like this. In closed national economies in which domestic producers serve domestic demand, capital is essentially national in character and immobile. It has no 'exit' option and must simply endure whatever levels of direct and indirect corporate taxation are imposed upon it by the state. At worst, punitive levels of taxation are likely to result in the decision to save rather than invest any profits made and to shed capacity and sell off plant and machinery where possible to augment such savings. Relocation to another less punitive tax jurisdiction is not an option. In such an environment, the state retains the capacity, if it so chooses, to fund generous welfare provision through a combination of income and corporate taxation. Capital is relatively impotent, save other than for its ability to hoard rather than to reinvest profits.

Under open economy conditions this is no longer the case. Capital may now choose where to locate its investments. This has the effect of bringing tax jurisdictions into competition with one another as they strive to attract and retain mobile investors. Mobility, in such a model, is the key to power – and capital is more mobile than labour. In other words, by playing off the regulatory regimes of different economies against one another, capital can ensure for itself the most favourable of investment environments.

Yet there is, of course, an additional assumption here – namely that economies characterised by high levels of welfare expenditure are unlikely to provide or, perhaps more importantly, are unlikely to *be seen by capital to provide* such an investment environment. For it is assumed in such models that capital will display a rational preference for low taxation regimes over high taxation regimes, welfare residualism over a comprehensive welfare state, and flexible labour markets, a largely un-unionised workforce and lapse environmental regulations over the converse. This brings us directly to the second element of the case against the welfare state.

The welfare state as a drain on profits

This, too, is simply stated – and it is likely to have a familiar ring to it. Capital is predicted to use whatever mobility it has in an era of globalisation to flee the high taxation environments with which generous welfare provision is associated *because such taxation represents a drain on profits*. Put slightly differently, whether they are mobile or not, businesses having to contribute through taxation to the costs of a generous welfare state are put at a competitive disadvantage by virtue of the additional costs they must bear relative to their competitors. Moreover, in a genuinely global market place they cannot pass such costs on to the consumer without a consequent loss in market share.

There is, of course, an intuitive plausibility about the claim that high taxation reduces profits, particularly where, as in a global market place, additional costs cannot easily be passed on to the consumer. But we need to proceed with a certain degree of caution here. For, to present the welfare state as nothing other than a drain on profits to business is to look only at the debit side of the balance sheet. As we shall see in far greater detail in Chapter 4, in a whole variety of ways the welfare state might be seen to contribute to economic performance. Such advantages to capital might include: (i) the ability of employers to rely on a healthy, educated and contented workforce; (ii) the stimulus to aggregate demand across the business cycle which comes from ensuring that there is redistribution from the most affluent to the least wealthy (who are more likely to spend rather than save any boost to their income); (iii) the macroeconomic stabilising effects of the stimulus to demand that comes in the form of benefits in times of recession; and (iv) the increase in the quality and supply of labour that comes with policies, such as the provision or subsidisation by the state of childcare, designed to broaden labour-market participation. In these and, indeed, many other respects, the welfare state may be seen to contribute to economic performance, particularly in economies that compete principally in markets that are more quality than price sensitive (see Hay 2011b). Whether, in the end, the welfare state is a net contributor to, or a net drain on, profitability, productivity and growth is likely to vary from case to case. It is an issue to which we return in far greater detail in Chapter 4.

As this already begins to suggest, is it useful to isolate the assumptions on which both variants of the incommensurability thesis are predicated and to consider how dependent its rather bleak vision of the welfare state is on such assumptions.

These assumptions are principally four-fold. They are summarised in Box 3.1.

The first thing to note about these assumptions is that the first three of them, at least, are fairly conventional in contemporary open economy macroeconomic theory (see, for instance, Obstfeld and Rogoff

BOX 3.1   The core assumptions of the 'incommensurability'
thesis

1. Capital is rational, profit-maximising and blessed with perfect information – consequently it can be assumed to invest where it can secure
   the greatest net return on its investment.
2. Markets for goods, services and investment are fully integrated globally. National economies must prove themselves globally competitive
   if economic growth is to be sustained and competitiveness is the ability to bring a given good or service to market for less than ones
   competitors.
3. Capital is perfectly mobile between national taxation and regulatory
   jurisdictions and the cost of 'exit' (or disinvestment) is either zero or
   can be discounted.
4. Since the welfare state increases the burden of taxation and since price
   is an index of competitiveness, the welfare state is a drain on both
   national competitiveness and the profits of business.

Source: Adapted and developed from Hay (2008).

1996; Rødseth 2000; Ugur 2001). Indeed, since the fourth is arguably
no more than a logical correlate of the other three, it might well be
argued that they are all conventional in neoclassical economic terms.
This might be seen to commend them to the analyst. But, it is important
to note that, somewhat perversely perhaps, such assumptions are
adopted in open economy macroeconomic theory not because they are
deemed to be accurate, but despite the fact that they are not. Their
appeal in fact lies in their simplicity. For this makes possible the
construction of the kind of formal models of the macroeconomy that
are the modern macroeconomist's *raison d'être*. In other words, the
inaccuracy of these assumptions is freely conceded by economic theorists whose justification for choosing them is purely technical. The
point is that such a defence is simply not available to proponents of the
incommensurability thesis in the literature on the welfare state whose
borrowings from neoclassical economics rarely if ever extend past the
assumptions to the algebra.

This is an important point in its own right, but it is by no means the
most important point here. Certainly no less significant than the accu-
racy of the assumptions is the sensitivity of the predictions that the
thesis generates to changes in such assumptions. Here it is useful to
differentiate between those assumptions that relate principally to the

conduct and motivations of capital itself and those which relate principally to the environment in which capital finds itself. In fact, the
predicted incommensurability between globalisation and the welfare
state is rather more sensitive to changes in the assumptions relating to
the latter than it is to changes in assumptions relating to the former. It
is useful to consider why this might be so.

It is, of course, unrealistic to assume that capital is blessed with
perfect knowledge of how best to maximise the return on any potential
investment it might make. But arguably this doesn't matter very much.
For, whether blessed with perfect information or not, it is credible to
think that capital will tend to project for itself a greater return on its
investment in low taxation regimes than high taxation regimes. Such
perceptions do not need to be accurate to be acted upon. Indeed, if we
want to predict the investment behaviour of capital, what we need to
know is not what its optimal investment strategy *might be*, but what it
perceives its optimal investment strategy *to be*. Whether we assume
capital to be blessed with perfect information or not, then, is likely to
have relatively little impact on our predictions as to the sustainability
of the welfare state under conditions of globalisation.

Yet this is most certainly not the case when it comes to assumptions
about the environment in which that investment is likely to occur. Here
our predictions are highly sensitive even to subtle changes in the
assumptions we use. Consider first the defining assumption of open
economy macroeconomics – that markets for goods, services and
investment are fully integrated globally. Clearly this is a simplifying
distortion, since no market – not even the smallest of national markets
– is perfectly integrated internally. But if we assume the global economy
to be perfectly integrated and if we assume competition for global
market share to be based solely on price then the so-called 'law of one
price' will hold (on which see Rødseth 2000: 261–6; Rogoff 1996).
What this means, in effect, is that the price dispersion for each good
traded on the global market will tend to zero with global market integration and a single world market price will emerge. Were this to mate-
rialise, it would be likely to prove the death knell of the welfare state.
For, funded as it surely must be, out of taxation receipts, it is almost
bound to place domestic producers at a profound comparative and
competitive disadvantage. In the world defined by such assumptions,
the welfare state is indeed a simple drain on (price) competitiveness,
profits and growth.

Yet, change either – or, indeed, both – of these assumptions and
things may pan out rather differently. If, for instance, rather than a

perfectly integrated global market we assume a series of regional economies, some more closely integrated than others, then the law of one price no longer holds – or, to the extent that it does, we are likely to see different prices in different regional economies. If, in addition, we allow competition at least in some goods and services markets to be determined not solely by price but by factors such as reputation and quality, then the prognosis for the welfare state – at least in some parts of the world economy – looks very different (for a more detailed discussion of the implications of this, see Hay 2011b).

The key point is that the viability of the welfare state depends crucially on the kind of world economy in which we find ourselves. Proponents of the welfare state have much to fear from a perfectly integrated world market in which price is the sole determinant of competitiveness and in which the law of one price holds. And if that is what we mean by globalisation, then globalisation and the welfare state may well be anathema. Yet proponents of the welfare state have much less to fear from a world economy that is far from perfectly integrated, in which there are many ways to establish competitiveness and in which the law of one price does not hold. If that is what we mean by globalisation, then the two might even exist in some kind of symbiotic relationship.

In the end, though, this is an empirical question. There is simply no substitute for a detailed examination of the evidence itself if we are to adjudicate between these competing images of the world in which we live and in which the welfare state's future (in Europe as elsewhere) will be determined.

Globalisation: an assessment of the evidence

As we have argued, the impact of globalisation on the viability of the welfare state in Europe is likely to depend greatly on what we take globalisation to mean. The less exacting our definitional standards, the more likely we are to find evidence of globalisation, but the less significant the confirmation of the globalisation thesis is likely to prove for European welfare states. Our task in this section, then, is to review the evidence for globalisation in Europe in recent decades in the light of this observation.

Such a detailed consideration of the evidence for globalisation is important, too, in evaluating the core claim of those who argue that the most generous welfare states in Europe (indeed, the world) contribute towards, rather than detract from, good economic performance under conditions of globalisation (see, for instance, Garrett 1993, 1998). For clearly some of the force of this argument is lost if it transpires, as many now contend, that these economies have simply not experienced globalisation (albeit by a pretty exacting definitional standard). Yet, conversely, any such lack of evidence for globalisation might reinforce the sceptics' view that the crises experienced by the social democratic welfare states in the 1990s had little or nothing to do with globalisation.

In the pages that follow we explore these questions empirically. We see how far the evidence will take us as we move from the least towards the most exacting of definitional standards for globalisation, considering the implications for the arguments already discussed in this chapter.

Globalisation – loosely defined

It makes some sense to start with the simplest and least demanding of definitions of globalisation. For many globalisation is merely a synonym for economic openness. Defined in this way, the greater the volume of trade, foreign direct investment and financial flows and the higher the level of migration between economies the more credible the claim that we have experienced a process of globalisation.

Once we have assembled the data, it is a relatively simple task to explore the degree to which, in recent decades, European economies have experienced a process of globalisation thus understood. The most conventional way to show such effects is to compare the rates of growth of trade (imports plus exports) and production, with both being expressed as standard prices or as shares of GDP. Figure 3.1. plots, on a logarithmic scale, such data for the economies of the EU since the late 1950s (for an equivalent plot for the world economy see Dicken 2003: 35, figure 3.2). Each data series is standardised at a value of 100 for 1995. Accordingly, a value of 1000 would represent a tenfold increase in trade or production relative to the 1995 figure; a value of 10 would represent a ten-fold decrease from the 1995 figure. Presenting the data on a logarithmic scale gives us something resembling a straight line where otherwise we would see an exponential growth curve.

The graph thus reveals an exponential increase in both EU production and trade since the late 1950s. More significantly it shows that, over this period of time, EU trade has increased at a far more rapid rate

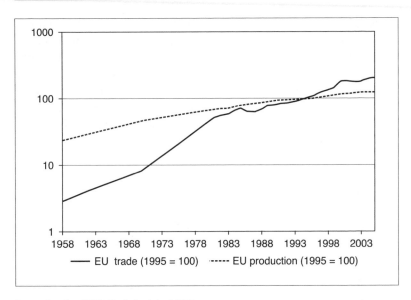

Source: Based on *WTO Trade Statistics* (2007).

FIGURE 3.1 *Rate of growth of EU trade and production (1958–2005)*

than that of EU production. Indeed, there has been a 260-fold increase in volumes of EU trade (at constant prices) compared to a more modest five-fold increase in EU production since 1958. This is an impressive statistic. It indicates very strongly that a greater share of EU production is being traded today than at any previous point (at least since the 1950s). In other words, the EU economy is producing more goods and a higher proportion of those good are being traded.

For many this is sufficient to demonstrate a decisive globalisation of the European economy, a view only reinforced by the data displayed in Figure 3.2. This shows the accumulated stock of inward and outward foreign direct investment to and from European OECD member state economies since 1990 (there is no reliable time-series data going back further).

Again, it shows the growing exposure of European economies to the broader international economy. Although Europe is a net exporter of FDI, over the period 1997–2006, seven out of ten of the world's leading importers of FDI and, less surprisingly, seven out of ten of the world's leading exporters of FDI were European economies. Moreover, since 2001, the ratio of research and development undertaken by affiliates abroad to that conducted in the domestic economy has exceeded 0.2 in

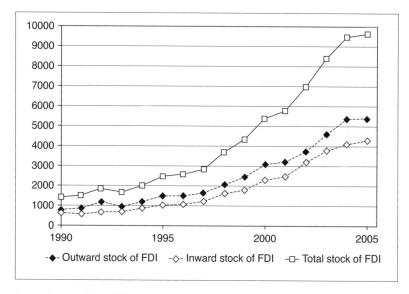

Source: Calculated from OECD (2005, 2006).

FIGURE 3.2   *FDI stocks for all OECD European economies, 1990–2005 ('000s of US$ millions)*

Germany (0.23), Finland (0.24), Sweden (0.41) and Switzerland (1.24) (OECD 2005). If the significance of cross-border economic flows is taken as an index of globalisation then there can be little doubt that, in terms of trade and foreign direct investment, the European economy has experienced a process of globalisation in recent decades.

Though it is more difficult to gauge such trends in financial markets by appeal to a single index, such markets would seem to reveal a common tendency. Figure 3.3 plots average daily turnover levels on foreign exchange markets since the 1980s.

The sums revealed here are staggering. What the data shows clearly is that turnover on European markets and the volume of transactions involving European currency have both grown as global financial market volumes have increased – if perhaps not quite at the same rate as the global trend.

Finally, though directly comparable time-series data is scarce or non-existent even for EU member states, it is important also to consider trends in labour markets. International migration has certainly grown in recent decades and many would see this as a further facet of globalisation. What is clear from the United Nations data is that a number of

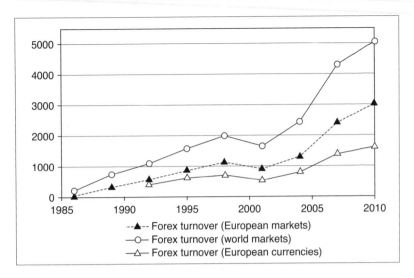

Source: Calculated from Bank for International Settlements (2002, 2005, 2008, 2011).

FIGURE 3.3   *Foreign exchange market turnover, 1986–2010 (average daily turnover, US$ billions)*

European economies are amongst the world's leading recipients of in-migrant labour. Most prominent amongst these are Germany (third in the world table with a migrant stock of 7.3 million in 2000), France (fifth, with a migrant stock in 2000 of 6.3 million) and the UK (eleventh, with a migrant stock of 4 million). Yet all three of these economies were in the UN's top ten in 1970 as well (United Nations 2003). Moreover, Eurostat data estimate that foreign residents in the EU-15 in 2000 represented less than 5 per cent of the total population. The European Labour Force Survey suggests a figure closer to 6 per cent and the, possibly rather more realistic, estimate of the International Organization of Migration for the size of the migrant population of western and central Europe is 8 per cent (International Organization of Migration 2006). But what all such estimates effectively show is how *non*-globalised, certainly in comparison to goods and financial markets, labour markets in Europe remain. Nonetheless, as the time-series data from the UK Census shown in Figure 3.4 demonstrate, levels of migration are higher today than at any point in the post-war period. And however small the aggregate figures may appear when expressed as a percentage of the overall population, net in-migration currently accounts for the 80–90 per cent of Europe's overall annual increase in population. Indeed, even though it is presently on the wane,

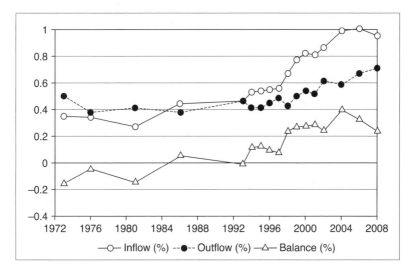

Source: Calculated from Office for National Statistics, *Population Trends* (various years), drawing on Census data and subsequent estimates.

FIGURE 3.4   *UK migration flows, 1973–2008 (% of total population)*

in societies like the UK it is largely responsible for preventing population decline. It also serves to hold up the ratio of net welfare contributors to net welfare recipients (with important consequences for the affordability of existing welfare commitments).

Globalisation or regionalisation?

As this suggests, understood simply (and in the least exacting of terms) as the tendency for cross-border flows of all kinds to increase, there is plenty of evidence of globalisation. European economies today – whether in terms of trade (imports and exports), foreign direct investment, financial transactions or, indeed, patterns of labour migration – are more deeply embedded in networks of cross-border flows than at any point in the post-war period and, arguably, than at any point in their history. There are, of course, those who have questioned such a view, especially for the former colonial powers such as Britain, France and the Netherlands (most notably, Hirst and Thompson 1996, 1999). Such authors have pointed to the, typically, greater degree of integration of these economies with the world economy in the period 1870–1914. In the mid to late 1990s when such interventions were made this was undoubtedly true. But, with continuing economic integration, it is no longer the case. The key point, however, is that the character of the economic interdependency of leading European economies in the late nineteenth century is very different to that today.

Yet, and altogether more significantly, this is to say nothing about the geographical character and composition of such flows. All flows have both a source and a destination and unless we define globalisation in a geographically more precise (and exacting) manner it is a term that can only hide the character of the flows that it is intended to describe.

An illustration perhaps serves to make the point. The aggregate evidence might well show that, between 1990 and 2000, the Hungarian economy became more open – the total value of its imports plus exports rose when expressed as a share of its GDP. If globalisation is synonymous with openness, then this is evidence of globalisation – regardless of whether that increase in openness was a consequence of a single bilateral trade agreement with a near neighbour, European economic integration or, indeed, a more general process of trade integration with the world economy. The point is that the consequences for the Hungarian economy and, indeed, the Hungarian welfare state, depend crucially on which of these processes are responsible for the increased openness we observe. We need to be able to differentiate clearly between processes of economic integration that are bipartisan and those that are multilateral, and those that are intra-regional, inter-regional and genuinely global in character; and we can only do so if we insist on a rather more demanding definition of globalisation. This we do by following David Held and his co-authors in defining globalisation as 'a process (or set of processes) that embodies a transformation in the spatial organisation of social relations and transactions, generating *transcontinental* or *interregional* flows and networks of activity, interaction and power' (1999: 16, emphasis added).

So, if we reassess the evidence for globalisation considered in the previous section with this rather more exacting definitional hurdle, do we find evidence consistent with the globalisation of European economies in recent decades? In short, not really; or, as least, certainly not for all European economies. Consider first trade.

Trade

Here, yet again, the absence of consistent and directly comparable time-series data going back to the 1960s hinders any simple attempt to gauge the globalisation of the European economy as a whole. However, such data does exist for the EU-15. What it shows is hardly the inexorable unfolding of a process of globalisation. Figure 3.5 plots, for all

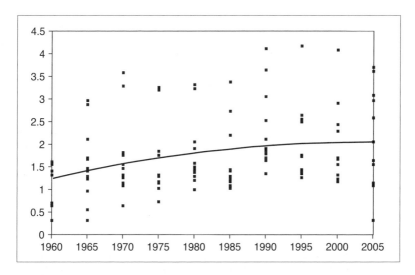

Note: EU-15: Austria, Belgium, Denmark, Finland, France, Germany, Greece, Ireland, Italy, Luxembourg, the Netherlands, Portugal, Spain, Sweden, UK.

Source: Calculated from IMF, *Direction of Trade Statistics*, various years.

FIGURE 3.5   *EU-15 economies' ratios of intra-EU to extra-EU exports, 1960–2005*

of the EU-15 for which data is recorded, the ratio of intra-EU exports to extra-EU exports at five yearly intervals from 1960. Where the ratio for a particular economy is 1, 50 per cent of its exports go to other EU-15 economies, 50 per cent to the rest of the world.

A number of aspects of this graph are interesting. First, throughout the entire period 1960–2005 only a handful of EU economies have, at any point, exported more to the rest of the world than they have to their EU neighbours (or those who would become their EU neighbours). Indeed, since 1980, every single EU-15 economy has exported more to the EU-15 than it has to the rest of the world. During this time the EU-15 average has risen from a ratio of intra-EU to extra-EU trade of around 1.25 to one to just over two to one. In other words, two-thirds of EU-15 exports are to the EU today; in 1960 the corresponding figure was 56 per cent. Conversely, EU-15 exports to the rest of the world have fallen from 44 per cent to one-third between 1960 and 2005. This is not a story of globalisation at all, but one of European economic integration; already highly regionalised patterns of trade have become more, not less, regionalised with each passing decade.

This is all very well for the EU-15, but what about the states that joined the EU in 2004 and 2007? Perhaps here we will see evidence of globalisation. The problem, as alluded to above, is a lack of reliable time-series data. But what data there is suggests very clearly that, for these economies too, regionalisation is a far more accurate description of recent trends than globalisation. The data that we have is from Eurostat, it is for some, but not all, of these economies from 1998 to the present day, and it is calculated in a slightly different way to the IMF Direction of Trade data. But, despite these caveats, it is nonetheless useful to overlay the data for the member states that joined in 2004 and 2007 on the data from Figure 3.5. This we do in Figure 3.6, the best fit curve shown being that for the entire set of data (the EU-15 plus the new states – that is, the EU-27).

A number of conclusions can be drawn from this interesting plot. First, overlaying the data for the 2004 and 2007 new members on the data for the EU-15 shows just how closely integrated with the EU economy these states were prior to their accession. Indeed, with the sole exception of Bulgaria, all of these states displayed, prior to accession, a more regionally concentrated pattern of export trade than the EU-15 average. Thus, although the shape of the best-fit curve changes a little with the introduction of the data from the new states, becoming steeper in the period since 1995, its positive slope remains unaltered. Despite the limitations in the data, then, it is clear that the new member states have, like their EU neighbours, experienced a process of regionalisation in recent decades. That process is ongoing and confounds any expectation of a globalisation of their trading relations. Though limits of space prevent a detailed consideration of the evidence, precisely the same inferences can be drawn from plots showing the ratio of intra-EU to extra-EU imports.

These findings are very important for arguments about the viability of European welfare states. For, put bluntly, they suggest that models that seek to derive the implications for the welfare state from all but the least inexacting of assumptions about globalisation are inappropriate. And that, in turn, would mean that most of the existing literature on globalisation and the welfare state is irrelevant to the situation of European welfare states today. That, of course, does not necessarily mean that the inferences, expectations and predictions drawn in this literature are actually wrong. But it does suggest the need to consider what happens to such inferences, expectations and predictions when we substitute for stylised assumptions about globalisation a set of premises that more accurately describe the highly regionalised patterns

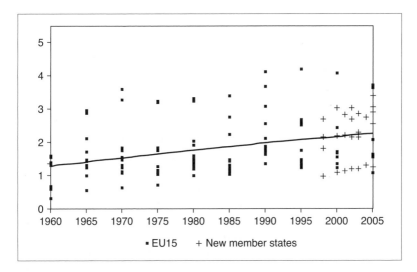

FIGURE 3.6   *Ratio of intra-EU to extra-EU exports, EU-15 plus new member states*

of economic interdependence of most European economies. This is the task we set ourselves in the final section of this chapter. But before turning to this, it is important to see whether the evidence of regionalisation with respect to trade is replicated when we move from trade to foreign direct investment, finance and patterns of labour migration.

Foreign direct investment

There are good *a priori* reasons for thinking that, even where we see very strong evidence of the regionalisation of trade, we might not expect to see an equivalent regionalisation of foreign direct investment (FDI) flows. Indeed, since inter-regional FDI invariably generates intra-regional trade, the globalisation of FDI may be a causal factor in the regionalisation of trade in Europe that we have observed. The point is a simple one and is well illustrated by considering the situation facing car producers in south-east Asia wishing to sell their products in the European market. Rather than incur the expense of shipping a valuable and potentially fragile commodity a large distance to market where it may well be subject to a variety of import restrictions (tariff or non-tariff barriers), they may decide to build an assembly plant within the

EU. This will have the effect of reducing transportation costs and of gaining the privileged access to the EU market that comes with being regarded as an EU producer. In such a scenario, the inter-regional FDI to set up and to maintain a European assembly plant gives rise to intra-regional trade, since any cars sold outside of the country in which the plant is located (but still within the EU) are recorded as exports from one EU economy to another.

Given the size of the European market and, within it, the EU market in particular, one might expect a rather more inter-regional pattern of FDI inflows and, indeed, outflows. Yet, again, any such expectation is largely confounded by the empirical evidence.

Again, access to reliable and consistent time-series data is a problem. Such data does exist for the EU economies, but only for the period since 1999. Moreover, since it is less prone to large swings from one year to the next, the data we use are for accumulated stocks of FDI, not annual flows. The data are shown in Figure 3.7. Here we plot, for outbound FDI, the ratio of investment within the EU to that invested in the rest of the world and, for inward FDI, the ratio of investment sourced from within the EU to that sourced from the rest of the world. The values of these ratios (all in the range 1 to 2.2) are shown on the left-hand axis. The graph also plots, again for both inward and outbound FDI stock, the ratio of investment sourced from, or invested in, the so-called 'triad' economies and that invested in, or sourced from, the rest of the world. The values of these ratios (all in the range 4 to 14) are shown on the right-hand axis. The term 'triad' in this context generally refers to the three largest regions in the world economy (ranked according to their share of world GDP) – North America, Europe and east Asia. Here, due to missing data, the 'triad' is defined more narrowly and refers only to the economies of the EU-25, other members of the European Free Trade Agreement (EFTA), the US, Canada and Japan.

Figure 3.7 is very interesting. It shows, just like the trade data considered above, the highly regionalised character of FDI inflows and outflows (and the accumulated stock of FDI to which they give rise). At no point between 1999 and 2003 has the accumulated stock of inward FDI sourced from within the EU itself not exceeded that from the rest of the world. Indeed, even in 1999, over 60 per cent of the EU's inward stock of FDI originated in other EU economies. Similarly, and despite the somewhat greater dispersion of FDI sourced from within the EU, at no point has the stock of FDI outflows invested in the EU not exceeded that invested in the rest of the world. Moreover, the trend in both cases would appear to be for the regional concentration of FDI

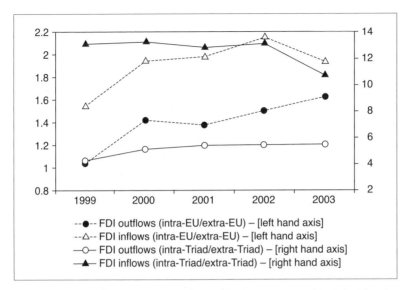

Notes: EU-25 for 2001–03; EU-15 for 1999–2000; triad: EU-25, plus EFTA, plus US, Canada and Japan.

Source: Adapted from European Commission (2006a).

FIGURE 3.7   *Ratio of intra-EU to extra-EU FDI stocks, 1999–2003*

to be growing, with ratios of intra- to extra-EU FDI stock almost as high as those for trade. This is, once again, a story of regionalisation not globalisation.

That having been said, levels of inter-regional FDI are by no means insignificant. But these too are highly concentrated geographically, as the ratios of intra- to extra-triad flows for both inward and outbound FDI show. Thus, on average for the period 1999–2003, for every US$100 invested in the EU economy from Europe, the US, Japan and Canada, only US$8 was invested from the rest of the world put together. Although the ratio falls for outward FDI sourced from within the EU – with US$20 invested in the rest of the world for every US$100 invested in Europe, the US, Japan and Canada – this is hardly indicative of a 'borderless' world economy in which geography no longer matters (Ohmae 1990; O'Brien 1991). Indeed, the trade and FDI data would both appear to suggest that the most accurate description of Europe's economic interdependence is in terms of regionalisation and 'triadisation' rather than globalisation (see also Frankel 1997; Hay 2006a).

Finance

Limits of space prevent a detailed consideration of the full complexity of financial market integration. Yet, as a number of commentators have observed, once one starts to examine the evidence, financial markets appear rather less globally integrated than is invariably assumed (see, for instance, Bayoumi 1997; Hirst and Thompson 1999; Watson 2001a, 2007; cf. O'Brien 1991).

One way of examining this is to look at the so-called 'home bias' of institutional investors such as pension funds. In a perfectly integrated global financial market we would expect such investors to select their equity and/or bond portfolios so as best to maximise the anticipated return on their investment. We would expect, as a consequence, their choice of equity and bond portfolios to show little or no preference (or 'bias') for government bonds or equities denominated in their home currency. Home bias thus provides an index of the extent to which financial markets remain national in character. Indeed, we can extend this kind of analysis to examine the degree to which financial markets are regionalised by looking, in effect, at 'regional bias' – the extent to which, say, French institutional investors' portfolios reveal a preference for government bonds and equities denominated in Euros (or, indeed, other European currencies). Again, lack of available data prevents a detailed analysis. But an interesting picture emerges from the data that is available. This we present in Tables 3.1a and 3.1b.

What is remarkable here is just how persistent home bias remains in markets that, in both political and academic debate, are invariably referred to as globally integrated. This home bias clearly varies considerably between equity and bond markets and between institutional investors in different economies. Moreover, and very much in keeping with the evidence for trade and FDI considered above, the data also reveals a pronounced regional bias in portfolio allocations. Thus, 88.4 per cent of eurozone institutional investors' bond portfolios and 83.5 per cent of their equity portfolios are in eurozone debt and shares respectively. Even UK institutional investors' bond and equity portfolios display a pronounced regional bias, with close to 80 per cent of their investments being in UK or eurozone debt and shares. Finally, as for FDI stocks, the ratio of intra- to extra-triad investment is exceptionally high – varying, in bond portfolio allocation, from 8.5 to 1 (for the UK) to 20.3 to 1 (for Italy) and, in equity portfolio allocation, from 2.5 to 1 (for Italy) to 14.1 to 1 (for the eurozone as a whole). Thus, insofar as this is a story of international integration at all, it is one of regionalisation and (some) triadisation, not globalisation.

87

TABLE 3.1a *Equity portfolio allocation, European institutional investors, 2003 (% of total allocation)*

Portfolio	France	Germany	Italy	Eurozone	UK	US	Rest
France	**73.6**	3.1	1.8	84.6	2.6	4.2	8.6
Germany	3.9	**62.9**	1.2	73.4	3.3	6.3	17.0
Italy	2.3	1.5	**58.2**	64.8	2.0	4.9	28.3
Eurozone	3.4	2.4	1.2	**83.5**	3.3	6.6	6.6
UK	2.3	1.5	1.0	8.1	**69.7**	8.9	13.3

TABLE 3.1b *Bond portfolio allocation, European institutional investors, 2003 (% of total allocation)*

Portfolio	France	Germany	Italy	Eurozone	UK	US	Rest
France	**65.2**	5.1	5.5	87.6	3.2	3.4	5.8
Germany	2.6	**74.3**	3.3	90.0	1.5	2.4	6.1
Italy	2.6	4.0	**80.0**	91.1	1.3	2.9	4.7
Eurozone	3.4	6.2	4.6	**88.4**	2.1	3.3	6.2
UK	3.4	4.1	4.3	18.8	**59.7**	11.0	10.5

Source: Adapted from International Monetary Fund (2005).

Labour migration

Finally we come to migration, an issue of great significance yet one seldom discussed in the literature on globalisation and its effects. As already noted, and unlike all of the other markets we have thus far considered, few if any authors suggest that there is a global market for labour. Yet levels of migration are undoubtedly rising. Again, the availability of good quality time-series data is a problem. But it does exist for a number of European economies from the mid 1990s and, in some cases, earlier. Data for the Netherlands, Italy, Norway and the UK are shown in Figure 3.8a–d.

Though there are substantial differences between these cases, there is precious little evidence of globalisation for any of them. Looked at in terms of composition, the UK looks the most globalised. For, at no time since the 1970s have EU nationals represented more than 30 per cent of the resident foreign population. But to describe this as globalisation (or the product of a process of globalisation) would be misleading, since such a large proportion of the UK's resident foreign population are in fact nationals of Commonwealth member states (see also Hay 2009b: 872–3). The EU proportion of the resident foreign population in each of the other cases is rather higher – around 35 per cent for the Netherlands, 40 per cent for Italy and 55 per cent for Norway. Again, it is difficult to see such data as a product of a process of globalisation.

But arguably more significant than the current composition of the stock of resident foreign nationals are the trends in the data over time – for it is these that reveal the process of change. Here again there is no evidence of globalisation. In the UK, the trend (such as one is discernible) would seem to be for Europeanisation (here, actually, EU-isation) rather than globalisation, with an accompanying fall in the proportion of in-migrants from the US and both the developing and, in particular, the developed parts of the Commonwealth. A similar if markedly stronger regionalisation trend can be seen in both the Dutch and Norwegian cases. Only in Italy has the pattern of migration proved more stable – but that, of course, is no evidence of globalisation.

Again, it is important to consider the position of the more recent member states. Yet the lack of reliable and comparable time-series data is a particular problem here. Hungary is a rare case for which we have limited time-series data for the late 1980s and early to mid 1990s as well as a more recent snapshot picture. This evidence is presented in Figure 3.9.

This data is again interesting. It shows very clearly the growing importance of internal EU labour migration to the Hungarian econ-

89

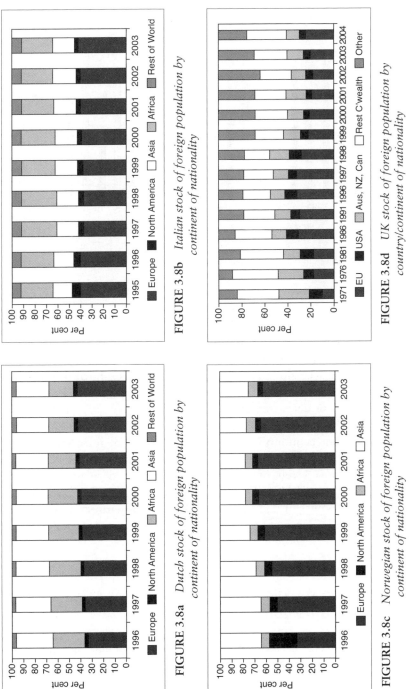

FIGURE 3.8a *Dutch stock of foreign population by continent of nationality*

FIGURE 3.8b *Italian stock of foreign population by continent of nationality*

FIGURE 3.8c *Norwegian stock of foreign population by continent of nationality*

FIGURE 3.8d *UK stock of foreign population by country/continent of nationality*

Source: Adapted from Migration Policy Institute, Country and Comparative Data, 2011 update.

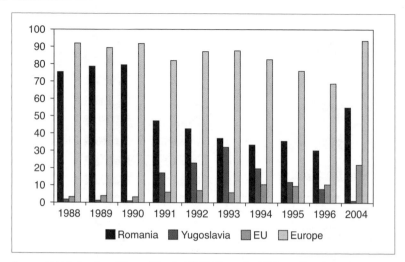

Sources: Calculations from Hárs and Kováts (2005); Hungarian Ministry of Interior, various years.

FIGURE 3.9   *Hungary – stock of foreign nationals registered to work, 1988–96, 2004*

omy, with in-migrants from the EU registered to work in Hungary rising from less than 4 per cent of the total in 1988 to some 22 per cent following accession to the EU in 2004. Yet it also shows just how high a proportion of labour migration is intra-regional rather than inter-regional in character. Indeed, it might well be suggested that whilst the 1990s witnessed a globalisation of labour migration into the Hungarian economy – with the proportion of intra-regional migrants falling consistently – the accession of Hungary to the EU has served to boost levels of intra-regional migration to previously unprecedented levels. If right, this would suggest that European integration is a powerful counter-tendency to globalisation – and one which, as the evidence of previous sections also shows, is currently in the ascendancy.

Reassessing the globalisation orthodoxy: the implications for the welfare state

It is tempting on the basis of the above evidence to conclude very simply that globalisation is not occurring in contemporary Europe and that rumours of the death of the European welfare state at the hands of globalisation are as exaggerated as the evidential claims about globalisation on which they rely. Yet that would be premature in a number of important respects.

It might, for instance, be that the predictions of the globalisation thesis for the viability of the welfare state in Europe are correct even in the absence of evidence for globalisation itself. Similarly, we might find that it is the extent of economic integration that is the important factor here, not the geographical character of economic interdependence. If so, then regionalisation and globalisation may well be essentially interchangeable terms (see, for instance, Hall 2001: 68) – in the sense that we might expect the predictions of the globalisation thesis for the welfare state to be borne out, despite a lack of evidence for globalisation itself. Conversely, we may find that the precise character and nature of the markets in which an economy competes matter greatly to the viability and sustainability of a comprehensive welfare state and that the predictions we might make for the welfare state are very different if we substitute regionalisation for globalisation. Finally, we might find that it is the premise that the welfare state is (or would be) a drain on good economic performance under conditions of globalisation, that is false. This might lead us to conclude that, whether we see evidence of regionalisation, globalisation, neither or both, there is likely to be a continued positive role for a comprehensive welfare state.

The task we set ourselves in this section is to choose between these options, by working through the implications of the evidence discussed in the preceding section for the viability and developmental trajectories of European welfare states. As we shall see, such implications may well vary from case to case.

Regionalisation versus globalisation: what difference does it make?

Much of the analysis of this chapter has assumed that it makes a difference – and a significant difference at that – whether European economies are exposed principally to a process of regionalisation or to a genuine process of globalisation. But, for many, these terms are essentially interchangeable. What is assumed to matter in such accounts is the extent of economic openness, not the specific character or geographical composition of that openness. So, when it comes to assessing the implications of economic integration and interdependence for the viability and sustainability of the welfare state in Europe are globalisation and regionalisation interchangeable? What difference – if any – does it makes if, having assumed that we live in a world of globalisation, we find instead that we live in a world of regionalisation?

The short answer to such questions is that it does matter and that globalisation and regionalisation are not simply interchangeable if we are to assess accurately the prospects for European welfare states. But, and this is perhaps the key point, the extent to which it matters is likely to vary considerably between European economies. In what follows we examine, first, why these terms might not be interchangeable, before turning to why this is likely to make more of a difference for our expectations in some contexts than others.

Consider two ostensibly similar economies, say Britain and France. These economies have close, though by no means identical, levels of productivity, taxation and welfare generosity – and they both produce a range of simple and more complex goods and services for domestic consumption and export. Both clearly stand to benefit from the removal of all barriers to trade in goods and services between them. In such a bilateral trading regime, each economy will tend to produce, over time, more of those goods and services in which it enjoys a comparative advantage. The result, all things being equal, is a series of so-called 'efficiency gains' as consumers in both societies benefit, in effect, from the comparative advantage each economy has in certain areas relative to the other. Yet, for the most part, consumers will simply find themselves in a situation in which they enjoy greater choice in markets in which producers and service providers in neither economy enjoy a clear comparative advantage.

The key point here is that free trade between such economies is unlikely to unleash a vicious war of competitive undercutting between Britain and France as producers squabble for precious market share. Reciprocal access to each others' markets is unlikely, then, to generate downward pressure on welfare state expenditure with producers entreating the state to reduce their costs in order that they might gain a (short-term) competitive edge. Indeed, when one considers that in relatively affluent societies like Britain and France price is by no means the sole (nor even the principal) determinant of consumer choice, generous welfare provision is likely to be quite compatible with good economic performance. This is an argument to which we return in more detail in Chapter 4. Suffice it for now to note that if the process of economic integration is one that involves reciprocal access to ostensibly similar economies, then it is unlikely to have a decisive impact on the viability or sustainability of the welfare state. It is but a short step to the suggestion that *European* economic integration holds no great threat to the most developed welfare states of northern Europe.

Yet consider what happens when an economy such as the British or French opens itself to a comparatively low wage, low skill, developing economy. Things now proceed rather differently. Typically such economies are capable of producing a range of staples and simple commodities (for which labour is the principal cost of production) for less than their northern European counterparts. Indeed, the price differential in such markets is likely to be significant in the absence of trade barriers. Reciprocal access is thus likely to generate substantial downward pressure on prices for British and French producers in these markets. This, in turn, will generate mounting pressure on governments, if market share is to be maintained, either to abandon their commitment to bilateral trade or to reduce the corporate tax burden and, with it, welfare generosity. It is but a short step to the suggestion that *global* market integration poses a very real and significant threat to the most developed welfare states of northern Europe.

Yet neat though this undoubtedly is, it is something of a simplification. There are a number of assumptions here that are likely to prove problematic. First, it is to distort significantly the process of European economic integration to assume that its sole (or even principal) effect is the removal of trade (and other) barriers *between ostensibly similar economies*. In the 1960s this might well have been the case. But with the expansion to twenty-seven members of the European Union (EU) following the 2004 and 2007 enlargements, is it certainly no longer the case. The EU is a diverse economic space with large variations in levels of GDP per capita, taxation and social expenditure – as Figure 3.10 shows very clearly.

This is a crucial point. For, it suggests that, for the last decade or so at least, the process of European economic integration has more closely resembled the textbook account of economic globalisation than it did in earlier decades. Yet we need to be careful here. For EU enlargement has certainly not resulted in a mass influx of cheap consumer goods and staples from the new member states undercutting producers in the 'old' EU. Indeed, prior to the global financial crisis, growth rates in the old and new EU alike have generally been good.

What this would seem to suggest is that, contrary to the expectations of the globalisation thesis, affluent economies with high levels of GDP per capita, high wages and high levels of skill are capable of surviving alongside less affluent, lower wage and lower skill economies even in an essentially free trade environment. But, in order to do so, they must

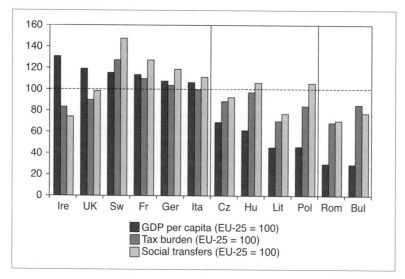

Note: Data for Romania and Bulgaria are for 2005.

Source: Calculations from European Commission (2006b).

FIGURE 3.10   *GDP per capita, tax burden and social transfers, 2003*

retain and indeed nurture a capacity to produce goods for international markets for which consumers are prepared to pay something of a premium. And this, in turn, implies the need to compete on the basis of quality, reputation and product innovation rather than cost, in markets which are less price sensitive than most (Hay 2007b, 2011b). In such a context, as we shall see in more detail in the following chapter, the welfare state may well prove a significant resource.

This is all very well for the most affluent and developed of high wage, high skill, high welfare economies, but where does it leave, for instance, the new members that joined in 2004 and 2007? And, indeed, where does it leave those 'old' EU member states that fail to retain their capacity to command a premium for their goods in international markets?

These are interesting and important questions and they are difficult to answer definitively. But our analysis thus far suggests the existence of two relatively stable models of growth in a diverse and closely integrated economic space, such as the EU today. The archetype of the first of these is perhaps the Nordic or Scandinavian model and it is characterised by a high skill, high wage, affluent consumer economy producing innovative goods and services of high quality for international markets. In such contexts high levels of welfare expenditure are likely to prove sustainable and indeed, to play an important role in ensuring a healthy, dedicated and skilled workforce. At the other end of the spectrum is the archetypal experience of many new membern states. Here we might expect to see, at least when set in the European context, low wage – though not necessarily low skill – economies competing largely on the basis of price in markets that are highly price sensitive. Such economies are likely to be characterised by welfare states that are both far less generous and which are also under constant pressure to justify their existence in terms of the contribution to economic performance that they make.

Yet this is unlikely to prove a static scenario. For it is surely credible to think that a number of the new member states, particularly those with higher levels of educational investment and attainment, high skill levels amongst the working population and technical and product innovation, will be able to make the transition from one growth regime to the other. Yet, by the same token, there will be those 'old' EU member states whose competitive advantage within EU product markets has traditionally rested more on price than quality who will struggle to compete in an enlarged Europe without reducing their cost base. Though it is a controversial claim, and though not all commentators would agree, Britain's large and growing trade deficit both with the EU and the rest of the world would suggest it may well be one such case. Spain, Portugal and Italy may well be others.

Conclusion

In this chapter we have covered a substantial amount of ground. We saw that, although widely associated with a variety of pressures for welfare retrenchment in Europe, as elsewhere, the impact we might expect globalisation to have on the viability and sustainability of European welfare states depends crucially on what we take globalisation to mean. We also saw that many of the most influential accounts of globalisation – which typically associate it with the need for welfare retrenchment – are based on the most inexacting of definitional standards, in which globalisation is merely a synonym for economic openness. Yet, having established the existence of globalisation by reference to such a low definitional threshold, much of this literature proceeds to derive a series of anticipated consequences of globalisation from the (untested) assumption of perfect market integration.

In seeking to counter the analytical unevenness of such a strategy, we proposed an alternative and somewhat more exacting definition of globalisation. This, we suggested, has the advantage of differentiating very clearly between globalisation and regionalisation and hence of sharpening our analytical purchase on the geographical character of the process of economic integration that European states experience. Armed with such a definition, we re-evaluated the evidence for globalisation in contemporary Europe, finding there to be rather greater evidence for regionalisation and rather less evidence for globalisation than is conventionally assumed – whether we are talking about trade, foreign direct investment, finance or labour migration.

In the final section of the chapter we re-assessed the view that globalisation is the source of significant pressures for welfare retrenchment in Europe today in the light of such findings. Yet, tempting though it might be simply to reject the idea that the welfare state in Europe today is in need of significant reform and retrenchment by pointing to the absence of systematic evidence of globalisation, to adopt such a view, we suggested, would be premature. Substituting regionalisation for globalisation certainly makes a difference to our expectations about the viability and sustainability of the welfare state in Europe, but the extent and nature of the difference varies from case to case. Indeed, it depends crucially on the domestic sources of competitiveness on which economies rely. For those competing in regional (or, indeed, global) markets principally on the basis of cost alone, the welfare state is likely to be a burden on competitiveness; yet for those competing in regional or global markets rather less on cost and rather more on the basis of the quality, reputation and innovation of the goods and services they provide, the welfare state may be a key source of competitiveness. It is to this crucial and complex relationship between the welfare state and competitiveness that we turn in the next chapter.

Chapter 4

Competitiveness and the Welfare State

Introduction

In this chapter we turn directly and in some detail to a complex set of issues present but largely undeveloped in the preceding chapters, namely the relationship between welfare provision and economic competitiveness. The welfare state – in the advanced liberal democracies in general and in Europe in particular – is increasingly judged in economic terms. For, in an era of economic interdependence and heightened competition between economies, it is invariably suggested that the welfare state must prove its value in an exhaustive competitive audit if it is not to reveal itself an indulgent luxury and an unsustainable burden on competitiveness. Given the powerful hold of such assumptions among policy-makers it is unremarkable that social policy goals are often subordinated to perceived economic imperatives – with, for instance, the reform of benefits and entitlements now routinely justified in terms of the labour-market incentives they generate. The more general privileging of economic considerations in social policy and labour-market reform is nowhere more clearly enunciated than in the so-called Lisbon agenda for the modernisation of the 'European social model'. This ostensibly commits EU member states to a programme of reforms designed to 'make Europe, by 2010, the most competitive and the most dynamic knowledge-based economy in the world' (Presidency Conclusions, Lisbon European Council, 23–4 March 2000).

As this perhaps already suggests, an evaluation of the relationship between the competitiveness of European economies (both individually and collectively) and patterns of welfare provision and expenditure is now integral to any adequate assessment of the developmental trajectory of the welfare state. Yet, as we shall argue, this relationship is often poorly understood, by academic analysts and practitioners alike, and is rather more complex and involved than is generally assumed. Building on the arguments and evidence of the preceding chapter, we examine the compatibility of high levels of welfare expenditure with an open and competitive economy.

In the process we present what is, in effect, a competitive audit of contemporary European welfare states, considering arguments for and against the contribution the welfare state might make to a nation's competitiveness in the light of the empirical evidence. We conclude that, far from being a simple burden on competitiveness, the welfare state may in fact be a competitive necessity for economies seeking competitiveness not purely on the basis of low labour costs in flexible labour markets.

Retrenchment re-assessed

That so many European policy-makers should regard the welfare state as corrosive of competitiveness at a time when competitiveness has become such an overriding concern of public policy might lead one to expect unequivocal and unambiguous evidence of systematic welfare retrenchment in recent years. Yet the empirical record, at least in aggregate terms, is likely to confound any such simple expectation. Moreover, as noted in the previous chapter, the positive correlation between social expenditure and economic openness first observed by Cameron (1978) in the 1970s has only strengthened in the intervening decades (Garrett 1998; Rodrik 1997). Open economies tend to commit a greater proportion of their gross national product in welfare spending than closed economies. This presents something of a paradox: a widely accepted conception of the *need* for welfare retrenchment that does not appear to be supported by the available empirical evidence.

So how might we understand this? In the pages that follow we develop a four-step argument of the following form:

1. that a focus on aggregate levels of welfare expenditure is distorting and, in fact, masks the actually degree of retrenchment we have seen since the 1980s;
2. that, once we control for demographic and other 'welfare inflationary' factors, significant welfare retrenchment can be observed;
3. that such retrenchment has been informed to a considerable extent by impressions of the 'competitiveness-corrosive' qualities of social spending; but
4. that, however paradoxically, such impressions have come at a time when evidence of the 'competitiveness-enhancing' qualities of the

welfare state have become ever more transparent in many, if perhaps not all, European economies.

The argument proceeds in four sections. In the first of these we assess the scale of welfare retrenchment in contemporary Europe before moving, in the second, to re-consider the orthodox view in the light of such evidence. In the third section, we attempt to draw up a more balanced assessment of the positive and negative externalities of the welfare state in the competitive environment of the contemporary global political economy. We conclude by considering the prospects for the welfare state in an era in which concerns as to competitiveness are increasingly to the fore. In particular, we focus on the consequences for the form and character of the welfare state of the stark choice currently facing European economies between cost competitive and quality competitive strategies.

The 'scope' and 'scale' of welfare expenditure: the aggregate evidence

The most obvious and direct way to assess the extent of welfare retrenchment is to look at evidence of aggregate welfare expenditure over time (see also Levy 2010; Obinger and Wagschel 2010; Stephens 2010). For the European economies there are basically two data series we might here consider and, since they measure social expenditure rather differently, they are not strictly comparable. The first is provided by the OECD and dates from 1960. This has the advantage of giving a long time-series, but it excludes many of the southern and east–central European cases. The raw data itself are shown in Table 4.1.

This is already interesting and its stands in some marked tension with the expectations one might generate from much of the existing literature. The period since the 1960s has seen the growth and consolidation, in Europe, of the largest welfare states (expressed as a share of GDP) the world has ever known. There is no evidence – certainly no systematic evidence – of welfare retrenchment here. Moreover, as the welfare state has grown there has been a pronounced divergence in social spending between European economies (the standard deviation has increased) – and, for the most part, that divergence has been sustained. Again, there is no evidence here of a convergence in levels of welfare state expenditure as, say, a more residual and competitively oriented competition state has emerged.

TABLE 4.1   *Social spending in northern Europe, 1960–2010 (% of GDP)*

	Den	Fin	Fr	Ger*	Ire	Ita	Neth	Swe	UK	Std dev
1960	10.6	8.8	13.4	18.1	8.7	13.1	11.7	10.8	10.2	2.90
1980	25.2	18.4	20.8	23.0	16.8	19.9	26.3	29.7	18.5	4.19
1984	24.9	21.7	22.6	23.1	17.1	20.5	25.4	28.8	19.3	3.50
1988	25.4	23.1	25.7	24.0	19.8	21.1	23.3	30.4	17.7	3.70
1992	26.8	33.4	26.6	25.7	17.1	20.7	24.9	35.0	20.3	5.88
1996	28.2	27.1	28.6	27.1	15.4	22.0	21.8	32.1	20.1	5.21
2000	25.8	24.3	27.6	26.6	13.6	23.2	19.3	28.8	19.1	4.93
2004	27.6	26.0	28.7	27.6	15.9	24.2	20.7	29.5	20.1	4.64
2007	26.0	24.9	28.4	25.2	16.3	24.9	20.1	28.4	20.5	4.07

*West Germany (until 1992 data).

Source: Compiled from OECD (1994a, 2006b, 2011).

It is nonetheless clear that, even prior to the turn to austerity since the global financial crisis (see Chapter 7), there has been some significant scaling back of the welfare state since a high point in the late 1980s or early 1990s. This has been most notable perhaps in the Finnish, the Swedish and the Irish cases. Yet even a momentary reflection on these cases shows that the steep rise and subsequent fall in aggregate levels of welfare expenditure that each exhibits is largely a product of the rise and fall in levels of unemployment.

Consider first Figure 4.1. This shows official levels of unemployment and levels of social expenditure (again, expressed as a share of GDP) between 1988 and 2010 for Finland and Sweden. These data are notable in two respects. First, social spending rises (at least at first) as unemployment rises, lending credibility to the claim that we simply do not need to invoke globalisation to explain changes in levels of welfare expenditure. Yet, a closer inspection of the data reveals that things are somewhat more complicated than this suggests. For note also that social spending reaches its peak, in both cases, some time before levels of unemployment start to fall. This is powerfully suggestive of a thesis that we will go on to explore in more detail presently (and further in Chapter 6) – that welfare states, often despite consuming a still growing proportion of GDP, are less generous in terms of both benefit levels and entitlements than once they were. In these two Nordic cases, it seems, had the generosity of the welfare state been maintained, aggregate levels of

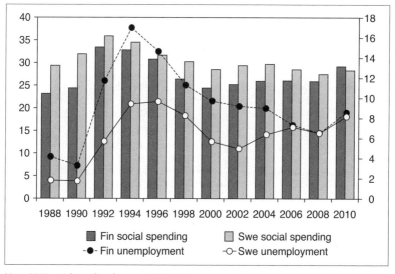

Note: 2010 social spending data are OECD estimates.
Source: Compiled from OECD (2011).

FIGURE 4.1   *Nordic social spending and unemployment, 1988–2010*

social spending would have risen further in the mid 1990s, before falling again (as, in fact, they did) in the late 1990s and early 2000s.

In one sense the Irish case is simpler. Here, as the data in Figure 4.2 show, unemployment fell consistently and precipitously from the 1980s until the bursting of the Irish consumer, housing and construction bubble with the onset of the global financial crisis. As a consequence, and for the duration of the so-called 'great moderation' prior to the crisis, there was rather less pressure on the Irish government to reign in on welfare benefits to the unemployed. Yet here too, there is an additional complicating factor. For during this time Irish growth rates were so extraordinarily high (in comparison to European, OECD or world averages) that to present social expenditure as a percentage of GDP is to make an ongoing expansion of the welfare state *in real terms* look like a marked retrenchment. Indeed, in seeming confirmation of this, as growth rates fell between 2000 and the onset of the crisis in 2007–08, so social spending as a share of GDP started to rise once more despite at that time still stable and comparatively low levels of unemployment. Yet that, of course, would not survive the crisis that – for the reasons we examine in some detail in Chapter 7 – has been particularly acute in the Irish case. The extent of the transformation of Ireland's economic

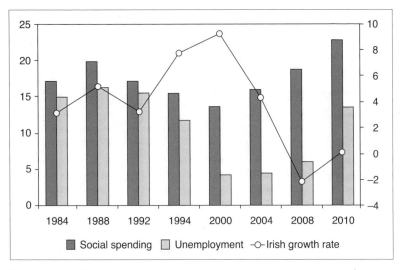

Notes: Social spending and unemployment shown on left-hand axis; growth on right-hand axis; 2010 social spending data are OECD estimates.

Sources: Compiled from OECD (2011); Irish Central Statistics Office.

FIGURE 4.2   *Irish social spending, unemployment and growth, 1984–2004*

fortunes is clearly shown in the data series – with a return to levels of unemployment not seen in Ireland since the early 1990s and a very deep recession at a time of already steeply rising social spending commitments. We return to the question of the viability of the Irish welfare state in such a context in Chapter 7.

In addition to the raw data itself, we can facilitate the comparison between cases by standardising the data – here at 1960 levels (see Figure 4.3). Precisely because this graph displays a standardised index of welfare expenditure (as a share of GDP), it is bound to show an initial divergence. Consequently, we can infer little if anything from this. It is what happens after this initial divergence that is interesting. For most stylised accounts of the development of the welfare state in recent decades would suggest a more recent process of convergence or, indeed, in the 'varieties of capitalism' literature dual or co-convergence. The simple convergence thesis (see, for instance, Gray 1998; Teeple 1995) would lead us to expect that initial divergence to be checked considerably by the 1990s and early 2000s. It would predict, in short, an oval shaped distribution. And the co-convergence thesis (see, for instance, Hall and Soskice 2001b) would predict the emergence of two clusters - one grouped around Germany, the other the UK.

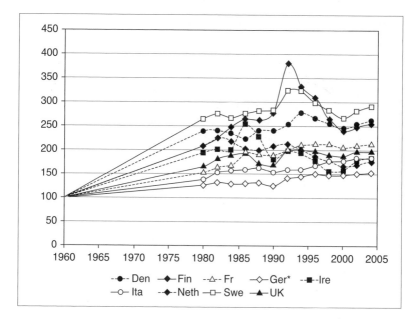

*West Germany (until 1992 data).

Source: Calculated from OECD (2006a).

FIGURE 4.3 *Trends in social spending in northern Europe, 1960–2004 (1960=100)*

As is clear to see, neither expectation is borne out by the evidence. What we do see, instead, is that consistent paths are mapped out from the 1960s that European welfare states continue to follow for the most part to the present day. There are really only two exceptions to this. They are, predictably, the Irish and Finnish cases which, for reasons we have already dealt with, criss-cross the paths of other welfare states at a number of points between 1985 and 2000. Putting these cases to one side, the wide initial variance in growth rates is largely sustained over time. Once again, this is not a story of systematic welfare retrenchment, nor is it a story of the diminishing distinctiveness of European welfare trajectories. If, as the conventional wisdom would have it, the period since the 1980s has seen an unprecedented intensification of competition between the advanced liberal democracies, then in northern Europe at least this has not come at great cost to the welfare state. In aggregate terms the most generous welfare states continue to thrive. This is a theme to which we return in much greater empirical detail in Chapter 6.

Instructive though the OECD data is, it can tell us nothing about many of the southern European welfare states, nor those of recent east–central European new member states. Here we have to turn to the European Commission's own data series. This records social expenditure in a rather different way, splitting it into two categories – (i) social benefits in kind; and (ii) social transfers other than in kind. Both are expressed as shares of GDP. Here they are combined to present an index of total social expenditure. Figure 5.4 plots this data for a series of geographical clusters of European welfare states since 1995 (the first date for which data for all of the EU-25 are available).

The European Commission's data series certainly seems to confirm the impression given by the OECD data. In recent years, social expenditure has been stable with little or no evidence of convergence either between geographical clusters or between individual welfare states (the standard deviation of social expenditure for the EU-25 remains almost constant over time). This is, above all, a picture of continuity rather than

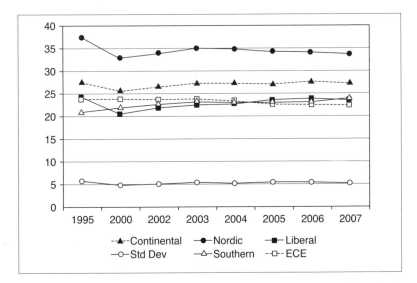

Notes: Social spending – the sum of 'social benefits in kind' and 'social transfers other than in kind' (% of GDP); Continental – Belgium, Germany, Luxembourg, the Netherlands, Austria; Nordic – Denmark, Finland, Sweden; Liberal – UK, Ireland; Southern – Greece, Spain, Italy, Cyprus, Malta, Portugal; ECE – Czech Republic, Estonia, Latvia, Lithuania, Poland, Slovenia, Slovak Republic; Std Dev – for EU-25.

Source: Compiled from EC (2007).

FIGURE 4.4   *Social spending of EU-27, 1995–2007*

change. Regimes in the Nordic cluster remain the most generous, those in continental Europe the next most generous, with little to choose between the Anglo-liberal, the southern European and east–central European in terms of total social expenditure. Much has been going on in the political economy of the EU-25 during this time, but their levels of welfare state investment have remained remarkably constant. Put slightly differently, if the welfare state is indeed a burden on competitiveness, then it remains just as much of a burden today as it was in the early to mid 1990s – in Nordic, continental, Anglo-liberal, southern and east–central European economies alike. And that of course begs a very significant question: is it any kind of economic burden on competitiveness at all? But before attempting to provide an answer, it is first important that we consider the extent to which continuity in aggregate terms may mask a somewhat different and more complex picture once we consider (and control for) variations in welfare need over time.

Relativising retrenchment

It is one thing to show that levels of aggregate welfare effort have remained relatively constant at a time when talk of European welfare reform is rife. It is another thing altogether to suggest that European welfare states have remained essentially unaltered. Much depends here on what we take retrenchment to entail. If we define retrenchment such that it refers to the scale of welfare effort (gauged as a share of GDP) then the evidence already presented may well be sufficient to reject the retrenchment thesis. Yet there may well be good reasons for preferring a somewhat different and more nuanced conception of retrenchment. If, for instance, we see the welfare state as an institution (or set of institutions) for responding to societal needs (see, for instance, Doyal and Gough 1991; Gough 2000; Gough and McGregor 2007), then we are unlikely to feel able to conclude, on the basis of stable or even increasing levels of expenditure alone, that no retrenchment has occurred. To be satisfied that retrenchment has neither occurred nor is underway, we would need to know, at minimum, that consistent levels of generosity and access to benefits for those in need have been maintained. And the point is that if we (re)define retrenchment in such terms, total welfare expenditure tells us next to nothing about whether retrenchment has occurred or not.

Indeed, the more one thinks about the changing distribution of need in contemporary societies, the more it seems likely that, despite stable or rising levels of expenditure, welfare retrenchment is underway throughout Europe.

In a more exhaustive survey than this (see, for instance, Barr 1998; Glennerster 1997, 2003, 2010), a vast range of issues might here be considered. To illustrate the point here, we concentrate solely on three of the most significant – (i) the trade-off between unemployment and inflation; (ii) demographic change; and (iii) the economics of public health insurance.

The trade-off between unemployment and inflation

In what is widely (if, as we saw in Chapter 2, arguably incorrectly) depicted as the heyday of the European welfare state in the 1960s and 1970s, levels of unemployment were invariably low, certainly by the standards of the 1980s and 1990s. Consequently, generous unemployment benefits with few qualifying restrictions for claimants did not prove particularly costly. A crucial element of this was, of course, that the predominantly Keynesian economic consensus amongst policy-makers of the time prioritised full employment as a key goal of macro-economic policy. It is for this reason, above all, that the welfare state of the post-war period is often referred to as a 'Keynesian welfare state' (Jessop 1980; Martin 1997; Offe 1983, 1984; C. Pierson 1998). Yet, with the rise of monetarism and supply-side economics out of the widely perceived crisis of Keynesianism in the 1970s, economic priorities were decisively reconfigured (Hall 1993; Scharpf 1991). A much greater emphasis would now be placed on inflation targeting, balanced budgets and fiscal austerity. The immediate effect in many European economies was a steep rise in interest rates to control inflation at a time when unemployment was already at its highest post-war level.

The irony is, of course, that this has placed a considerable additional burden on the welfare state. Were it not then for a widely observed tightening of eligibility criteria, a greater emphasis upon means-testing and the more general targeting of benefits, we would expect to have seen a rather more pronounced rise in social expenditure since the 1980s than that observed (Esping-Andersen 1996c; Ferrera 1998; Hagen 1992; Jordan 1998; Ormerod 1998; Rhodes 1997; Stephens 1996; Stephens, Huber and Ray 1999). Or so, at least, the argument goes.

The proposition is presented schematically in Figure 4.6. for a hypothetical economy experiencing a rapid rise and more gradual decline in unemployment. The difference between expected welfare expenditure (assuming consistent income replacement ratios and eligibility criteria)

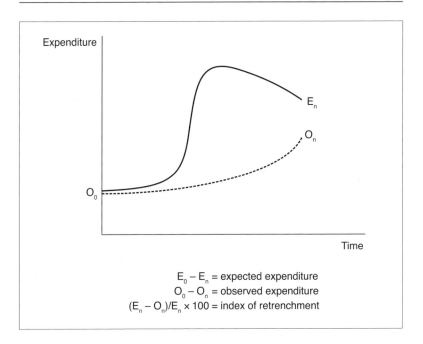

FIGURE 4.5 *Expected and observed expenditure on unemployment benefits*

and that observed provides an index of the extent of effective welfare retrenchment pertaining to the unemployed.

The problem with Figure 4.5 is that, however much it may conform to the experience of many European economies from the late 1970s onwards, it is ultimately a *stylised* depiction of a *hypothetical* case. The actuarial complexity of calculating expected expenditure given observed patterns of unemployment (with different levels of entitlement for different family experiences and so forth) has prevented graphs like that shown above being populated by real data.

Yet even in the absence of such data there are still ways of exploring the generosity of welfare states over time more directly. Chief amongst these is to look at actual benefit levels as *income replacement ratios*. These express the value of welfare entitlements (such as unemployment, sickness and disability benefits) as a percentage of the average net (post tax) working wage. The OECD data for unemployment benefits since the 1960s is shown for a number of European welfare states in Figure 4.6.

What is interesting about this data series is that although it does show a modest decline in unemployment benefits expressed as income replacement ratios, in most cases this is a very recent phenomenon –

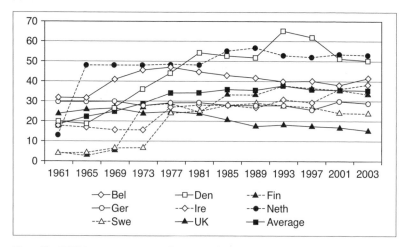

Notes: The OECD's summary measure of income replacement is shown here and is defined as 'the average of the gross unemployment benefit replacement rates for two earnings levels, three family situations and three durations of employment'. For full details, see OECD (1994b).

Source: Compiled from OECD, Tax-Benefits Models (www.oecd.org/els/social/ workincentives).

FIGURE 4.6   *Unemployment benefits as income replacement ratios, 1961–2003*

which has really only taken effect from the mid 1990s. In fact, until 1993 the average level of income replacement grew consistently and it has fallen back by only a couple of percentage points in the ensuing decade. Yet we would almost certainly be wrong to conclude from this that, even looking only at benefit levels and coverage, European welfare states are as generous today as they have ever been. The above data considers only unemployment benefits and it does so by constructing a compound or summary index which largely fails to take account of trends in the duration of unemployment and in its distribution across family structures. Moreover, it also fails to take account of the significantly stricter enforcement of official eligibility criteria for benefits in many European welfare states in recent decades (Nickell, Nunziata and Ochel 2005). It is for this reason that, in Chapter 6, in which we present a far more detailed picture of trends in the generosity of benefit levels over time, we use instead the *Social Citizenship Indicator Programme* data series (sadly only available at present for the period 1947–2000).

Overall, then, it is difficult to be definitive about the extent to which changes in eligibility, access and levels of benefit have contributed to welfare retrenchment. It does nonetheless remain the case that aggregate social expenditure has not risen as much as we might have expected given exhibited trends in the level of unemployment in many European economies. And that, in turn, is certainly suggestive of this as an element of welfare retrenchment (see also Esping-Andersen 1996c; Hagen 1992; Stephens, Huber and Ray 1999).

The 'demographic timebomb'

The increase in the rate of unemployment in Europe since the post-war period is not, however, the only demand-side factor which might lead us to expect rising levels of social expenditure (at least where levels of generosity and entitlement have been maintained). The most obvious of these is demographic change and here the empirical evidence is overwhelming.

The problem facing European welfare states is simply stated. Most European societies have rapidly ageing populations; and the elderly have always consumed, on a per capita basis, the largest share of the public goods the welfare state provides. Consequently, all things being equal, a rapidly ageing population equates to rapidly increasing social expenditure. Indeed, somewhat ironically, the positive correlation between the level of social spending and both life expectancy and increases in life expectancy means that the welfare state has contributed to its own escalating costs (Barr 2006; Crepaz and Crepaz 2004; Timmons 2005).

Yet alarming though this might already be, it is only part of the picture. The problem is exacerbated by an ongoing decline in birth rates in many European societies (Italy, Spain and Portugal in particular) and by the legacy of an earlier decline in birth rates in others (such as France, Ireland and the Netherlands). In short, the demographic projections for European societies are rather bleak, at least when their implications for welfare state expenditure are considered (Franco and Munzi 1996; Rhodes 1997; Rodríguez-Pose 2002). Figure 4.7 describes the rapidly changing demographic profile of European societies. It shows, the so-called 'support ratio' – the ratio of net contributors to the funding of the welfare state to net recipients of welfare benefits and services (in fact, the proportion of the total population aged 65 or over divided by those of working age – it being assumed that the former figure gives a rough index of the pool of net welfare recipients and the latter figure a rough index of the pool of net contributors to the funding of the welfare state).

What alarms policy-makers in Europe (and elsewhere) is that the 'support ratio' is rising and it is not projected to begin to stabilise until at least 2050.

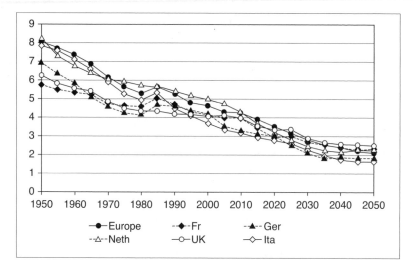

Source: Calculated from UN Department of Economic and Social Affairs (2007).

FIGURE 4.7   *European support ratios (15–64/65+) – actual and projected,*
1950–2050

It is not difficult to see why this might concern policy-makers. In 1950, on average, each elderly potential recipient of state welfare benefits was supported, in effect, by 8 tax-paying citizens of working age. By 2005 that support ratio had fallen to just over 4:1 and, by 2050, it is projected to fall to 2:1. In other words, assuming that the needs of the over 65s relative to the rest of the population remain constant and that the welfare state retains its current form, the purely age-related costs of the welfare state are set to double in the next four decades.

Of course, this might seem likely to overstate the extent of the problem. For, it might be argued, those in the early years of retirement are often no more reliant on welfare services and/or benefits than they were in their pre-retirement years. This is undoubtedly true, but it is likely to be more than offset by the escalating costs associated with a rising population of those aged 80 or above, whose longevity is often a product of medical intervention and who may well require intensive and expensive community or institutionalised care. At present less than 4 per cent of the European population are aged 80 or over; by 2050 that figure is estimated to rise to 10 per cent.

Concerns about demographic trends are often couched in terms of the metaphor of the ticking 'time-bomb'. Yet legitimate though such discourse may seem, it may inadvertently serve to divert our attention from the extent to which we have *already* witnessed significant demographic change. As Figure 4.7 in fact shows very clearly, the implications of such change for the welfare state and for levels of social spending in particular are already profound. In the last decade alone, the aggregate European support ratio has fallen by some 15 per cent. Yet during this time aggregate European welfare state expenditure, as we have seen, has scarcely grown at all. This is, again, highly suggestive of retrenchment – since welfare state spending has failed to keep pace with demonstrable increases in the single most significant determinant of need (longevity).

As this suggests, whilst we might take some legitimate pleasure from envisioning longer and healthier lives, demographic trends are not good news for governments anxious to appease the preferences of tax-averse populations and businesses. The inauspicious combination of declining birth rates and greater life expectancy has already served to increase significantly the ratio of net welfare recipients to net welfare contributors since the 1950s. That ratio is higher than ever before and is rising steeply. The fiscal predicament this has generated is already reflected in significant welfare retrenchment, though such retrenchment to date is only really visible once we start to control for the significant increase in demand for both welfare benefits and services associated with an ageing population (an argument set out in greater empirical detail in Chapter 6).

The escalating costs of health provision

A related tendency, closely linked to demographic change, but by no means reducible to it, is escalating health care demand. Much, but certainly not all, of this can be attributed to an ageing population and, indeed, to a population whose ageing is to a significant extent made possible by new medical interventions and procedures which are, invariably, costly – in terms of drugs, care, or both. Figure 4.8 shows health expenditure expressed as a share of GDP at current prices for a number of European economies, selected here simply on the availability of time series data over consecutive decades.

As this demonstrates, from an average of just under 4 per cent of GDP in 1960, health care expenditure has risen to around 10 per cent of GDP for European OECD member states today. OECD projections suggest that it is set to double again in the next ten to fifteen years (OECD 2006c; see also Oxley and Macfarlan 1995).

As Martin Rhodes is surely right to note, quite apart from the demographic change to which public health care may well be contributing,

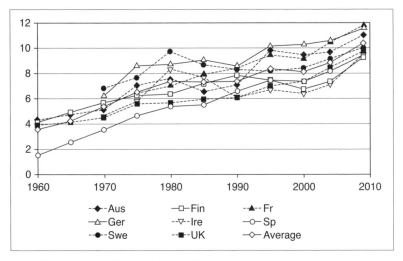

Source: Compiled from OECD Health Data, 2010.

FIGURE 4.8   *Health expenditure (% GDP), 1960–2009*

'the health care sector, broadly defined, contains its own inflationary dynamic' (1997: 64). Almost all modern health care systems, whether private or public, are based on the principle of collective insurance against individual risk. In effect, the risk of ill health and the associated costs are pooled and managed collectively. The financial viability of a private health care system relies on the average premium paid by the members exceeding the average cost of delivering the level of care specified in the insurance contract. Thus, in a financially sound private health care regime, the majority of policy-holders (assuming that they pay for their own insurance) will consume fewer health care resources than their policy premium might purchase for them in a pay-as-you-go system. But, typically, they are prepared to bear the additional cost of a health insurance policy for the peace of mind which comes from knowing that their medical costs (as specified in the terms of the policy) will be borne if, as and when required. This sounds all well and good, but it does leave the consumer with the potentially difficult choice as to what level of cover to opt for. Premiums vary greatly between, on the one hand, fully comprehensive health insurance which might bring considerable peace of mind and, on the other, minimal levels of cover offering merely a contribution to the costs of health care and far less confidence that ones needs will ultimately be met. There is, quite literally, a considerable premium to be paid for peace of mind.

In public systems, things work rather differently. As in the private system, public healthcare is only likely to prove sound financially if that proportion of taxation receipts earmarked for health expenditure covers the full costs of providing for the population. But, in contrast to the private system, there is no need for the system to generate a surplus (profit). The other major difference to almost all private insurance schemes is that a common level of entitlement and service ('cover' in insurance parlance) is ostensibly offered to all. It is tempting to see this as the equivalent of a fully comprehensive health insurance scheme, but that is in fact somewhat misleading. For, in effect, all public health care systems are also health care *rationing* regimes. National health care systems must, in effect, specify a level of cover appropriate for the entire population that is fundable out of taxation receipts. And herein lies the difficulty. For the level of cover that such a system can credibly provide is likely to fall some way short of that delivered by a fully comprehensive private insurance policy – whose per capita premium is likely to be very much higher than the per capita share of GDP invested in a public healthcare system.

In a world in which vast (public and private) resources are invested in the search for new drugs and procedures, in which medical innovation occurs at an almost exponentially increasing rate, and in which pharmaceuticals companies demand an ever higher price for the highly specialised drugs they are increasingly able to supply, such rationing is likely to become highly politicised. Patients, who may well have previously been encouraged to regard their national health care system as akin to a fully comprehensive insurance scheme, are likely to respond very negatively to being told that they cannot have access to the latest therapies, drugs and techniques to diagnose and treat their condition. And whilst those responsible for health care rationing within the system may have periodic successes in suppressing expectation amongst citizens about appropriate 'cover', it is difficult to see how they can prevent pharmaceutical and therapeutic costs rising year-on-year in real terms. Add to this the problem of an ageing population, whose life expectancy might be further enhanced by access to the newest and most expensive drugs, procedures and techniques, and the problem of escalating demand and the escalating costs of satisfying that demand become clear (for estimates of the size of this effect in the UK, see Glennerster 2010).

This might be seen as a good argument for the privatisation of health care. Yet, it is here chastening to remind ourselves that private insurance systems (such as operate in the US) invariably prove more expensive, on a per capita basis, for a given level of care than public systems. They also tend to leave a significant proportion of the population either totally uninsured or dangerously under-insured (see Aaron 1991; Barr 1998: 277–318; Evans, Barer and Hertzmann 1995). It might also be noted that non-mandatory occupational health insurance schemes tend to have the effect of suppressing labour market mobility and hence the capacity of employers to respond flexibly to changing demand in international or domestic markets.

Overall, then, when contextualised in terms of both demographic trends and self-reinforcing cost-inflationary pressures, it is remarkable that health care expenditure in Europe in recent years has not risen more rapidly. Stable or even rising aggregate welfare expenditure may well mask an ongoing process of retrenchment. Our welfare states, though costing us more, are in fact failing to deliver the levels of access, care and service that we were previously accustomed to expect.

Reassessing the conventional wisdom: a competitive audit of the welfare state

As the above paragraphs reveal, once we begin to control for variations in demand (and need) for welfare services and benefits, it is difficult not to conclude that Europe has witnessed, in recent decades, a quite significant process of welfare retrenchment. Moreover, a quite plausible and compelling narrative of welfare retrenchment (or at least of the pressures for welfare retrenchment) can be told without reference to exogenous factors relating to the terms of international competition so much as to endogenous factors widely experienced. So where does this leave the conventional view so frequently voiced by politicians and academics alike? This view suggests that: (i) it is the transition from closed to open economies that has exposed European welfare states for the burden on competitiveness that they now are; and (ii) it is the corrosive character of welfare expenditure on competitiveness that has led to such pressures for reform as we have seen. Is it little more than a convenient alibi, offered as a post hoc rationalisation for a long-term retrenchment already underway and precipitated by rather more immediate and parochial factors?

In order to answer these questions we need, in effect, to develop a competitive audit of the contemporary welfare state. In so doing we develop, adapt and extend the work of Ian Gough (though see also Atkinson 1999; Mares 2010). In a particularly thorough and perceptive way, he assesses the full range of arguments that have been brought to bear upon the complex relationship between the welfare state and international competitiveness (1996, 2000: 177–202; see also Pfaller *et al.* 1991).

As we shall see, and as Gough demonstrates well, things are considerably more complex than most public discourse and, indeed, almost all of the academic literature would lead us to believe. For a breathtaking variety of both positive and negative economic effects (or 'externalities' as economists prefer) of welfare state expenditure have been identified at various times in relevant bodies of literature. At the very least, this suggests that the orthodox account that presents welfare expenditure simply as a drain on competitiveness is a gross and distorting simplification of a far more complex reality. Whether, in the end, it suggests that the welfare state is competitiveness-enhancing is a more nuanced judgement, requiring a detailed consideration of the evidence.

It is precisely such an audit of the welfare state that Gough develops. This he does by considering, in turn, the potential economic effects which might be seen to follow from: (1) the cost of the welfare state (as reflected in levels of taxation of capital and labour); (2) its direct social and economic consequences; and (3) its indirect social and economic consequences. Each of these is further assessed in terms of the likely consequences for: (1) the cost and/or supply of capital; (2) the cost and/or supply of labour; and (3) levels of economic productivity.

In what follows, the case against the welfare state (in terms of its supposedly competitive-corrosive consequences) is considered first, before we turn to the case in favour of the welfare state (in terms of its supposedly competitive-enhancing consequences). We attempt to draw up an overall balance sheet in conclusion.

Negative externalities: the 'competitiveness-corrosive' consequences of the welfare state

As we have sought to demonstrate, the conventional orthodoxy tends to posit a simple trade-off between, on the one hand, the kind of goals associated with a comprehensive welfare state – most significantly, equity and equality – and, on the other, economic efficiency. In such accounts welfare expenditure, particularly that associated with redistribution to correct market-generated inequalities, comes at a significant cost in terms of economic competitiveness since it impedes the efficient operation of the market. In addition to the arguments reviewed above, a variety of negative (or 'competitive corrosive') exter-

TABLE 4.2　*The competitive-corrosive consequences of welfare expenditure*

	Cost/supply of capital	Cost/supply of labour	Productivity of capital and labour
Expenditure/ taxation (indirect effects)	1. Borrowing crowds out investment; 2. Social costs encourage capital flight	3. Direct taxes increase labour cost and reduce supply	——
Social programmes (direct effects)	4. PAYE (pay-as-you-earn) pensions reduce savings	5. State pensions, unemployment and sickness benefits reduce labour supply	6. Public sector social provision less efficient

nalities of welfare expenditure – both direct and indirect – are identified in this literature.

These are summarised in Table 4.2. Though they constitute an impressive list of ostensibly competitive-corrosive economic consequences of welfare expenditure, the evidence on which they are based, as we shall see, is by no means unequivocal. In the following paragraphs we consider each entry in the table in turn.

Borrowing crowds out investment

The 'crowding-out thesis' as it is invariably known, is a classic argument against comprehensive and costly welfare states. It became extremely influential in the 1970s at a time of low growth, rising inflation and rising unemployment. Though largely discredited by economists in recent decades – both theoretically and empirically – it does still have a certain caché in debates about the future of the welfare state.

The argument itself is relatively simply stated (for the classic exposition, see Bacon and Eltis 1976). It is premised on the assumption that costly welfare states are likely to be associated with high levels of public debt and hence public borrowing. Debt financed government spending, it is argued, has the effect of diminishing (or 'crowding-out') both private spending and, more significantly, private investment. Two mechanisms are here pointed to. The first is the more direct. Public borrowing serves to reduce bond prices and to drive up interest rates, thereby increasing the returns to savings and decreasing the propensity to both private consumption and private investment (particularly that funded out of borrowing). The second mechanism is based on expectations. Businesses are likely to take deficit financing as evidence of the government's willingness to trade inflation for employment. Consequently, the former will seek to adapt itself to anticipated inflationary pressures by saving, rather than reinvesting, profits.

There are a number of theoretical and empirical problems with such an argument today. But perhaps the key point is that the assumptions made in the crowding-out thesis about government preferences are no longer plausible, if ever they were. In a sense, it is Keynesianism not the welfare state itself that is in the dock in the crowding-out thesis; and the close association of Keynesianism with the welfare state is now long since over. In an era of monetarism, central bank independence and, indeed, EMU, few if any contemporary European governments are either willing or able to trade inflation for employment. Nor (whether subject to the Stability and Growth Pact or not) are they likely to plan concertedly to run budget deficits as a means of sustaining demand – witness the rapidity of the turn to austerity in the face of the global financial crisis. In short, there is no longer any evidence of the assumed correlation between the welfare state expenditure and public borrowing which is the thesis' central premise. It is, then, at best an irrelevance – a warning about the dangers of a practice long-since abandoned.

Or so one might well have argued prior to the global financial crisis. For, as we shall see in rather more detail in the final chapter, the crisis has brought with it a severe deterioration in the state of the public finances and the return of current account deficits across Europe. This, in turn, has prompted a wave of austerity, targeting welfare state expenditure. In such a context, the 'crowding- out' thesis may well seem destined to make a return. But that does not make it any more accurate today than before the crisis. For it is very difficult credibly to attribute the deficit to welfare state expenditure. Moreover, current account deficits have typically grown most rapidly in economies characterised not by their comparative welfare generosity but by their welfare residualism. And finally, though investment is undoubtedly being squeezed today, this is not a result of high interest rates, but despite low interest rates – it is product of a credit crunch and the deleveraging of the banking sector following the crisis, certainly not of high interest rates borne of welfare profligacy (Hay 2011c).

Taxation encourages capital flight

Rather more intuitively plausible in an age of much-vaunted globalisation is the thesis, familiar from Chapter 3, that the high levels of domestic taxation associated with the welfare state are likely to result in disinvestment and capital flight. Footloose multi-national investors, in other words, are quite literally likely to take their business elsewhere, choosing the more lightly regulated business environments and less punitive taxation burdens of economies unencumbered by costly welfare commitments.

Plausible though this may seem, the principal problem with such a thesis for current purposes is that it assumes that which we are seeking to assess here – namely that the welfare state is a burden on competitiveness. And it makes this assumption precisely because it equates competitiveness with simple price competitiveness – the ability to bring a good or service to market for less than ones competitors. If we acknowledge that there is more to 'meeting the test of international markets' than the price for which one can produce a given commodity (see, for instance, Hay 2011b), then the investment behaviour of footloose investors becomes rather less predictable. It is perhaps for this reason that there is precious little evidence of the kind of disinvestment predicted by the thesis (as shown by Cooke and Noble 1998; Dunning 1988; Traxler and Woitech 2000; Wilensky 2002: 654–5). Of course this might also be because: (i) the cost of 'exit' to mobile investors is by no means negligible; (ii) such investors are, as a consequence, somewhat less footloose than is often assumed; and (iii) proximity to market is a rather more significant factor in determining investment behaviour than the character of the business environment and levels of taxation in the host economy (Hay 2008). In other words, that there is little evidence of disinvestment from high welfare spending societies cannot necessarily be taken as evidence that the welfare state enhances an economy's competitiveness. But it is certainly difficult to reconcile with the thesis that it provides an unequivocal burden on competitiveness.

The cost and supply of labour

Despite a dearth of confirming empirical evidence (for an impressively comprehensive review, see Atkinson and Mogensen 1993), the conventional wisdom has it that high levels of direct taxation represent a disincentive to full and effective labour-market participation. Workers envisaging a large proportion of their nominal wage disappearing in direct taxation, so the argument goes, will be less highly motivated than they would otherwise be. Workplace effort is, effectively, disincentivised.

It is, of course, very difficult to assess directly such a proposition. But what evidence is available seems to suggest that the European economies with the most generous welfare states and the highest levels of direct taxation are (in general) also characterised by high levels of product innovation, long employment tenure, co-operative industrial relations, impressive productivity and, above all, high levels of employee satisfaction (Eskildsen, Kristensen and Westlund 2004). The partial 'decommodification' of labour, in Esping-Andersen's terms, may well lead workers to participate more enthusiastically, flexibly and co-operatively in the production process – securing higher returns for business on its investment in labour, despite higher non-wage labour costs. Indeed, it may well be that individual remuneration for employment is rather less significant a factor than is widely assumed in determining the degree of motivation of workers; and it may well be less significant still in more co-operative societies and amongst those employed in the public sector (Heintzmann and Marson 2005). One might go further still and suggest that, whilst sizeable *increases* in the burden of taxation may well be disincentivising (certainly in the short term), stable levels of taxation (even if high) are likely to be rather less of a disincentive to workplace effort.

Yet even accepting this, all taxation on labour has the effect of placing, as Gough puts it, 'a wedge between the cost of labour to an employer and the value of the goods workers can buy with their labour' (1996: 216). But this does not, in and of itself, make the welfare state a simple burden on competitiveness. What it does suggest, however, is that societies characterised by high levels of welfare expenditure are more likely to *need* to prove themselves competitive in international markets. For domestic demand alone may be insufficient to sustain economic growth at full employment.

PAYE (pay-as-you-earn) pensions reduce savings
The superficial plausibility of the view that public pension provision funded through some kind of national insurance scheme serves to reduce levels of savings within the economy is again deceptive. As Gough notes, highly abstract neoclassical models do indeed suggest that 'a state pension scheme financed by a payroll tax will displace all or a large part of private savings' (1996: 219). If it is further assumed that any changes in savings will be mirrored by changes in investment, we would expect this central pillar of the welfare state to suppress the long-term rate of investment in, and consequent growth of, the economy.

Yet, despite this rather gloom-laden theoretical prognosis, the empirical evidence is at best ambiguous, with generous welfare states typically being associated with high and stable levels of investment (Atkinson 1995; Saunders and Klau 1985). There are two potential explanations for this – the first is that the size of the effect, though real, is small and is simply swamped by other factors. The alternative is that, in a more financially integrated market for investment, domestic savings and investment correlations have fallen to such an extent that the suppression of domestic levels of saving by public pension provision matters far less than it once did.

Moreover, and perhaps more significantly, even if PAYE pensions may have some adverse consequences for levels of domestic investment, this should not lead us to overlook the potentially perverse consequences of the transition from state-guaranteed to privately-funded pension schemes. For, as even the briefest of glances at the speculative activities of pension funds in capital-market based financial systems reveals, any significant addition to the volume of portfolio assets circulating in capital markets is only likely to intensify further corporate fears of takeovers. This is, in turn, likely to suppress levels of investment irrespective of any independent boost to savings within the domestic economy (Pollin 1995; Watson and Hay 1998). As this suggests, here as elsewhere, the story can be told rather differently.

State pensions and welfare benefits reduce the supply of labour

For those keen to emphasise the negative externalities of welfare provision, state pensions schemes stand indicted not merely for their effects on the supply of capital, but also for their adverse effects on the supply of labour. A generous state-guaranteed pension, it is argued, is likely to act as an incentive for workers to take comparatively early retirement, thereby reducing the supply of labour (and hence increasing its cost in a self-equilibrating labour market). Yet whilst there is some evidence for this claim in the US, where the demand for the labour of workers nearing retirement age is relatively high (and unemployment somewhat lower), in Europe (where that demand is rather less and unemployment higher) the relationship simply does not hold (Esping-Andersen 1994).

Similar arguments are made about the effects of unemployment and sickness benefits on the supply of labour. Once again the case made is one based on economic incentives. If the income replacement ratio is high then, it is argued, individuals will have perverse incentives – to prolong periods of unemployment and, on occasions, to opt for 'voluntary' unemployment where market compensation is poor. The consequences are clear: a diminished supply of labour and a less competitive and flexible labour market.

Again, however, whilst arguments based on incentives acquire relevance under conditions of near full employment, the problem in contemporary European labour markets is not perverse incentives (implying a conscious choice to exclude oneself from the labour market) so much as structural unemployment (the forcible exclusion from the labour market). Moreover, as we have seen, the onus in contemporary welfare state is now much more upon the benefit claimant to demonstrate that she or he is genuinely worthy of receipt of benefit – and this increasingly involves satisfying benefit agencies that claimants remain active in the search for work. As this suggests, welfare state restructuring may already have counteracted any tendency for access to benefits to provide a disincentive to labour-market participation. Insofar as this is the case, what might once have been a credible argument against the welfare state is no longer.

Public sector social provision is inefficient

The final argument on the debit side of the balance sheet, as it were, is that the public provision of welfare is costly and inefficient, certainly when compared to more market-oriented forms of provision. This, again, is a difficult claim to explore empirically and commentators' preferences for market or public forms of provision tend, perhaps as a consequence, to reflect rather more their normative/ideological preferences than they do any dispassionate attempt to assess the empirical evidence – such as it is.

Limits of space prevent any detailed assessment of the arguments, both theoretical and empirical, on this point (though see, for instance, Barr 1998; Ringen 1987). But it is certainly instructive to reflect on the costs of market-based provision. Consider health care. As already discussed, private health insurance schemes need to return profits to both the insurer and the primary health care provider. Moreover, since there are invariably those who cannot afford even the most basic of cover almost all societies in which private systems predominate are backed by some (often residual) public health care system. In effect, then, there is a problem of duplication. This we see very clearly if we compare the per capita cost of the US's largely privately delivered health care system and, say, the British National Health Service (see also Brailer and Van Horn 1993). Figure 4.9 shows, as a percentage of GDP, total health care costs in the US and the UK since 1960.

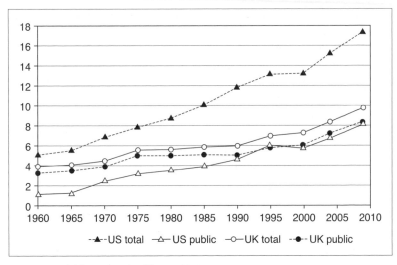

Source: Compiled from OECD Health Data, 2010.

FIGURE 4.9   *Health care spending in the US and the UK, 1960–2009 (% GDP)*

It demonstrates very clearly that, despite leaving a significant proportion of the population either completely uninsured or under-insured, the US health care system consumes almost twice as much as its UK equivalent as a share of GDP. US GDP per capita is, of course, rather higher than UK GDP per capita (as it has been throughout this period the graph shows). In 2009, according to OECD statistics, US health care expenditure was US$7,960 per capita, UK healthcare expenditure merely US$3,487 per capita (at purchasing power parity). Yet what is perhaps most staggering about Figure 4.9 is the size of the US *public* health care system – which consumed, in 2009, 8.3 per cent of GDP in comparison to the (UK) NHS's 8.2 per cent. In fact, on a per capita basis, the US spent significantly more on its public health care system in 2009 (US$2,727) than the UK spent on the NHS (US$2,164). This is hardly compelling evidence of the greater efficiency of a privately funded health care system.

Different welfare states, different effects?

On the basis of the above discussion, the economic case for the corrosive impact of the welfare state on competitiveness does not look terribly compelling. But thus far we have tended simply to assume that a common story can be told for all European welfare states. That is, in fact, rather unlikely.

Of the supposedly competitiveness-corrosive qualities of the welfare state considered above perhaps the most compelling argument is that the taxation revenues out of which the welfare state is funded increase the cost of labour and decrease the willingness of firms to take on new labour. Yet such tendencies are likely to be unevenly distributed amongst welfare states. For clearly the non-wage labour costs that businesses bear will have less of an impact on competitiveness in economies that compete primarily in capital-intensive and quality competitive sectors. By the same token, however, they will have more of an effect in economies that compete in labour-intensive sectors that are highly price sensitive. In the Nordic cases, for instance, labour costs represent a small proportion of the overall costs of production and it is quality and innovation rather than cost that are most likely to confer a competitive advantage. Yet in many east–central European cases, minimising non-wage labour costs is a rather more credible strategy for enhancing (cost) competitiveness.

What this suggests is that the balance between competitive-enhancing and competitive-corrosive externalities is mediated powerfully by institutional factors (the 'contingency viewpoint' in Ian Gough's terms). Principal amongst these is what might be termed the 'regime of competitiveness' of the economy as a whole. For economies competing solely (or even principally) on the basis of cost in low-skill, labour-intensive industries, the welfare state is a clear burden on competitiveness, whilst for those seeking to pave a high-tech, high-skill route to competitiveness in capital-intensive sectors, any such negative externalities are significantly attenuated. That this is so becomes rather more transparent if we turn from the debit to the credit column of the welfare state's competitiveness audit.

Positive externalities: the 'competitiveness-enhancing' consequences of the welfare state

Given the now pervasive orthodoxy, we might expect to find little in the way of hypothesised competitive-enhancing externalities associated with inclusive social provision. Yet what is immediately striking, given the ascendancy of the conventional wisdom, is the sheer range and diversity of factors, even in quite mainstream economic analysis, pointing to the potential contribution of the welfare state to competitiveness in export markets. These are summarised in Table 4.3 and considered in more detail in the following pages.

TABLE 4.3   *Positive externalities of welfare expenditure*

	Cost/supply of capital	*Cost/supply of labour*	*Productivity of capital and labour*
Macro-economic effects	1. Macroeconomic stabilisation effects		
Social programmes (direct effects)	2. Public housing provision boosts consumption	3. Support for women's employment increases supply of labour	4. Human capital enhanced through education and training
Welfare outcomes (indirect effects)	5. Social inclusion tempers criminality; crime deters investment	6. Reduced costs of ill health	7. Contribution to internal work-place flexibility (trust and reduced trans-action costs)

Macroeconomic stabilisation effects

Here the argument is a traditional one, closely associated with Keynesian economics. High levels of social expenditure, it is argued, will tend to promote economic stability insofar as they have counter-cyclical economic effects.

This is particularly the case with unemployment benefits whose aggregate value rises in times of recession and falls in times of sustained economic growth as levels of unemployment fluctuate. Unemployment benefits provide a boost to demand at all points in the business cycle, but they provide the greatest boost in times of recession when it is needed most.

Unemployment and other transfer payments are also highly efficient ways of injecting demand into the economy. For recipients of benefits tend, almost by definition, to be drawn from the poorest sections of society. They are, as a consequence, more likely to spend (rather than save) any benefits they receive, thereby ensuring that such benefits are effectively recyled to appear as demand within the domestic economy (see also Esping-Andersen 1990: ch. 2). Such benefit recipients are also rather more likely to consume locally sourced staple goods than they are luxury imports. Consequently, demand injected into the domestic economy in the form of social transfer payments is more likely to provide a stimulus to domestic producers and service providers and less likely to fuel import penetration. As this suggests, social transfers are certainly a more effective means of stimulating demand than tax concessions to the more affluent, who will tend to save a greater proportion of any tax rebate they receive and to use a higher proportion of what they do spent on imported goods. In each of these respects, welfare expenditure contributes to macroeconomic stability

Public housing provision boosts consumption

Even ten years ago, this might well have looked one of the weaker arguments on the credit side of the welfare state's balance sheet. But arguably today, in the wake of the global financial crisis, things look different.

The thesis itself is a simple one. The subsidisation or direct public provision of housing, it is argued, holds down both public and private rents and, in the process, frees capital for consumption, thereby raising the aggregate level of demand within the economy. The logic is impeccable though the effect is likely to be small.

But things were never perhaps as simple as this implied. For, however real the effect to which it points, this was never the argument for the mass public provision of housing that it might at first seem. As the British, Irish and, indeed, Hungarian experiences in recent years show, steep and sustained rises in house prices may well have the effect of driving the poor out of the housing market and of suppressing labour-market flexibility. But, crucially, they may also have contributed in no small part to raising aggregate demand in the domestic economy (see Hay, Smith and Watson 2006; Hay, Riiheläinen, Smith and Watson 2008; Hay 2011a). For what has happened in such economies, in the 1990s in particular, is that house price inflation has allowed home owners to release portions of the equity stored in their homes as prices have risen – increasing their personal indebtedness by securing new borrowing against the appreciating value of their property. This they have used to fuel direct consumption, contributing to an impressive trajectory of growth – the 'Anglo-liberal growth model' that we identify and explore in the final chapter.

There have, of course, always been concerns about the sustainability of such a growth dynamic as house prices and levels of personal debt have risen to previously unprecedented levels during a sustained period of low interest rates (see, for instance, Hay 2006b; Hay, Smith and Watson 2006). Such anxieties would seem to have been vindicated by the bursting of the housing bubble that led to the global financial crisis. But, for as long as it lasted, house price inflation sustained by easy access to mortgage finance and rising levels of personal debt produced real wealth effects, a process Colin Crouch (2008) usefully refers to as 'privatised Keynesianism'.

In sum, then, in rather different ways, for rather different constituencies and at rather different times, the private and public provision of housing can both contribute to raising levels of demand within the domestic economy. But, as the global financial crisis brutally reveals, whilst the former might be seen as macroeconomically stabilising, the latter has proved profoundly macroeconomically destabilising in ways that now challenge the very viability of public welfare provision in the most exposed economies. This is an issue to which we return in much greater detail in the final chapter.

Support for women's employment increases the supply of labour

Rather less controversial is the claim that the support for women's employment invariably provided in the most inclusive of welfare states, serves to increase women's participation in the labour market, yielding a series of positive economic consequences.

Quite simply, the provision of nursery places and pre-school care is likely to facilitate access (particularly that of women) to the labour market and hence to improve the supply and quality of labour with consequent benefits for the productivity of the economy. Moreover, where access to the labour market can be facilitated in this way (as, for instance, in many Nordic countries in recent decades), the ratio of net welfare contributors to net welfare recipients has increased, easing fiscal pressures generated by demographic change.

Human capital is enhanced through education and training

As Gough notes, most contemporary variants of the view that the welfare state has the potential to enhance competitiveness focus on its supply-side contribution (1996: 222). Human capital theory is by far the most influential current strand of thought in this area (Allmendinger 1989; Ashton and Green 1996; Bosworth, Dawkins and Stromback 1996: 211–52; Finegold and Soskice 1988; Lucas 1988; Prais and Wagner 1987).

In an era of heightened competition, it argues, the skill level of the economy is crucial. Here the welfare state has a central role to play, ensuring flexible, high quality training and re-skilling programmes oriented directly towards the requirements of the economy (see, for instance Gradstein and Justman 2002). The implications of such a theory are that welfare retrenchment, though frequently couched in terms of competitiveness, may come at a considerable price in terms of the ability of the domestic economy to compete on any basis other than cost alone in international markets. With the turn to public austerity across Europe, this is a very important point.

Social inclusion tempers criminality; crime deters investment

An altogether different perspective on the positive externalities that may follow from significant welfare expenditure is given by a consideration of the wider societal consequences of inclusive social provision.

The logic of the argument is impeccable. Inclusive welfare regimes serve to generalise community membership, preventing the emergence of a disenfranchised and, frequently, criminalised 'underclass'. It is certainly the case that there is a strong and negative correlation between incarceration rates and levels of social spending, as shown in Figure 4.10.

Consequently, a cost–benefit analysis of welfare retrenchment that fails to take account of the likely cost (both substantive and qualitative) of heightened levels of criminality is wholly inadequate. Costs that must be considered include the expense of incarceration and law enforcement, the (social) cost to child development of crime and social dislocation and the cost to capital of excessive insurance premiums in high crime areas. Once such costs are factored into the equation, the suggestion that competitiveness may be enhanced by welfare retrenchment is significantly problematised.

A further point might also be noted – and here the US provides a chilling example. For, as an impressive body of research now demonstrates, if the incarcerated are counted among the ranks of the unemployed, the US male jobless rate rises to a level above the European average for most of the period since 1975 (Western, Beckett and Harding 1998; Western and Beckett 1998). Moreover, since the job prospects of ex-convicts are significantly eroded such that they invariably leave prison to join the ranks of the long-term unemployed, the impressive employment performance of the US in the 1980s and 1990s has in fact depended in large part on a high and increasing incarceration rate (Western and Beckett 1999). This suggests an intriguing trade-off for advanced liberal economies between costly welfare states, on the one hand, and no less costly carceral and security states, on the other.

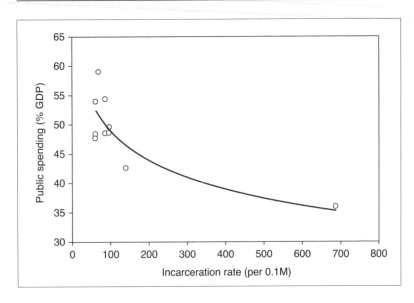

Source: Compiled from OECD *Economic Factbook* (various years).

FIGURE 4.10　*Incarceration rates and public spending, 2003*

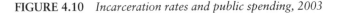

The reduced costs of ill health

Here again the argument is simple and intuitively enticing. Poor health, arising from under-insurance or non-insurance in a (primarily or exclusively) privately financed system, is likely to disrupt production. It is also likely to impose unnecessary costs on a residual public health care system which will be left to treat those whose insurance policy has failed to provide for them, and often only at the point at which they are in need of hospitalisation. Like most public goods, health is most effectively provided by the public sector and is most efficient when it contains a significant preventative component (see, for instance, the Wanless Report of 2004). Moreover, a redistributive welfare state, contributes significantly to a softening of social stratification – and this is, in itself, closely correlated with poor health (Wilkinson 1996a, b). An inclusive state-funded national health service may, then, both decrease the volume of health care demand (through preventative medicine) whilst minimising the cost of satisfying that demand; and, quite apart from this, it may also secure better and more equitably distributed final outcomes.

Welfare enhances flexibility via greater trust and reduced transaction costs

Finally, inclusive welfare states, particularly where associated with encompassing labour-market institutions (high levels of union membership and coverage), encourage relationships of co-operation and trust. Significantly, this facilitates internal flexibility — in which workers adapt themselves and their working practices to new demands and new technology. And this in turn prevents the need to resort so frequently to external flexibility (flexibility achieved by recourse to the labour market). This fosters co-operative relations between managers and labour, with consequent reductions in the rate of labour turnover (see, for instance, Eskildsen, Kristensen and Westlund 2004; Nickell 1997). It may also be reflected in higher levels of investment in human capital as workers are less likely to depart with their newly acquired skills (skills acquired at the company's expense) to the competition. In short, the welfare state may have a key role to play in nurturing the kind of co-operative industrial relations that best reward a strategy of investment in human and physical capital – and hence a regime competitiveness predicated on innovation and quality, not on cost alone.

With each of the above observations, the competitiveness balance sheet of the welfare state moves further into credit.

Conclusion

What the above discussion serves to suggest is that the relationship between competitiveness and the welfare state is far more complex (and perhaps rather more contingent) than the orthodoxy would have us believe. Nonetheless, this cannot and should not serve to hide the fact that significant welfare retrenchment has occurred and continues apace. That this is so is due, in no small part, to the predominance of a view of the competitiveness-corrosive impact of the welfare state that is at odds with much of the empirical evidence we have considered.

As the analysis of this chapter reveals, however, even this is to present an overly simplified picture. The specific consequences of welfare provision will vary on a case-by-case basis, mediated by a range of institutional and cultural factors. Not the least of these are the scope and scale of welfare provision itself and the 'regime of competitiveness' of the economy as a whole. Low cost–low skill competitiveness in labour-intensive industries places a considerable premium upon externally flexible labour markets and cheap labour. The welfare state in such a scenario is likely to represent little more than an expensive indulgence – though the social and economic cost of its retrenchment (in terms of the criminalisation and marginalisation of an underclass) should not be underestimated. Whether out-and-out cost competitiveness represents a viable competitive strategy for any contemporary European economy is debatable. What it does suggest, however, is the stark choice that European economies now face and the significance of that choice for the continued viability of the welfare state. Yet one thing should perhaps be made clear. Europe's most open economies have, throughout the post-war period, always sought competitiveness on the basis of quality not cost. They have thus sought to promote internal flexibility within the firm rather than external flexibility in the labour-market, permanent innovation in production as opposed to productivity gains on the basis of hire-and-fire and the elimination of supply-side rigidities, high and stable levels of both human *and* physical capital formation, and inclusive and encompassing labour-market institutions. Within such a model, far from representing a supply-side rigidity, the welfare state is not only a competitive advantage, it is a competitive necessity.

Chapter 5

European Integration and Welfare Capitalism

That the European Union is – or should be – more than an economic entity has been a recurring ideal in the history of integration: aspirations for a 'social Europe' have long been articulated within the integration process, while the protection of the 'European Social Model' (ESM) has been an important theme over the past twenty years. For much of this period, the Commission and member states have also poured huge effort into benchmarking social policies through the 'open method of coordination' (OMC) and the Lisbon process – an effort continued through the 'Europe 2020' agenda. Although employment issues lie at the core of this 'social dimension', European integration also touches on other aspects of social and welfare policy, ranging over areas including poverty alleviation, education and health care. It also implicates more abstract issues like solidarity and equality. In their own terms they may be effective, but these processes, policies and engagements have not been the main influences on social provision in Europe.

Instead, a broad consensus exists that the European Union privileges economic over other concerns – and is biased towards market liberal forms of economic integration. The idea of a *structural* bias in the EU towards liberal economics over social welfare is associated with a variety of theoretical and political positions. Thus, Majone's market liberal concept of the EU as a 'regulatory state' (1996), a number of social democratic elegies to welfarism (Liebfried 1992; Streeck 1995, Sharpf 2002; Habermas 2001) and a rich vein of neo-Gramscian analysis (for instance, Rhodes and van Apeldoorn 1998; van Apeldoorn 2002) all share this basic claim. If European integration has widely been seen to enhance the structural priority of liberal market economics over social and political objectives during the 1990s and early years of the new century, the economic, political and social conditions since the financial crisis of 2007–08 appear to have entrenched this power much more deeply, as public austerity cuts deep into social programmes across Europe – especially in southern Europe, east–central Europe, the UK and Ireland.

We agree, in broad terms, that the EU tends to privilege economic over social priorities and has generally promoted market liberalism. However, we believe that this consensus risks 'naturalising' the EU and the 'European' economy on which it is based, depicting it as the automatic upshot of a wholly impersonal structural logic. This view downplays the conscious efforts made to create and design any such logic (Rosamond 2002), which has drawn on a variety of political, administrative and legal elements and tools. But while European integration has clearly been the product of conscious strategic effort, it has hardly been an entirely controlled process. Rather than following a single blueprint, 'integration' is the upshot of diverse and often contradictory pressures. To the extent that it naturalises the process, the consensus view may also distract our attention from the sharp disagreement and contestation that has always surrounded its existence and – particularly – the form it has taken. Disputes and struggles over individual policies and the overall shape of the EU continue. For example, it is easy to speak of the EU as a whole – and even easier to talk of particular institutions like the European Commission as if they were unified and coherent. But we should not forget Europe's complexity: the divergent perspectives and objectives of various member states; differences between European institutions; and even divisions within individual institutions, such as the Commission's functional Directorates-General (see Cram 1994 on the Commission as a 'multi-organization').

Moreover, integration has influenced European welfare capitalism in a variety of different ways – by constructing EU-level institutions, by regulating and in the process reshaping European states, and through economic as well as social policies. Although it is not always easy to draw clear boundaries between them, these influences include:

1. The construction of EU level social policies – in principle these might add up to a 'European welfare state', but in practice EU level social 'policies' typically take the form of social regulation (Cram 1993; Majone 1993) and have tended to focus on employment policy.
2. The creation of an EU framework for the protection, development and/or reform of member state social policies – the value of the OMC for this purpose has been heavily debated in recent years, but state social regimes could also receive forms of constitutional or legal protection within the EU system.
3. The direct impact of EU policies in other fields (such as economic

integration, competition policy or monetary policy) on social policies (as discussed, for example, in Scharpf 1999).

4. The indirect impact of economic integration: whether by generating the economic basis for the development of the welfare state (Milward 2000) or intensifying general competitive pressures and thereby eroding the foundations of existing social policy settlements (deliberate strategies of regulatory competition would have a similar impact).

While generally endorsing the idea of a structural bias towards market liberalism, then, we seek to develop a more nuanced and open-ended historical analysis of its development. We argue that it is heuristically useful to view the European and state levels together as an overall social (or socio-economic) regime – albeit one that has encompassed a number of different varieties of European welfare capitalism.

This chapter has two main sections: the first traces the history of the social dimension of integration, analysing the development of the EU's structural bias towards market liberalism, while the second focuses on the period after the early 1990s. Each large section is itself subdivided. The first section begins by considering an initial period of integration in the late 1950s and 1960s, noting the reluctance of states to allow the EU to acquire major social policy competences even at this early stage amongst its original six members (West Germany, France, Italy, Belgium, the Netherlands and Luxembourg), but noting the balance struck between developing state social policies and European level economic integration.

Next, we analyse alterations to this balance in European institutional and policy developments between the late 1970s and the early 1990s. Rather than being the consequence of a natural unfolding of political and economic forces, the conscious crafting of the European economy was contingent on these other developments – and in particular the construction of a new legal system. From the point of view of economic and political integration, these developments in the legal sphere were improbable – they are effectively without parallel in the modern world. Indeed, key legal developments were often resisted by member states. The legal system was consolidated during the 1980s and early 1990s as a key foundation of the European economy.

Our historical analysis leads us to a paradox. We see the 1980s as a key decade in the consolidation of market liberalism in Europe. But others depict the decade as the heyday of 'social Europe'. Guillén and Palier, for instance, argue that Brussels was 'more oriented to the development of public social policies in the 1980s' (2004: 206). Indeed, although the notion is somewhat elusive, influential commentators hint that the possibility of a European Union Welfare State was seriously considered in the late 1980s and early 1990s (Majone 1998: 13–14). Thus, Wolfgang Streeck discerns at this time processes leading to the creation of 'interventionist-federal institutions capable of superseding both national states and free markets, and legitimating the former by doing the latter' (Streeck 1995: 396). In fact, as we shall see, key aspects of the EU's market liberal structure were created during the 1980s and early 1990s and the idea of the European Social Model (ESM) emerged within EU discourse only later.

Reference to an EU welfare state emerged in academic analysis in the early 1990s, but the term was almost always used to emphasise its implausibility (Leibfried and Pierson 1992; Streeck 1995). Leibfried (1991) hinted that social integration might be a 'forcing mechanism' for political union (a theme explored further in Kleinman and Piachaud 1993: 12, 13, 17), while Ross (1995: 357) makes some allusions to the fleeting attachment of colleagues to such claims. Perhaps the impression that the EU was set to develop as a welfare state may result from the noisy conflict between British prime minister Margaret Thatcher and Commission president Jacques Delors, in which Thatcher presented herself as a bulwark against the socialism or statism of the EU. However vaguely articulated and lacking in historical substance, this image of the late 1980s and early 1990s, contributes to the impression of a turning point in European integration, marking the 1990s and 2000s as a distinctively neoliberal phase for European integration. Our second major section addresses this conventional claim, through an analysis of European integration since the early 1990s.

The second part of the chapter thus focuses on the three processes that dominated the integration agenda between the early 1990s and the financial crisis of 2007–08: eastern enlargement; a massive extension of policy co-ordination (notably for social policy); and monetary union. We see clear evidence of the imprint of market liberalism in all three areas. First, we analyse eastern enlargement during the 1990s, to reveal the very low priority the EU placed on social policy concerns within it. Matters are a little more complex with respect to social issues although these were also articulated within the OMC and the Lisbon policy co-ordination process. Indeed, the idea that social provision could be a 'productive factor' potentially parallels our analysis of competiveness and the welfare state (in Chapter 4). Equally, however, policy co-ordination could be – and arguably increasingly *was* – aimed at reconstructing social policies so as to subordinate them to economic priorities. Finally, the blueprint for EMU clearly followed a highly orthodox and market liberal design – and influential analysts depict the euro as the centerpiece of a disciplinary neoliberal economic constitution for Europe (Gill 1998; Cafruny and Ryner 2003). Yet a moment's reflection on the developing discourse of sovereign debt in the aftermath of the crisis of 2007–08 – particularly in relation to southern European eurozone countries – suggests anything but the effective imposition of a disciplinary monetary orthodoxy over the previous decade. Arguably, eurozone membership *weakened* the orthodox discipline of some member states during the early years of the twenty-first century, with tragic social implications since 2007–08. So, in contrast to the increasing market-orientation of the Lisbon Process, we suggest that process of economic integration during the 1990s and early 2000s in fact saw the disciplinary liberal model of EMU decisively weakened.

Tracing market liberal bias in European integration

Economic integration and social Europe: the early years

Core aspects of the framework provided by the Treaty of Rome (1957) were filled in during the 1960s and a balance was set between economic integration and social concerns. Its economic core was made up of the Custom's Union and Common Market alongside developing provision in such areas as competition law. The Common Agricultural Policy (CAP) became more a matter of subsidising agricultural incomes than of creating an integrated market. The Treaty also included a European Social Fund, some general statements of principle on social questions and two or three substantive articles (the basis, in revised and renumbered form, of articles 117, 118 and 119). These defined limited areas of social policy competence in which the EC could pass law in the form of 'Directives'. Key social policy articles (117, 118) were added 'very late' in the Treaty debates after labour representatives intervened directly with Paul-Henri Spaak, a key Belgian negotiator (Hoskyns 1996: 48). These articles were also weak; by contrast the equal pay article was clearer and provided strong Commission powers. Originally in part of the Treaty on distortions to competition (which was deleted), the provisions on equal pay had a longer history, and strong backing from the French delegation. But equal pay notwithstanding, social policy was marginal to the original design of the Treaty of Rome. It is easy to imagine the European Economic Community coming into existence *without* Treaty provision for social policy or equal pay for women and men.

As early as 1958, however, the Commission was already arguing that 'the sphere of action of the institution in social matters has no strict limits' and 'the problems listed in Article 118' are 'in no way exclusive' (Commission First General Report 1958: 78). The following year the Commission identified 'the comparative lack of precision in the Treaty' on social policies as giving it no choice but to interpret these articles, and it had no 'intention that the interpretation shall be restrictive'. As it went on to explain, '[we] cannot conceive that the Community has not got a social purpose' (Commission Second General Report 1959: 107). Prefiguring its later practice, the Commission seized upon a Council decision to accelerate 'the first stage' of the EU's internal economic liberalisation, by removing internal tariffs ahead of schedule as an 'excuse . . . to increase its push on social policy'; the member states faced 'a sudden embarrassment when it was found that nothing had been done to honour the commitment . . . to ensure the application of the principle of equal pay during 'the first stage', and very little on social policy generally' (Hoskyns 1996: 61, 60).

The Commission's 'push' focused on the *harmonisation* of state social systems, in particular social security. Again, adopting an approach that would later become a mainstay of its action in the entire social policy field, the Commission sought to draw trade union and employer associations as well as government representatives into joint deliberations (as this stage largely through various ad hoc committees). It also sought to assert its own prerogatives, arguing that it should itself 'keep the Council and member governments informed of what the Treaty implied for the Commission' (Commission Sixth General Report 1963: 21). This approach 'suggested that governments might be bypassed and action encouraged which was unwelcome to them' (Collins 1975: 191). The 1962 European Conference on Social Security was typical: while it included a multiplicity of private and public actors, member states participated only as observers. Nonetheless, on the basis of the Conference conclusions, within a year the Commission had completed a draft programme for the harmonisation of social security schemes, and issued recommendations on the employment of young workers and the rationalisation of invalidity costs, both opposed by employers and member states on grounds of cost (see especially Cram 1997: 31–4).

The original six member states are usually considered to share both similar social institutions and a commitment to European integration.

Yet fully five of 'the six' perceived the Commission's strategy as high-handed and over-reaching its practical and legal competence. Aside from Italy, all member governments expressed their discontent with the Commission and refused to co-operate with it on social policy. Prefiguring French president de Gaulle's famous 'empty chair' policy (1965–6) of withdrawing his ministers from the Council, no meetings of the Council of Ministers for Social Affairs were held between October 1964 and December 1966. Eventually the deadlock was broken by the 'Veldkamp Memorandum' – whereby the Council sharply restricted the Commission in social policy: even the relatively strong Treaty provision for equal pay remained largely a dead-letter throughout the 1960s. Veldkamp also reinforced the dominant 'economic' interpretation of the Treaty (a reading promoted by the member states) against a more 'social' alternative (promoted by the Commission) (Collins 1975: 161; Holloway 1981: 57; Hoskyns 1996: 51).

As this powerfully suggests, even when EU membership was restricted to a small number of relatively similar states, the barriers to a 'supranationalisation' of social policy were already significant. Even here the Commission's 'social' position may have been more instrumental than ideological: more a vehicle for expanding the Commission's competence than a reflection of a principled advocacy. Initially it adopted a stance that served potentially to maximise its role and influence. The Commission then learned about the difficulties facing social policy harmonisation and the weakness of the tools at its disposal.

In retrospect, the thirty years after 1945 have been widely described as the 'golden age' of the welfare state. Yet, as we saw in Chapter 1, the key expansive phase for many continental European states was during the 1960s – and even the 1970s – rather than the late 1940s. Even for the 'original six', the idea that a dynamic domestic policy field should be surrendered to supranational control was unacceptable. But, as Alan Milward (2000) has argued, the integration process promoted the further deepening and development of the core European economy – and this helped to generate the resources necessary for welfare expansion. Arguably, the result was a 'workable balance' between European economic integration and the 'social' sovereignty of the member states – but this was a product of serendipity; it was not consciously planned.

Negative integration or the European regulatory state?

The creation of the pan-European market is central to the story of the EU's impact on welfare. During the 1990s analysts writing from a variety of perspectives converged on the broad idea that something about the structure of the EU privileged liberalisation as the means of creating that market (Leibfried 1991; Streeck 1995; Rhodes and van Apeldoorn 1998; Habermas 2001; van Apeldoorn 2002). Here we will focus on two influential versions of this thesis – Fritz Scharpf's analysis of 'negative' and 'positive' integration (1999, 2002); and Giandomenico Majone's account of the EU as a 'regulatory state' (1996). Scharpf's influential analyses provide a downbeat assessment (from a broadly social democratic perspective) of the prospects for the ESM. He argues that Europe's political and legal structures are structurally suited to 'negative' integration – that is, to the tearing down of policies and practices seen as barriers to the internal market in Europe; but that 'positive' integration – the construction of European level institutions and policies – is a much more difficult task. The European Court of Justice (ECJ) and the centrality of internal market and competition law to the EU treaties – often understood as an 'economic constitution' – lie at the heart of this dynamic: 'a court-driven process of market liberalization undermining the social policy competence of the Member Sates' (Armstrong 2010: 189). Scharpf (1999: ch. 2) provides a detailed and sophisticated analysis of the application of EU competition law to public services – particularly utilities – showing how they have been subjected to a logic of European competition.

Describing the EU as a 'regulatory state', Majone (1996) also notes its market orientation, but provides a significantly – if subtly – different analysis. While 'negative integration' treats the European market as a natural consequence of the tearing down of national economic and social barriers, Majone (1992, 1993, 1996) insists that markets require regulation, and hence points to positive (re)regulation at the European level. We push this argument further, emphasising that the European market had to be constructed and needs to be maintained. Two instances of positive integration through the creation of common institutions are, we suggest, particularly important: the constitution of the European legal order and the process of monetary union. While both have made major contributions to the marketisation of Europe, whether either represents a pure victory for neoliberalism is a matter for empirical analysis. We will return to a detailed consideration of each presently.

Majone's analysis amounts to a sophisticated form of economic liberalism – that acknowledges (at least some of) the 'positive' institutional prerequisites of the market. Indeed, Majone recognises that social aspirations may lead to the creation of positive EU social policies

(1993). But where Scharpf's analysis hinges on the distinction between positive and negative integration, Majone's turns on the difference between regulatory and redistributive policies (1996: 54–6). So, for Majone, while the EU can legitimately and effectively engage in social *regulation* it lacks both the capacity and legitimacy to make traditional welfare policies (1993). Practical factors are at play here: the EU lacks bureaucratic capacity and budgetary resources to deliver the traditional range of state social provision (education, health care and so on). But Majone's regulatory theory also includes more explicitly normative elements.

One concerns the absence of a European 'demos'. Redistributive policies move resources between individuals, so Majone associates them with 'majoritarian' democracy, which is notably absent at the EU level. Sometimes Majone seems to suggest that the EU should be based on a 'workable division of responsibilities between supranational economic integration and national social welfare' (Armstrong 2010: 188). Here, however, there is an important ambiguity in the regulatory analysis. For at times Majone also argues that the displacement of the (Keynesian) welfare state by the regulatory state is a general phenomena across Europe, occurring across all levels of government, though with the EU as its cutting edge (1996: i, 55–6, 285–8, 296; for a critical review, see Wincott 2006). On this analysis, the 'workable balance' between supranational regulatory liberalism and redistributive state welfare is disrupted.

While the legitimacy of redistribution and social policies is depicted as somewhat tenuous, Majone has taken a bullish view of regulatory legitimacy, whether at the EU or the domestic level. This is based on his view of the 'Pareto efficiency' of the putative benefits of regulation at this level (which, in short, are assumed demonstrably good for all). As a result, regulatory policies lead to a general enhancement of 'welfare' and, in effect, generate their own legitimacy. At times Majone entertains the idea that positive developments in regulation follow normative assessment of where it is needed. This notion – summed up in the phrase 'normative analysis as positive theory' (or NPT, see Majone 1992, 1996: 33–4; see also Peltzman 1989; Joskow and Noll 1981) – fully reveals the functionalist character of this kind of regulatory analysis. And here, Majone's confidence about regulatory legitimacy swamps any anxieties about legitimacy problems generated where supranational liberalisation undermines democratic state welfare.

The regulatory theory of the EU pivots on distinguishing between regulation and other policy forms. In effect, regulatory policies are defined in contrast to redistributive policies, macro-economic stabilisation and the provision of 'merit goods' (Majone 1992, 1996, 1998). The former are *defined* as efficiency enhancing and the latter, by implication at least, as a drain on economic performance. Both these claims can be contested (as we saw, in effect, in the preceding chapter). It is by no means clear that regulatory policies are efficiency-enhancing (indeed, most neoliberals would want to make the opposite argument), while we have argued that the welfare state – merit goods, redistribution and all – *can* make a positive contribution to economic performance. If this is the case then why should regulatory market liberalism systematically win out over the welfare state?

The distinction between regulatory and redistributive policies is a powerful heuristic device, and a vast literature has taken off from 'Majone's great insight' that the EU's 'distinctive character' is captured in the term regulatory state (see, for instance, Moran 2002: 404). Yet for all its descriptive value, the normative and explanatory foundations of the 'regulatory state' thesis are problematic and difficult to disentangle from his ostensibly descriptive account. Rather than providing an independent or external framework for the analysis of market liberalisation and the emergence of the EU as a regulatory state, Majone's account amounts to a normative argument, or effort of persuasion. He becomes, in effect, an advocate of a sophisticated form of (regulatory) market liberalism. Ultimately, the argument depends on a prior commitment to a market ideology (as Majone sometimes himself seems to concede 1996: 50, 52–4).

Latterly, Majone's confidence in the legitimacy of EU-level regulatory liberalism seems to have been shaken – albeit for seemingly contradictory reasons. Optimism about the future of the EU is, he has now come to argue, 'not sufficiently supported either by hard economic data or by an adequate analysis of the challenges facing the Union today'. The most significant of these challenges, he goes on, are the (presumably unanticipated) 'consequences of decisions taken during the fifteen years since the fall of the Berlin wall … in particular … monetary union and … eastern enlargement … two endogenous shocks [that] could have far-reaching consequences for the future of the Union' (2006: 1). By moving monetary policy far from the reach of democratic political control, EMU appears as the apotheosis of regulatory liberalism. Yet, noting the 'decision to sacrifice the democratic legitimacy' of the ECB 'for the sake of monetary (and political) integration', Majone has also expressed concern about the Bank's 'extremely high degree of independence' (2006: 8–9). Yet his reasons for doing so – *both* because the

EU has become 'over-extended' *and* due to the failure to develop an 'economic government' – are in some tension with one another.

The signal contribution of Majone's work is its emphasis on the importance of positive integration in the creation and maintenance of the European market. Majone also directs attention to the roles of ideas, deliberation, persuasion and evidence in the (regulatory) policy process (1992, 2006). We take up and build on these insights in what follows. Yet ultimately we offer a different explanation, which is at once more institutional and which places greater emphasis on the role of ideas. Instead of treating the rise of regulatory liberalism in Europe as the product of functional and efficient processes – or even as the victory of norms which generate these processes – we see the increasing influence of regulatory liberalism on the theory and practice of the EU as intimately related to the idea of market liberalism.

While regulatory analysts tend to emphasise the role to be played by 'independent' regulatory agencies, the most significant institutional prerequisite for market liberalism – the rule of law – remains relatively neglected. In fact, the law is so fundamental to market liberalism that it can easily become taken for granted in some of its key features. For example, Scharpf (1999: ch. 2) offers a detailed and highly influential account of the role of law in European integration. He develops a persuasive analysis of the crucial ways in which law has helped to structure the EU in such a way as to grant systematic advantages to priorities of economic liberalisation over social concerns. Yet, in equating this Court- and law-focused system with *negative* integration, Scharpf directs our attention away from the fact that the construction of the European legal 'order' was – as it remains – itself the (ongoing) outcome of a complex process of *positive* integration. To be fair, Scharpf does draw heavily on influential analyses of the history of legal integration (in particular, Weiler 1982; Burley and Mattli 1993). Yet, *from the perspective of the EU's bias towards market liberalism* even these analyses largely miss two key implications of treating the EU legal system as an instance of positive integration.

First, the ability to embark on a deep and wide-ranging process of market integration from the mid-1980s required, and was predicated upon, the existence of a reasonably effective and broadly respected EU legal system – and *before the early 1980s such a system had not yet been fully constructed.* Standard legal accounts obfuscate this issue by treating 'direct effect' (the idea that EU laws are binding on individuals as well as states – in contrast to standard international law) and 'supremacy' (the idea that EU law trumps domestic law) as the twin foundational doctrines of the European legal order. But if they are twins, direct effect and supremacy are so intimately connected as to be conjoined. We prefer to view supremacy as the underlying principle, and direct effect as a kind of technique for achieving that principle. In fact, direct effect is a series of techniques, not just one. Accordingly, it takes rather different forms in relation to (some) Treaty rules than it does for secondary laws (in particular directives).

From the perspective of the role of the law and courts in a system biased towards market liberalism, the European Court of Justice (ECJ) had not developed key features of 'direct effect' *that turned the law into a viable tool for substantive negative integration in the economic domain* by the mid-1970s. For example, the principle that Treaty provisions could have a 'horizontal' direct effect – that is, that they might regulate relationships between individuals as well as 'vertical' relationships between individuals and states – was introduced by the Court in 1976 (*Defrenne v SA Belge de Navigation Aerienne* (SABENA) [1976] 43/75, 567). *Van Duyn v Home Office* (Case 41/74) [1974] ECR 1337), also in the mid-1970s, was the landmark case with respect to the direct effectiveness of secondary legislation (Directives) – and this issue remained contentious and unclear throughout the 1980s (particularly regarding 'horizontal' effect – whether individuals could rely on Directives in their relationships with one another). In *Marshall v Southampton and South-west Hampshire Health Authority* (Case 152/840 [1986] ECR 723), the ECJ rejected the horizontal direct effect of Directives – a decision criticised for failing to provide individuals with legal certainty). The Court later dramatically strengthened the liability of states where they failed to implement a Directive fully and accurately. In Francovitch (Joined Cases C-6/90 and C-9/90 [1991] ECR I-5357), the Court decided that the Italian state had to provide workers with compensation on the insolvency of their employer, to which they would have been entitled if Italy had implemented Directive 80/987/EEC.

The ECJ continued to develop the structure of EU law into the 1990s and beyond, but by the early 1980s a reasonably robust overall framework of law was in place. The creation of this legal framework fundamentally transformed the possibilities for economic liberal market integration in Europe. The 'Cassis de Dijon' decision (Case 120/78, *Rewe-Zentrale AG v Bundesmonopolverwaltung für Branntwein* [1979] ECR 649), has rightly received attention from political analysts (Burley and Mattli 1993; Alter and Meunier-Aitsahalia 1994; Garrett 1995; Mattli and Slaughter 1995) and has generated a vast legal literature. The former is primarily focused on whether the ECJ exercised autonomous political power in this case, or remained essentially constrained by the preferences of the member states. So, what is for us the key issue remains somewhat out of focus or blurred.

In itself, the ECJ's decision in Cassis had no direct policy implications: if anything, it narrowed the scope of the 'mutual recognition' principle set out by the Court five years earlier (see Case 8/74 *Procureur du Roi v Dassonville* [1974] ECR 837). It established the principle that state regulatory requirements are essentially equivalent – if a product has met the regulatory requirements to be sold legally in one state, it can be marketed throughout the EU. The 'mutual recognition' of domestic regulatory requirements creates a presumption in favour of product market integration across the EU and was the idea at the heart of the internal market. Why is this principle, then, so widely linked to the Court's decision in 'Cassis', which actually restricted its scope, rather than to 'Dassonville'? Some integration theorists suggest that it indicates that the member states remained in ultimate control of the process (Garrett 1995; Moravcsik 1995) while others stress the entrepreneurial Commission decision to promote mutual recognition after 'Cassis' (Alter and Meunier- Aitsahalia 1994; Wincott 1995). But this discussion misses the key point: *other decisions made by the Court between 1974 and 1979 fundamentally transformed the EU legal system.* The full significance of the 'Cassis' decision includes its status as a symbol of that change. Whatever the contributions of supranational institutions and member states to the wider development the EU's legal system, it involved the construction of a set of institutions and norms: that is, it was a major achievement of positive integration. Had the EU's wider legal system not developed in this manner, the internal market programme would have been unimaginable – and so too would be both Majone's 'regulatory state' and Scharpf's 'negative integration' theses.

Political analysis of EU law took off after 1993, motivated by a desire to explain the 're-launching' of an integration process previously perceived as being moribund or sclerotic. It offers a heroic image of the ECJ, steadfastly committed to 'ever closer union' – a Court with a political mission to promote European integration. Given that an 'Economic Community' provided the core of its legal jurisdiction – as well as the structural bias of the Court towards negative integration – legal promotion of integration would be expected generally to enhance liberalisation. As the scope and depth of the EU increased, areas of traditional state social provision were drawn into the ambit of EU law and the ECJ.

The Court was confronted with cases on the relationship between 'social' insurance and the economic market for insurance or the social provision of health care and the marketing of health services. On the one hand, this process often unsettled domestic systems of welfare. On the other, facing cases with a significant 'social' dimension may have introduced new elements into the jurisprudence of the Court. Particularly since 1993, these new elements include a conception of 'solidarity' as a basis on which *social* and *economic* insurance can be differentiated and the former defended from the latter (Cases C-159/91 and C-160/91 Poucet et Pistre [1993] ECR I-637) and a willingness to treat certain 'restrictions on competition' as 'necessary in order to enable undertakings to perform services of general interest' (Armstrong 2010: 202, see Case C-320/91 Criminal Proceedings Against Paul Corbeau [1993] ECR 1-2533). These decisions establish legal principles that (partially) restrict the scope of economic integration in order to preserve aspects of the social system of member states. This would seem to contradict the standard political account of a relentlessly pro-integration Court.

While the general thrust of ECJ decisions over the history of European integration has promoted liberalisation, what analysts describe as the *preferences* of the Court may not be best described as either relentlessly pro-integration or pro-market. Instead, the ECJ seems to regard itself as a Constitutional Court (Granger 2005), a role within which it has begun to look for a balance between EU economic integration and state-level social solidarity and public service, albeit at a relatively late stage. Far from being the heyday of 'social Europe' (as, for example, Guillén and Palier suggest (2004: 206), it was in the 1980s that the framework for the 'court-driven process of market liberalization' was consolidated, while the Court introduced certain limitations to liberalising economic integration only later.

The 1990s: eastern enlargement, the ESM and EMU

Analysts from a variety of different theoretical perspectives view the structure of the EU as privileging economic liberalisation over social concerns (compare Majone 1996; Gill 1998; Scharpf 1999; Habermas 2001; Cafruny and Ryner, 2003). Our analysis of EU law, or 'legal integration', and of the history of early attempts at social policy integration both broadly confirm the image of the EU as a strategic terrain that privileges integration on a liberal economic model. But alongside this general analysis, there is also a tendency in EU studies to see the early 1990s as a turning point – when European integration moved decisively in a neoliberal direction. While some of those sceptical about eastern enlargement saw a risk that 'widening' of this kind would undermine the prospects for a 'deepening' of integration (in which they might have included a social deepening), for most analysts it was EMU – and particularly the seeming constitutionalisation of a strictly orthodox form of monetary governance – that was the key move in the neoliberalisation of Europe. Whether or not it is right to see the early 1990s as the moment when the EU crossed a critical threshold for neoliberalisation is a theme we will pick up as we consider EMU, the 'Lisbon Strategy' and the ESM, and eastern enlargement.

Social policy and enlargement

When countries of east–central and south-eastern Europe joined, the EU changed massively in territorial scope as well as political, social and economic composition. This process of enlargement occurred alongside the development of the ESM. If the ESM – and the social dimension in general – are indeed fundamental features of the EU, this importance should be reflected in the terms negotiated with the incoming member states (cf. Hill and Smith 2005: 3, on foreign policy). In fact, during the 1990s, the EU generally deferred to the 'Washington' institutions (the World Bank and the IMF) on social policy. These institutions sought 'to implement radical changes in various fields of social policy' in east–central Europe. 'Not the European Union, but the World Bank is identified as the most influential regional agenda-setting actor in economic and social policy making in the region' (Potsůček 2004: 263–4; see also Ferge and Juhász 2004; Orenstein and Haas 2002). In other words the EU largely failed to address social issues in the enlargement process.

Despite the fact that the Copenhagen Criteria for enlargement were elaborated in 1993, alongside the Commission's Social Policy Green Paper and its White Paper *Growth, Competitiveness and Employment*, the two processes took place largely in isolation from one another. The Copenhagen Criteria included political and economic headings (plus a 'legislative alignment' category):

> Membership requires that candidate country has achieved stability of institutions guaranteeing democracy, the rule of law, human rights and respect for and, protection of minorities, the existence of

a functioning market economy as well as the capacity to cope with competitive pressure and market forces within the Union. Membership presupposes the candidate's ability to take on the obligations of membership including adherence to the aims of political, economic and monetary union. (Conclusions of the European Council, Copenhagen, June, SN 180/1/93 REV 1 1993: 13)

Social concerns did not merit consideration on an equal footing with economic, political and legal ones. Of course, new members were expected to implement the full body of existing EU rules – the *acquis communautaire* – as the allusion to taking 'on the obligations of membership' indicates. And these did include certain social elements. Some social issues – such as the social dialogue – were addressed in the enlargement process. But attention focused on 'the very existence of the main pillars of the Social Dialogue' rather than on 'the quality of their functioning' (Lendvai 2004: 324).

Overall, the EU's priorities clearly focused on the effective operation of the market economy, while also taking the legal prerequisites of the market into account. They also set out basic features of democratic institutions and practices. 'Rights' and 'social' concerns receive attention, but in a 'human rights' rather than social policy framework. Where human rights spill over into social concerns most explicitly, the results prove problematic. For example, the EU's concern with the treatment of minorities can appear as rather presumptuous and paternalistic. The EU's credibility in this domain is questionable: it is charged with operating a double standard, as it has sought to instruct aspirant members on the terms of appropriate conduct, without first having developed and implemented clear and coherent internal procedures (Lendvai 2004: 323).

So, viewing EU social policy through the lens of enlargement reinforces the conclusion that the social dimension has, at best, a secondary status. It is worth noting that the adoption of the 'Lisbon Strategy' in 2000 seems to have raised the profile of social issues for the incoming member states. But, it was 'only in 2002, when the preparation of the new member states ... to enter the EU had just finished [that] the Lisbon Strategy was presented to them as a strategy they should also adhere to' (Potsůček 2004: 263). Only at this late stage, after the completion of the enlargement process, did the internal EU discourse and politics of the ESM begin to be reflected in the relationship between the EU and its new members.

The European Social Model, part 1: Lisbon and the Open Method of Co-ordination

For more than a decade after 2000, EU social policy reform focused on the 'Lisbon Strategy'. Dating from the March 2000 extraordinary European Council meeting held in March 2000, the Lisbon social policy agenda was rooted in the idea of the European Social Model (ESM), seen as in need of protection and modernisation. Despite (or perhaps because of) its centrality, the ESM was never defined precisely. The Lisbon Strategy also had another strand – concerned with economic competitiveness, which was arguably more prominent at the Summit itself. At least initially, the Lisbon Strategy focused mostly on establishing the knowledge-based economy (KBE) as the basis for enhancing European competitiveness. The key 'strategic objective' published in the 'Presidency Conclusions' included both elements, envisaging that that European Union would, by 2010, become 'the most competitive and dynamic knowledge-based economy in the world capable of sustainable economic growth with more and better jobs and greater social cohesion'. The two strands were presented as interdependent: a vibrant KBE would provide the resources necessary to sustain the ESM; as well as offering a basis for social inclusion and cohesion the ESM was a 'productive factor' for the economy (and perhaps especially for the KBE).

The Lisbon meeting also created – or at least named – a new form of 'soft', non-legislative form of policy co-ordination: the 'Open Method of Co-ordination' (OMC). European integration had long featured various forms of 'soft law' and policy co-ordination, but Lisbon broke ground by identifying and christening the OMC as a new 'method', in contrast to the traditional 'Community Method' (focused on the production of legally binding rules, particularly in the form of Regulations and Directives, see Presidency Conclusions 2000; Commission 2001; See Wincott 2001b for an analysis). Conceiving of (some forms of) 'soft law' and 'policy coordination' as the OMC seemed to place it on something like an equal footing with the Community Method. Prior to the 1990s, a good deal of European 'soft law' – particularly that initiated by the European Commission – could be seen as preparing the ground for the later development of 'hard law' through the Community Method (analysed by Cram 1997: 99 as a 'softening up' process). By contrast, the Council was permanently to hold the strategic role in the OMC (although the Commission also had an important role). While the OMC might lead to greater convergence in policy or performance (the Presidency Conclusions discussed 'greater convergence towards the main EU goals', para. 37) – and could help to sustain integration in other domains (or even the legitimacy of the overall multi-level European policy mix) – the naming of the OMC did not enhance the prospects of bringing the policy domains to which it applied under the Community Method.

At Lisbon, the European Council identified four key elements of the OMC. It was to involve:

1. fixing guidelines for the Union combined with specific timetable for achieving the goals set in the short, medium and long terms;
2. establishing, where appropriate, quantitative and qualitative indicators and benchmarks against 'the best in the world' and tailored to the needs of different member states and sectors as a means of comparing best practice;
3. translating these European guidelines into national and regional policies by setting specific targets and adopting measures, taking into account national and regional differences;
4. periodic monitoring, evaluation and peer review organised as mutual learning processes (para. 37, Lisbon Council Conclusions).

The Lisbon meeting identified several substantive policy domains in which to use the OMC. They were: the information society (para. 8), research and development (para. 13), enterprise and innovation (para. 15), education (para. 27), social protection (para. 31), and social inclusion (para 32). Each was seen to be implicated in some way in the building of either the KBE or the ESM, or both.

The relationship between the economic and social strands of the strategy proposed at Lisbon can be understood in at least two ways: *either* as a subordination of social policy to the demands and imperatives of the economy *or* as a repudiation of the 'big trade off' (to use Okun's 1975 classic phrase) assumption that social provision is necessarily a drain on economic performance (precisely the two approaches that we have contrasted in Chapter 4). As reflected in the published Presidency Conclusions (2000), the emphasis of the original agenda set at Lisbon was more on the economy than on social concerns. Equally, however, an optimistic mood prevailed at the Lisbon meeting in March 2000, based on confidence that the new economy could be linked in a virtuous circle to 'more and better jobs' and a renewal of the ESM. The optimism was reinforced by the explosion of investment in the new 'dot.com' economy, which appeared to offer a new phase of economic growth grounded in the spread of novel technologies. The Lisbon Strategy seized on the *possibility* of reconciling different ideological positions, policy models and priorities by creating a virtuous circle of economic growth and social cohesion, that would minimise the need for hard choices to be made. Lisbon was a triumph of hope, but did it live up to expectations?

After Lisbon, the emphasis seemed to shift. Within fifteen months of the meeting, explicit 'OMCs' had been adopted for social inclusion (at the Nice Council in 2000), pensions (Stockholm 2001) and health care (Gothenburg 2001) (Armstrong 2010, Citi and Rhodes 2007). The OMC for research and innovation followed at the 2003 Spring European Council (although processes similar to the OMC were also created for such areas as enterprise and e-business, education and the information society, and 'new' governance approaches have also been developed for climate change policy, (see Citi and Rhodes 2007). Aside from suggesting that rather than representing a single policy 'type', a variety of OMCs exist (as Armstrong argues convincingly (2010)), these developments show how 'Lisbon' and particularly the OMC became closely associated with 'social Europe'. Two reasons for this change relate directly to the substance of the Lisbon Strategy itself.

First, building on the experience of the European Employment Strategy (EES – of which more below) 'socially-oriented' actors mobilised vigorously to make use of the OMC for social policy. These actors included the then Commission Directorate-General V (Employment and Social Affairs) and subsequently the Employment Committee and Social Affairs Committee (Palier 2006: 9, see also de la Porte and Pochet 2002) as well as various social NGOs – not least as organised through the European Anti-Poverty Network. Second, the Lisbon Strategy was conceived at the height of an episode of irrational market exuberance about the KBE. The key market for new economy investment – NASDAQ – peaked on 10 March 2000, less than a fortnight before the Lisbon Council met (23–4 March). By early April it had become clear that a speculative investment bubble had blown up into a 'dot-com' boom – indeed the bursting of that bubble is usually dated to developments in a legal case against Microsoft on 3 April (when the company was declared to be a monopoly). Of course, the bursting of this bubble undermined the overly optimistic Lisbon assumption that the KBE would inaugurate a new era of sustained economic growth (Watson 2001b critiques the idea that the Lisbon Strategy could be based on the 'new economy'). As a result, the immediate appetite for new KBE-linked OMCs was weak – although some did eventually emerge in 'new economy' policy domains.

The collapse of the 'dot.com' dream pushed the economic debate back to familiar discussion of structural reform and competitiveness. 'Economically-oriented' actors sought to re-focus the Lisbon Strategy as a whole, rather than developing particular 'economic' OMCs. Renewed emphasis on the economic dimension of integration was evident within a couple of years of Lisbon, especially in the July 2002 terms of reference for André Sapir's high-level independent expert group. The Sapir group was invited to 'propose a strategy for delivering faster growth together with stability and cohesion in the enlarged Union' (Sapir *et al.* 2003: i). The 2003 Sapir Report was followed swiftly by (former Dutch prime minister) Wim Kok's 'mid-term' review of the Lisbon Strategy. Highly critical, the Kok Report (2004) argued that the Lisbon Strategy should concentrate on 'actions that promote growth and jobs'. It set the tone for the Commission's re-launching of a streamlined and economically oriented Lisbon Strategy in February 2005. For a period it seemed possible that the new networks, institutions and practices associated with the 'social' OMCs and the Lisbon Strategy might collapse. In the event 'socially-oriented' actors and networks mobilised to ensure that this did not happen, but they were not able to resist a significant downgrading of social priorities relative to economic ones.

The Lisbon Strategy is widely regarded as a failure: well before its 2010 deadline it was clear that Europe was not about to become 'the most competitive and dynamic knowledge-based economy in the world capable of sustainable economic growth with more and better jobs and greater social cohesion'. Shortly before taking up the EU Council Presidency, on 2 June 2009 Swedish prime minister Frederik Reinfeldt and finance minister Anders Borg published a joint article in *Dagens Nyheter* arguing that 'the Lisbon Agenda, with only a year remaining before it is to be evaluated, has been a failure'. Yet a broadly similar approach – involving attempts to set targets at both the EU and national levels – has been adopted for the successor EU strategy: 'Europe 2020'. The overall themes sound eerily familiar: a 'smart, sustainable, inclusive' economy delivering 'high levels of employment, productivity and social cohesion'. The means for achieving these ends also echo the Lisbon Strategy, featuring EU-wide and national targets in employment, innovation, education, social inclusion and climate/energy (see www.ec.europa.eu/europe2020/index_en.htm).

Thus far, we have addressed the Lisbon Strategy largely on its own terms. This reflects the mainstream approach adopted by social policy analysts, which treats the Lisbon Strategy as a turning point for European governance. But by isolating the strategy from the wider context of EU economic and social policy, we end up with a somewhat distorted perspective both on Lisbon and the overall economic and social character of Europe. Two inter-related aspects of the wider economic and social context of the Lisbon Strategy have an immediate significance here: first, the patterns of policy co-operation that had developed during the 1990s and second, the history of monetary union in Europe. Some systems of policy co-operation were created explicitly to serve EMU – most obviously the Stability and Growth Pact (see below) – while in a sense all were created in the shadow of monetary union. The enlargement of the EU to include countries from the former communist bloc was an equally important development over this period, although it was arguably less visible in the debate about the economic and social future of Europe (at least until the Sapir Report).

So, far from having been invented at Lisbon in 2000, policy co-ordination has a long history in European integration – perhaps going back to the strategies adopted by the Commission in the 1960s after its initial attempt at social policy harmonisation was defeated. The six or seven years before the Lisbon meeting had been a particularly intense phase of 'process' creation. Starting with the economic policy co-ordination introduced by the Treaty of Maastricht, widely known as the Broad Economic Policy Guidelines (BEPGs), subsequently 'processes' were introduced at – and named for – European Council meetings. They include the Essen Process (1994), the Luxembourg Process (1997), the Cardiff Process (1998) and the Cologne Process (1999). Essentially, the BEPGs and the Cardiff and Cologne Processes focus on structural economic reform, while the Luxembourg Process is concerned with employment (Luxembourg superseded Essen, after the Treaty of Amsterdam in 1997 provided a legal foundation for the European Employment Strategy (EES)). Perhaps showing some weariness with the remorseless creation of 'processes', the Lisbon Council stated: 'No new process is needed. The existing Broad Economic Policy Guidelines and the Luxembourg, Cardiff and Cologne processes offer the necessary instruments, provided they are simplified and better coordinated' (para. 35). In retrospect, the idea that the Lisbon Strategy aspired to simplify policy co-operation appears risible.

The re-launch of the Lisbon Strategy, with its narrowed focus on economic competitiveness, coincided with the reform of the SGP. It seems paradoxical that the Lisbon Strategy – where the 'social' element had been stronger – experienced a neoliberalisation in 2005, while (as we shall see below) the orthodox character of core institutional instruments of disciplinary liberalism and economic constitutionalism – EMU and the SGP – weakened. These events reflect the ongoing struggle between different political formations – but they also suggest that it may be premature to regard Europe has having a settled economic or social regime.

The European Social Model, part 2: origins

The ESM connotes something that merits, but also requires, preservation and modernisation (Commission 1993a: 46, 95, 1994: 1; Presidency Conclusions 2000). As a result, we might assume that the phrase and the institutions and practices to which it refers have been with us for a long time. In fact, although almost ubiquitous in EU debate by the turn of the twenty-first century, the ESM was established as a term only in the early-to-mid 1990s, and even then almost accidentally. It was absent from landmark EU social texts of the late 1980s and early 1990s (including the 1989 Social Charter and the Social Agreement attached to the Maastricht Treaty). The ESM subsequently featured in key Commission texts, including the 1993 White Paper on *Employment, Competitiveness and Growth* as well as the Green and White Papers on Social Policy issued in 1993 and 1994 respectively. On investigation, the origins and development of this element of EU discourse prove revealing.

Unswerving in his commitment to the Single Market, Commission President Delors also displayed a sustained interest in the EU's social dimension – referring to 'social Europe' or Europe as a 'social space'. Indeed, he chose to pursue the Single Market because it commanded sufficient support across the member states (and might, as a consequence, restore dynamism to the integration process) rather than giving priority to the economy as a matter of principle. George Ross, a close observer of the Delors Commission, described it as 'Russian Dolls' strategy, with social objectives nestled inside economic reforms (1995). Ultimately Delors believed strongly that economic dynamics had to be counterbalanced by social concerns, or contained within a social framework. Dissatisfied with his earlier attempts to augment the social dimensions of European integration, the 1993 White Paper was Delors' final official statement; probably best seen as a final throw of the dice rather than a triumphant culmination of his tenure in office. From the

'Val Duchesse' talks to Maastricht's Social Chapter, by way of the Social Charter, Delors' ambitious attempts to construct a social corner-stone for the EU largely met with criticism and failure at the hands of European business organisations and the British government (although other governments may have sheltered behind British opposition to 'social Europe' during this period). The ESM concept emerged in EU discourse after, and perhaps partly in reaction to, the failure of these earlier efforts; it certainly followed the collapse of aspirations for the emergence of a supranational welfare state.

Alongside continued advocacy of economic efficiency, the 1993 White Paper on *Growth, Competitiveness and Employment* finds Delors (still) searching for a means of counterbalancing the (apparent) imperatives of the economy: But by 1993 the environment – particu-larly in the idea of 'sustainable development' – had replaced 'social Europe' as his prime candidate for this role. Before the White Paper, the environmental emphasis emerged with particular clarity in Delors' presentation to the Copenhagen European Council meeting in June 1993 (*Entering the 21st Century: Orientations for Economic Renewal in Europe*). Although it considered active labour market policy, this document did not mention the ESM. Nevertheless, 'social Europe' was destined to return in the White Paper itself. The use of the ESM idea in a general strategy document, rather than in a specialist social policy paper (1993a, especially 46, also 95), was both unusual and taken up with alacrity by Commission social policy advocates. Building explic-itly on the *Growth Competitiveness and Employment* paper, the ESM was a pivotal organising concept tying together employment and social policy in the Commission's Social Policy White Paper the following year.

The ESM may have entered official Commission discourse as a muta-tion of another idea: the quintessentially Delorsian concept of the 'European model of society' (EMoS). Although used less often in Commission documents, Delors himself deployed EMoS more often, and earlier, than the ESM (see for example, in Delors 1992: 157–8 – originally published in French in 1988); it also seems to be the preferred terminology for close observers of Delors (Ross 1995; Drake 2000: 26, 40). Published shortly before the White Paper on *Growth*, the Commission's 1993 *European Social Policy* Green Paper appears to be the pivotal document here. A little more than one hundred pages long, this paper is replete with references to 'models'. Alongside EMoS and the ESM, it alludes to sustainable development models, 'western' and European socio-economic models as well as American and Japanese models. The ESM emerged from this rich discursive stew to become a term of art in EU discourse.

Delors's original usage of the 'model of society' concept was within a specifically French context (see Delors 1992). The emphasis on *society* seems to have been intended to redress what Delors saw as three major 'imbalances' in post-war France: the 'tentacular' state, 'excessive' individualism, and the more inhuman sides to capitalism' (Drake 2000: 26, citing *Le Monde*, 24–5 May 1981). Delors later added the reference to Europe to his 'model of society' concept, again in an intervention within French political debate to reject any 'mental reservation regarding ... the opening to Europe' by placing emphasis on 'the solid foundations of our Europe', calling for a 'switch' in 'the political debate, unequivocally on to what unites us and gives us strength'. That is, Delors was seeking to focus this debate on the 'European model of society to which the great majority of Europeans are committed', the 'spirit and political foundations' of which 'most people want to retain' (1992: 158, 157).

Just as Delors used 'model of society' ideas to motivate social and political change in France, the ESM has been used in EU political discourse (whether by the Commission or the European Council) as a political tool more than a descriptive category or analytical concept. This helps to explain why the ESM, rather than EMoS, became entrenched in Commission discourse. Placing the accent on *society* tends to displace policy and politics. In the French context Delors associated the 'model of society' concept with a critique of 'tentacular' state power. But the European Commission was seeking precisely to extend its political influence in the realm of social policy. Here the idea of a 'social model' appears less specifically *societal*, and so focuses attention on policy and politics. Arguably its primary reference is to a *policy* model. Indeed, recent commentary on the ESM leans heavily on the policy-oriented idea of welfare state regimes (Sapir 2006). Drawing heavily on 'worlds of welfare' literature (discussed in Chapter 2) the ESM has gradually evolved into the idea that there are several European Social *Models*. While implicitly acknowledging that its key features were located in national welfare states, the ESM also suggested a significant *European* dimension. In contrast to the EMoS idea, the ESM offered an attractively ambiguous discourse for a Commission keen to extend its social role.

The 1993 White Paper emphasised employment – particularly job creation and the reduction of unemployment. These themes were reinforced by the 1995 enlargement (adding Austria, Finland and, especially, Sweden to the EU). The appointment of Swede Allan Larsson to run the Commission's Directorate-General for Employment and Social Affairs was particularly significant. Larsson was familiar with the notion of a social 'model' which linked employment and social policies. The White Paper's Employment agenda was pushed ahead under the banner of the ESM and given a legal basis in the Amsterdam Treaty (1997). The election of Tony Blair's New Labour Government meant that the UK embraced these developments as well as signing up to the Social Chapter agreed by the other member states at Maastricht in 1992. In the late 1990s social democrats were swept into government across much of Europe. The European Employment Strategy developed ahead of the Amsterdam Treaty timetable. It was a major focus of the European Summits held in Luxembourg (1997 – where elaborate National Action Plans were initiated, to be reviewed by the Commission and the Council), Cardiff (1998) and finally Cologne (1999, where the European Employment Pact was agreed). Against this backdrop the Lisbon Strategy is better seen as the culmination of six or seven years of development rather than a new start for Europe.

European Monetary Union

That monetary union in Europe was based on a highly orthodox economic model has rightly been stressed by academic analysts. The institutional design for the European Central Bank (ECB) laid out in the Maastricht Treaty gave it an unusual degree of formal independence in the conduct of monetary policy. The ECB was closely modelled on the German *Bundesbank*, widely regarded as an exemplar of orthodox monetary policy, while arguably enjoying an even greater measure of formal independence. EMU also made controlling inflation the overwhelming priority for the ECB. Moreover, the Maastricht Treaty also set out demanding standards that states would have to meet in order to qualify for EMU. These 'convergence criteria' covered inflation performance, public finances, interest rates and exchange rate policy. They mandated the following:

1. inflation rate: within 1.5 per cent of the three EU countries with the lowest rate;
2. budget deficit: below 3 per cent of GDP;
3. public debt: below 60 per cent of GDP;
4. long-term interest rates: within 2 per cent of the three lowest interest rates in EU;

5. exchange rates: within 'normal' fluctuation margins of Europe's exchange-rate mechanism.

The Stability and Growth Pact (SGP – agreed in 1997) was essentially a continuation after monetary union of the public finance elements of the convergence criteria. Pressure for the conclusion of the SGP came primarily from Germany, with finance minister Theo Waigel the Pact's main instigator: its German origins strengthen the impression that the SGP amounted to a strengthening of the orthodox nature of EMU.

It is, however, possible to interpret the SGP in another way. In retrospect, it seems odd that the system for managing public finance after the creation of the euro had not been set out the Maastricht Treaty itself. Perhaps this was simply an oversight. Alternatively, the actors responsible for the orthodox monetary policy architecture believed that Maastricht was a comprehensive victory. In particular, the Treaty and convergence criteria implied that EMU would have a restricted membership. Only those countries with an established 'stability culture' could meet the convergence criteria and hence qualify for monetary union. The application of tight public finance rules during the qualification period might allow some states to establish and entrench such a culture – and evidence exists of new patterns of economic and social governance emerging in several states during the 1990s. In the next chapter we will explore how state welfare systems changed through this period, helping to assess how far the convergence criteria actually induced retrenchment. The convergence criteria were treated as a significant constraint on domestic policy, placing pressure on public finances and hence also on national social programmes. This represents the orthodox face of a stability culture.

Equally, however, some states attempted to manage fiscal pressures, including the convergence criteria, in creative ways during the 1990s. So-called 'new social pacts' were a particular focus of attention (Regini 2000; Ferrera, Hemerijck and Rhodes 2000; Rhodes 2001; Grahl and Teague 2003; Hanké and Rhodes 2005; Donaghey and Teague 2005; Avdagic, Rhodes and Visser 2005). The Netherlands, Ireland and Finland are usually identified as exemplars (Italy, Spain and Portugal were also included in the 'new pacts' group). Looking back, the argument that these pacts entrenched domestic stability cultures is hard to sustain – some states then depicted as leaders are now among the hardest hit by the post-2008 economic difficulties (considered in our final chapter). But between the mid-1990s and mid-2000s, at least in some states, these pacts seemed to offer a novel means of maintaining – or even improving – state social commitments while meeting the budgetary challenges linked to EMU.

If we dig beneath the surface of the SGP, a different picture emerges. Rather than representing a decisive consolidation of EMU's orthodox design, the SGP is better seen as a rearguard action by the proponents of orthodoxy. By the mid-1990s the fragility of the Maastricht design for EMU was becoming increasingly clear. The Maastricht design had been premised not just on Germany – and particularly the *Bundesbank* – as a model of institutional orthodoxy, but also on the day-to-day practice of orthodoxy in Germany – to an extent that may not have been fully appreciated at the time (hence the absence of rules to govern public finances after EMU). The key – and wholly unanticipated change – was that Germany itself 'lost control' of its public finances. Between 1991 and 1996, German public debt rose from just over 40 per cent to just over 60 per cent of GDP (Bundesbank 1997: 18). Of course, the unification of Germany was a major cause of these changes. Nevertheless, by 1996 Germany was in breach of the key public debt criterion – if only marginally – and hence was formally failing to qualify for a monetary union constructed in its (former) image.

Set in the context of a clear weakening of German 'stability culture', the negotiation of the SGP takes on a rather different character. First, it might be seen – at least in part – as a move within German politics. The guardians of monetary orthodoxy (in the Finance Ministry and *Bundesbank*) could seek to use European constraints to bind other parts of the German state. Secondly, and more significantly, Germany's failure to fully meet the convergence criteria had major consequences for the overall character of EMU. The option of abandoning or significantly delaying EMU does not seem to have been seriously considered, despite the fact that only France and Luxembourg formally met the full convergence rules. Equally, EMU without Germany was impossible to imagine. But if Germany could join EMU while being in breach of the convergence criteria, then their character – and that of EMU itself – would change fundamentally: from providing an apparently objective economic standard, they might become (and arguably did become) a matter of political negotiation. Once the formal criteria were relaxed for states that might have been regarded as 'core' eurozone members – such as Austria and the Netherlands – it became difficult to exclude Belgium, the seat of the EU institutions, despite its very high levels of public debt. Such recent member states as Spain and Portugal were regarded as having taken significant steps to stabilise their budget deficits. Consequently, with Belgium in they were hard to exclude. Italy was also regarded as having made significant efforts at public finance stabilisation. The same logic applied: if Spain, Portugal and Belgium were to be granted EMU membership, exclusion of Italy – an original signatory of the Treaty of Rome – seemed impossible (its continued public indebtedness notwithstanding). In the event, of states actively seeking EMU membership, only Greece was excluded in the first round. And (even) the Greeks joined in January 2001. Within two years of its creation every country that had sought membership had been allowed to join.

It is difficult to overstate the difference between the eurozone that came into being around the turn of the twenty-first century, and that imagined by the proponents of monetary policy orthodoxy who had dominated the design of that system only a decade earlier. The SGP was concluded in 1997, just as it was becoming clear that Germany would not meet the letter of the convergence criteria, with the possible consequence that the eurozone would have a wide membership. Viewed in this perspective, Theo Waigel's SGP proposals look more like an attempt to re-establish a fading orthodoxy, than the consolidation of that orthodoxy by a hegemonic actor. Once states had gained membership of the eurozone, the pressure of qualification was eased and the management of public finances relaxed, with possible consequences for the credibility of the euro. Of course, the fact that all the aspirant members signed up to the SGP in 1997 is itself testament to the continuing influence of orthodox monetary policy ideas within the nascent eurozone.

The operation of the SGP after 1999 broadly confirms our analysis. By 2002 Portugal had exceeded the 3 per cent deficit rule. The next year, 2003, Greece, Italy, France and Germany had all exceeded this level. And by this time, Austria, Belgium, France, Germany and Italy all also had public debt over 60 per cent of GDP. While punitive proceedings were begun against some of these states (notably Portugal (2002) and Greece (2005)) the larger member states (France and Germany) largely escaped sanction, despite persistently breaching the SGP. Ironically, the same large states that had been strong proponents of the SGP in 1997 later led demands for greater flexibility and the reform of the system. These were to bear fruit in 2005. While the basic ceilings for budget deficits and public debt remained unchanged, the circumstances in which a breach of these levels might trigger punishment (for example under the 'excessive deficit procedure') were clarified and, in the process, relaxed.

Despite dominating the initial period during which EMU was designed, economic constitutionalists and disciplinary neoliberals failed to control the implementation process. The resulting hybrid led to a decade of stagnation in Germany alongside unsustainably rapid growth (blown up by public and private debt) in the eurozone periphery. This peripheral growth vanished after 2007–08, while the (relative) economic performance of the German economy improved. The result appears catastrophic for the countries of southern Europe that the original EMU design implicitly excluded: they now face vicious retrenchment in what were already comparatively ineffective social systems (see, for example, Sapir 2006). The failure of implementation of what was (in its own terms) a coherent neoliberal plan for EMU, did not result in an alternative architecture for the eurozone. As a consequence, Europe is left with inadequate institutions and no guiding model to deal with the aftermath of the credit crunch. Almost by default, deep cuts in public spending are presented as the only solution to economic collapse in the periphery. Not only is wave-after-wave of retrenchment likely to prove socially and politically unbearable for peripheral countries; it also risks a deep deflation for Europe as a whole.

Conclusion

Social policy has been a consistently contentious issue within European integration. During the 1990s, scholars from a number of distinct analytical traditions converged on a shared broad view of the EU's structural orientation towards economic liberalism. For some, a deregulatory bias in the EU, associated with its capacity to engineer 'negative integration' (Scharpf 1999) is its source, while others have emphasised elements of 'positive integration' in the creation and maintenance of the European market (Majone 1996). Both approaches share – and our analysis broadly confirms – the vanishingly small prospect of anything like a European welfare state. The institutional capacity to supply social services, such as education, health care or childcare is effectively absent at the European level. However, from the 1960s struggles over social security harmonisation onwards, it has proven impossible to construct directly redistributive level policies at the EU level. The 'workable balance' (Armstrong 2010) between supranational regulation of economic integration and member state 'social sovereignty' that emerged from the mid-1960s was neither consciously designed nor the product of consensus. As our historical analysis has shown, this balance emerged from a fierce struggle in which the early proponents of a supra-nationally 'harmonised' system of social security were decisively defeated.

Why, then, are the early 1990s so widely identified as a key moment in the emergence of neoliberal Europe? We think that there are three main reasons. The first and second are well known and widely acknowledged: respectively, the establishment of an ultra-orthodox policy design for EMU and the market liberal terms established for the eastern enlargement of the EU. The final reason is less widely or precisely recognised, but arguably the most important. Building on the positive integration emphasis in 'regulatory' analysis, we argue that the establishment of a reasonably encompassing and robust legal framework was a necessary prerequisite for European market integration. Our analysis has shown that most of the basic elements for such a legal framework were more or less in place by the early 1980s, although some key features (especially related to secondary legislation) were constructed through the 1980s and into the 1990s. It was only during this period, then, that the 'positive' prerequisites for 'negative' integration were firmly established. Putting these conditions in place, of course, meant European law could threaten the 'workable balance' between market integration and state social policy, largely along the lines Scharpf (1999) analyses in terms of 'negative integration'.

A major lesson of our analysis, then, is the misguided nature of the suggestion that the 1980s were a golden age for 'social Europe'. EU level social policy interventions before the 1990s were largely superficial and/or ineffective – with the partial exception of some elements of 'social regulation' (Cram 1993; Majone 1993). Despite the widespread view of the 1990s as a period of neoliberal dominance, our analysis of the relationship between EMU and the modernisation of the ESM reveals their paradoxical relationship during the 1990s and 2000s.

EMU is often seen as the apotheosis of European disciplinary neoliberalism – and rightly so in many respects. But rather than bearing witness to the triumph of efficiency – the factor to which functionalist regulation theory attributes the rise of market liberalism and the EU regulatory state – the design for EMU represents the victory of a particular neoliberal vision of market society. But EMU appears to have become significantly less orthodox in the decades after its design and inception. Initially this change was an unanticipated product of historical contingencies – the manner in which German unification forced a loosening of the convergence criteria and produced a much wider EMU membership than its designers had envisaged. Later, however, the erstwhile guardian of monetary orthodoxy and chief proponent of the 'stability culture' led the reformist drive to introduce greater flexibility into the SGP. This raises important questions about how and when the EMU process imposed fiscal and budgetary pressures on European states. Broadly speaking, the most significant pressure was exerted during the 1990s, while states were complying with the convergence criteria to qualify from euro membership. The next chapter will analyse the patterns and causes of welfare policy change in Europe during this period, assessing whether convergence did indeed take place.

The massive retrenchment imposed on peripheral eurozone countries after 2008 throws the putative 'disciplinary' character of EMU into stark relief. Recall that for much of that decade, Germany was seen as Europe's failing economy, while Ireland, Spain and others were heralded as growth champions; these roles have been decisively reversed in the years after 2008. Although it is too soon to draw final conclusions, egalitarian welfarism appears to be an advantage rather than a burden through the economic crisis: at least the 'most egalitarian' Nordic and northern continental European states (Sapir 2005, 2006) seem to be weathering hard times better than the inegalitarian southern states (or the Anglo-liberal cluster which the credit crunch has also hit particularly hard). Recent developments raise difficult questions about the ultimate consequences of the 'inclusive' form of EMU that emerged through the 1990s. Some of the peripheral countries that managed to gain entry may well leave EMU, or be expelled from it. Ironically, the *failure* of orthodox model EMU is devastating southern European social provision. The countries originally seen as forming its core face the choice of bankrolling the periphery or attempting to reconstruct EMU after (enforced) departures or a collapse.

If EMU became less orthodox in the years before 2007–08, the Lisbon Strategy moved things in the opposite direction. Having developed a strong social profile during its initial phase, since the mid-1990s major strategic efforts have been made to emphasise the economy and competitiveness within the strategy. Moreover, the growing emphasis on the economy was explicitly at the expense of 'social' Lisbon. Although it was the culmination of a series of initiatives dating back at least to the Sapir Report of 2003, the timing of the re-launch of the Lisbon Strategy refocused on economic competitiveness is striking: it was done by the same European Council meeting – held in Brussels in March 2005 – that reformed the SGP. Perhaps the renewed emphasis on the economy in the Lisbon Strategy provided some cover for the relaxation of the SGP.

It is also important to recognise that the ESM emerged in EU discourse only during the 1990s. This discourse, and the institutional processes to which it has given rise – first the European Employment Strategy/Luxembourg Process and latterly the various 'social' OMCs – strengthened the legitimacy and role of 'socially-oriented actors' (de la Porte and Pochet 2002; Palier 2006) within the European institutions, in some national governments and in various social and political organisations across Europe. The promotion of social issues up the EU's agenda after Lisbon is reflected in the enlargement process. While both eastern enlargement and the EU's discourse on the ESM originated during the early 1990s, the ESM had little or no impact on the terms of enlargement. When social policy matters *were* raised as part of the broader 'transition' process that the states of east–central Europe were subject to through the 1990s, it was under the auspices of – and on the terms set by – the 'Washington consensus' institutions (the IMF and the World Bank). These issues only began to form part of the EU's agenda in relation to east–central Europe in the context of the Lisbon Strategy after 2000 – only at the very end of the enlargement process.

The position of social issues within the Lisbon Strategy has been contentious and contested. Although it dominated the Strategy's initial launch, the KBE agenda rapidly ran out of steam, so Lisbon and the OMC came to be closely associated with social concerns. The re-launching of the Lisbon Strategy in 2005 certainly involved a relegation of the 'social' OMCs from this central position, might be seen as an attempt to refocus Lisbon exclusively on economic matters, eliminating almost entirely its social agenda. However, the concerted efforts of the 'socially oriented actors' managed to defend the legitimacy of 'social Lisbon'. And even after 2010, when the Lisbon Strategy drew to an ignominious end, social policy co-ordination has retained a presence within the follow-on: Europe 2020.

Alongside the Lisbon Strategy, further developments have taken place in the EU on the basis of 'hard law', particularly through the decisions of the ECJ. On the one hand, as we have seen, the concept of solidarity has entered the lexicon of the Court, as a means of protecting some state policies from the full neoliberalising force of European market rules. On the other, the Court continues to make rulings that cut into other aspects of state social sovereignty. The introduction of solidarity represents a significant move away from the image of an unflinchingly intregrationist and neoliberal Court (Granger 2005). But how are we to reconcile it with the latter set of developments? Armstrong concludes that the Court has a rather narrow vision of how solidarity can be expressed. Because of their democratic legitimacy, the Court can more easily accept manifestations of solidarity when expressed in general laws imposing, for example, universal public service obligations than it can when those rules are either not publicly promulgated laws but collective bargains or, when those laws or agreements are not 'universal' but sectoral or particularistic. (2010: 227).

What does this analysis suggest about the emergence of a European social policy regime? It is tempting to argue for a modified version of the EU as a regulatory polity. In principle, Lisbon-style policy co-ordination provides a means of trying to address shared social policy challenges across Europe, while respecting the social sovereignty of the member states (on the compatibility of the Lisbon Strategy with the regulatory analysis see Wincott 2003). Alongside certain forms of supra-national social regulation – for example in relation to equality treatment – the main thrust of European integration through the 'Community Method' remains economic. The boundary between supra-national economic integration and the social sovereignty of the member states remains a difficult and contested issue. Nevertheless, alongside some judgements that drive the logic of economic integration into traditional social policy domains, the ECJ now sometimes acts as a constitutional court that protects state social prerogatives over supra-national economic integration.

We are, however, still at an early stage of the development of social policy co-ordination and – particularly – of the ECJ's jurisprudence on solidarity. Even over the ten-year span of the Lisbon Strategy, patterns of social policy co-ordination and their relative status have been subject to considerable changes. Only time, and a further development of the case law, will clarify how much protection the Court's solidarity jurisprudence can offer to member state social policy systems. But any such developments seem set to take place in unpropitious circumstances, dominated by the social implications of economic hard times.

Chapter 6

Convergence and Divergence in European Welfare Capitalism

In this chapter we evaluate critically the literature that suggests that welfare regimes across Europe (and more generally) are converging, whether on a 'best practice' Anglo–US model of welfare residualism or on something altogether more encompassing and inclusive. We argue that such convergence theses tend to be characterised by the rather casual appeal to the concept of convergence – in which convergence and movement in a common trajectory are typically conflated – and by a tendency to ignore the 'path dependent' character of processes of welfare reform. Due recognition of such processes and greater conceptual precision, we suggest, may serve to diminish the expectation that common pressures should produce convergent outcomes. Indeed, as we show, there is plenty of evidence of path dependent institutions reinforcing diversity in welfare trajectories even in the face of ostensibly common challenges. We examine the means by which different welfare regimes respond to such common pressures for reform as they face. In the process, we consider the contribution to our understanding of convergence, divergence and diversity made by so called neo-institutionalist scholars. Finally, we consider a range of principally quantitative indices of welfare convergence, differentiating between aggregate indices of welfare effort and more disaggregated measures of welfare generosity and assessing, in conclusion, the developmental trajectories and viability of distinct welfare regime clusters today.

Our conclusions are, in the context of the existing literature, quite challenging. For, in effect, they invert the established orthodoxy, suggesting that it is the period of welfare state expansion and consolidation that is characterised by convergence and that, since the turn to retrenchment in the 1980s, there is powerful, mounting and pervasive evidence of welfare divergence. What is also clear from our analysis of the available data is that retrenchment to date has served to reinforce rather than diminish the existing diversity in welfare regimes. Divergence *between* regime clusters has been combined with convergence *within* clusters.

The concept of convergence

As we have already seen, there is a vast and still growing literature on the impact of both exogenous pressures (such as globalisation and European integration) and endogenous pressures (such as demographic change, the rise of the service economy and change in familial structures) on contemporary welfare trajectories. Almost all of that literature, whether obliquely or more explicitly, makes some reference to the concept of convergence. Indeed, alongside retrenchment, convergence is the term most frequently used today to characterise welfare trajectories (in Europe as elsewhere). Yet despite the centrality of the concept to contemporary debates about the current and future trajectory of welfare reform, the precise meaning of the concept is rarely considered (though for notable exceptions see Brady *et al.* 2005; Holzinger and Knill 2005; Knill 2005; Montanari *et al.* 2007). As a consequence, the term has come to be used in a multitude of rather different, and often incompatible, ways – even in the space of a single text. As this already suggests, when it comes to questions of convergence, confusion abounds. And it is not at all difficult to identify the source of that confusion.

As is so often the case in such matters, it is instructive first to seek advice from the Concise Oxford Dictionary. This informs us that convergence – from the Latin *vergere* (lit. 'to incline') – is the process of coming together from different directions so as eventually to meet. This is immediately significant, because it stands in some significant tension to most contemporary appeals to the concept in the literature on the welfare state. For in this literature, convergence is almost invariably used to refer to movement *in a common direction* – as, for instance, in the phrase 'neoliberal convergence', especially when it is used as a synonym for 'neoliberalisation'. It is, of course, important to be able to identify movement in a common trajectory (as the term 'neoliberalisation' implies) and, indeed, to be able to differentiate this from movement in different trajectories. But however we choose to label this, it is *not convergence* in and of it itself, it is *no guarantee of convergence* and it is most unhelpful to refer to it as if it were. To identify and to document empirically the growing influence of neoliberal ideas on policy trajectories in a number of European welfare states over a given period of time is not to show convergence.

That said, and so as not to risk substituting one source of confusion with another, movement in a common direction can of course produce convergence – but the point is that there is no guarantee that it need do so. Thus, just as it would be wrong to infer *divergence* from evidence of welfare states moving along different trajectories, so it would be wrong to infer *convergence* from evidence of a common trajectory. In order to establish convergence, or indeed divergence, we need to know not just about the direction of movement, but the relative pace of change and the initial starting positions of the units in question. As this suggests, neoliberal convergence is by no means an impossibility, but it would require that neoliberalisation proceed at a greater pace in those (welfare) states initially with furthest to travel to be seen as genuinely neoliberal in character (at least relative to existing neoliberal exemplars). Needless to say, the evidence to satisfy such an exacting empirical standard rarely if ever accompanies claims to have identified neoliberal convergence in the existing literature (for by no means particularly egregious examples, see McBride and Williams 2001; Crepaz and Moser 2004).

The sense of frustratation that comes from acknowledging this all too casual (and, by now, almost universal) appeal to the language of convergence is well expressed by Torben Iversen and Jonas Pontusson:

> Suppose that we are interested in some unidimensional and readily measurable feature, such as the level of social spending. Clearly it is perfectly conceivable that two countries would partake in a common trend (decline) without becoming more alike ... convergence presupposes that *the rate of change is greater in the country that started with the higher level of social spending.* (2000: 3, emphasis added).

This may seem like a remarkably obvious observation – and, in a sense, it is. But it is precisely because such a self-evident and unobjectionable comment needs to be made that it is so important. For, however mundane, the implications for the literature on European (and other) welfare trajectories are profound. Thus, if we are to insist (which doesn't seem unreasonable), that evidence of convergence must actually show convergence, then the adoption of neoliberal economic and social policies in a number of contemporary European polities will not suffice.

Thinking about this in graphical terms (as in Figure 6.1) may help to clarify things further. If, as in the Iversen and Pontusson quote considered above, we are able to identify a single unidimensional index to capture the element of welfare effort or generosity that we are interested in, then we can trace trends in our data over time for a number of countries. For the sake of simplicity, let's assume that we are interested in only two countries, A and B, and that we are able to secure data for each on aggregate expenditure on child care provision (say, as a proportion of GDP) for the two-decade time frame of our analysis. Let's assume, also, and for the sake of simplicity, that the initial direction of change in spending on child care in A and B remains constant over the duration of the study. Within this, admittedly rather stylised and unrealistic general framework, expenditure on child care in A (as a share of GDP) can either rise, remain constant or fall; the same is, of course, true for B. And if A and B are assumed to be capable of exercising any kind of domestic control over social policy choices, then we cannot assume that what happens in A will be duplicated in B. This gives us a range of potential scenarios – each of which is depicted schematically in Figure 6.1.

A number of points emerge from this. First, in only four of the ten scenarios shown is there genuine convergence (scenarios 1, 3, 5 and 7); and in only one of those (scenario 7) is convergence the result of a common trajectory of change (such as one might associate with, for instance, neoliberalisation). Similarly, though there are three scenarios in which a common trajectory of change arises (scenarios 2, 7 and 9), in only one of those (scenario 7) does such a process result in convergence. As this shows very clearly, movement in a common direction is no guarantee of convergence. Indeed, in order for movement in the same direction to result in convergence, the rate of change needs to be greater in the state with the lower initial value where the overall trend is upwards, or lower where the overall trend is downwards.

Yet a third point perhaps also needs to be noted here. For if a more sustained reflection on the concept of convergence cautions against the casual conflation of convergence and movement in a common direction so typical of the existing literature, then it does not leave the dictionary definition of the term with which we started unscathed either. For, and although it is just as likely to result in continued diversity (scenario 9) or divergence (scenario 2), movement in a common direction *can* (as scenario 7 shows) result in convergence.

In fact, if there is a single conclusion to be drawn from this kind of mapping exercise, it is surely that, contra both the dictionary definition and the conflation of convergence with movement in a common trajectory, convergence is independent of the direction of change.

This kind of conceptual clarification is undoubtedly very helpful – and it certainly cuts through plenty of confusion in the literature. Yet there is, of course, one important objection to all of this. For thus far at least we have only looked at how we might attach labels, in a logical and consistent manner, to a purely *hypothetical* set of examples. Is it

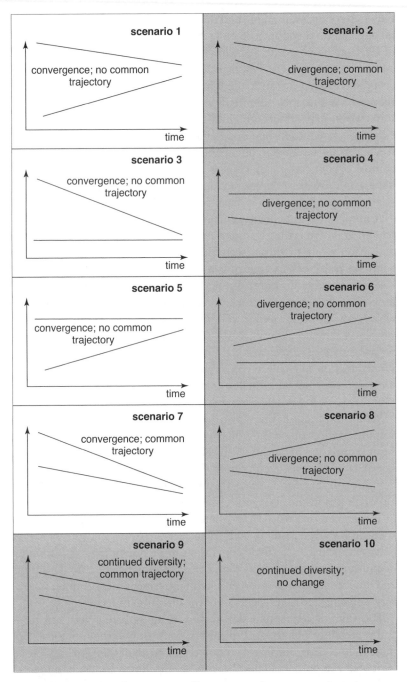

FIGURE 6.1 *Convergence, divergence and common trajectories*

not bound to be the case that some of these scenarios are more likely to arise in real world situations than others? And, more particularly, is it not the case that welfare reform in a common trajectory *in the real world* is more likely to generate convergence than this purely hypothetical and largely semantic exercise would suggest? There is certainly something to this, and it would undoubtedly be wrong to infer that since convergence arising from movement in a common direction is but one of ten possible scenarios here, that this renders it unlikely. Indeed, the point is that nothing can be inferred about the relative probability of any one of these scenarios from the exercise summarised in Figure 6.1.

Yet there are theoretical reasons for suggesting that in the 'real worlds of welfare capitalism', as Robert Goodin and his colleagues would have it (1999), convergence is both less likely than we tend to assume and more likely to arise amongst welfare states moving in opposite directions (as in scenario 1) than amongst those exhibiting a common trajectory (as in scenario 7). The point is a relatively simple one and one to which we will return in more empirical detail later in the chapter. It is well-illustrated by reference to the process of neoliberalisation. As a number of institutionalist scholars have noted, neoliberalising tendencies might be expected to be strongest where existing welfare institutions are either the most residual or already exhibit the most pronounced liberal or neoliberal characteristics – in short, where market-based systems of welfare allocation already feature prominently in the welfare mix (see, for instance, Hall and Soskice 2001a; Swank 2001). Where, in other words, neoliberalisation runs with the existing grain, it is likely to prove easier to establish and sustain. Insofar as this proves to be the case, we might expect neoliberalisation to proceed at a more rapid pace in the more residual welfare states and to be more difficult to establish and to proceed at a slower rate (certainly initially) in more encompassing and inclusive welfare systems. That, in turn, suggests that neoliberalisation, insofar as it can be identified as a common reform trajectory, is perhaps more likely to be associated with divergence (scenario 2) or at least continued diversity (scenario 9) than with convergence; and, conversely, that convergence is more likely to arise where welfare leaders and laggards are moving in opposite directions (in all likelihood in response to rather different imperatives). In the end, however, these are open empirical questions – and we will need carefully to survey the evidence available to us later in the chapter before coming to any kind of a considered conclusion.

Types of convergence

In the hypothetical situation discussed above we have concerned ourselves with convergence, divergence and diversity amongst only two cases, A and B. But when it comes to the real worlds of welfare capitalism we are typically interested in a much larger number of cases. This, of course, complicates things. For where, with two cases, we can simply gauge convergence or divergence by comparing the arithmetic distance between welfare states A and B on a common index at different points in time, that will not suffice with a larger number of cases. Indeed, as soon as we move beyond two cases, a variety of different ways of gauging convergence/divergence present themselves. For present purposes, and in the specialist literature on welfare state convergence that has emerged in recent years, we are principally concerned with three – what have been termed *sigma* (σ), *beta* (β) and *delta* (δ) convergence (see Barro and Sala-ì-Martin 1992; Sala-ì-Martin 1996; Castles 2004; Heichel *et al.* 2005; Starke *et al.* 2008).

Sigma-convergence is perhaps the most intuitive and direct sense of convergence – that most likely to correspond to the everyday sense of the term. A test of sigma-convergence is satisfied if there is a fall (invariably, a statistically significant fall) in the dispersion of the cases (here welfare states) with respect to the variable in question (say, social spending as a share of GDP). There are, of course, different ways of gauging dispersion. The principal measures of dispersion used in the existing literature are, from the simplest to the most complex: the range (the difference between maximum and minimum); the standard deviation; the coefficient of variation; and the Gini coefficient (Sala-ì-Martin 1996: 1326). It might seem odd that the Gini coefficient is included here since it is usually encountered as a measure of inequality. But it is in fact simply a statistical measure of dispersion that just happens to have become closely associated with the analysis of income inequality. Its advantage over other measures of dispersion such as the standard deviation and the coefficient of variation is that it is independent of the arithmetic mean, less sensitive to outliers and correspondingly more sensitive to changes in the middle part of the distribution (Montanari *et al.* 2007: 304–5).

Beta-converegence is a rather more specific sense of the term that relates to what might be termed, 'catch-up' – the propensity of laggards or late adopters to grow, with respect to the variable or index in question, at a faster rate than leaders or early adopters. A test of beta-convergence is satisfied if an inverse relationship (usually one that is also statistically significant) is found between the initial value of the variable in question and its subsequent rate of growth. As Peter Starke, Herbert Obinger and Frances Castles explain (2008: 980), the standard test of beta-convergence is 'to regress the starting value of the policy indicator on its subsequent growth rate (or change) for the period of interest – if the coefficient [in the regression equation] for the initial value has a negative sign and is significant' the test is passed. Beta-convergence is a necessary, but not in itself sufficient condition of sigma-convergence.

A third, and for our purposes final, sense of convergence widely debated in analyses of welfare state reform is *delta*-convergence. Tests of delta-convergence seek to gauge the distance, with respect to a particular variable or index, to a particular case, often seen as some kind of exemplar. In the literature on the welfare state, the US is sometimes seen as a model of welfare residualism towards which many other welfare states are gravitating. Similarly, the rather more sophisticated 'varieties of capitalism' approach sees both the US and Germany as exemplars of what it terms liberal and co-ordinated market economies respectively, positing a process of dual or co-convergence (see, for instance, Hall and Soskice 2001). Both imply some form of delta-convergence that can, of course, be tested for empirically.

Such statistical measures of convergence undoubtedly help to clarify what precisely we mean by convergence whilst providing a basis for operationalising the term empirically. Yet it is important to acknowledge that the statistical tests for convergence that they give rise to are, of course, only directly applicable to quantitative empirical indicators. And the point is that much of the literature on convergence is, quite appropriately, concerned at least as much with the subjective and qualitative aspects of the process of convergence as it is with those that are more readily quantified. Being able to point to statistical tests for convergence is all well and good; but it should not be taken to imply that all claims to identify convergence need – nor necessarily can – be defended in such a manner.

Convergence in and of what?

If it is important to establish what, precisely, we mean by convergence and how we might differentiate empirically between convergence, divergence and development along a common trajectory, it is perhaps no less important that we are clear about the potential *referents* of convergence – about what is being said to converge. Confusion and conflation again abound, especially in the more general literature on welfare reform and development which typically makes reference to the concept but whose core research interest is not the attempt to gauge empirically the extent of convergence itself. The point is that, even where authors are clear and precise about what is meant by convergence – and, as we have seen, that isn't always the case – they can nonetheless proceed to talk past one another by appealing to different aspects of welfare reform when describing such reform by reference to the concept of convergence. To say, for instance, that the German and Dutch welfare states have converged can mean a host of rather different things, depending on what specific aspects of the welfare state are the focus of attention. Here the more specialised literature on convergence is again helpful (see especially Bennett 1991: 218; Coleman and Grant 1998; Heichel *et al.* 2005: 828–31; Holzinger and Knill 2005; Seeliger 1996). For this tends to differentiate between a variety of potential objects or referents of convergence, noting that convergence in one need not imply convergence in any of the others.

This literature throws up quite a number of potential objects of convergence. In the interests of clarity and in an attempt to inject some order into this, we here differentiate between six. These are summarised in Box 6.1.

BOX 6.1   The potential objects and referents of convergence

1. Convergence in the pressures and challenges to which welfare regimes are exposed (*input convergence*).
2. Convergence in the policy paradigms in and through which such pressures and challenges are identified and understood (*paradigm convergence*).
3. Convergence in the policies pursued in response to such pressures and challenges (*policy convergence*) – this category might be further subdivided by differentiating between convergence in policy goals, policy content and policy instruments (as in Bennett 1991: 218).
4. Convergence in the ideas used to legitimate such policy choices (*convergence in legitimatory discourse*).
5. Convergence in policy outcomes, usually gauged in terms of indicators of policy performance (*outcome convergence*).
6. Convergence in the process in and through which challenges are translated into policy outcomes (*process convergence*).

The first thing perhaps to note about this list is that it is not ordered randomly. For each potential object of convergence can be seen to relate to a different stage in the process of policy-making. This certainly applies to the first five entries in the list (the sixth relating to the character of the overall process itself), with policy inputs, the translation of such inputs into policy and its implementation, the legitimation of policy and the outcomes arising from such policy forming some kind of a sequence. Yet in much of the general literature on welfare reform, these rather different referents of convergence are simply conflated in the casual appeal to 'welfare state convergence' as if it were a single undifferentiated thing.

This, of course, is extremely problematic. For, as a moment's further thought reveals, though linked in the policy-making process, each has a certain autonomy from the others. Input convergence need not necessarily imply policy convergence, policy convergence need not necessarily imply outcome convergence, and neither need necessarily imply process convergence. Each is at least relatively autonomous of the others.

Indeed, one of the advantages of presenting the potential referents of convergence in this sequential and disaggregated way is that it serves to draw attention to the rather complex and involved process in and through which common external pressures (such as economic interdependence) and/or common challenges (such as demographic change) are translated into specific policy outcomes. This exercise in *process-tracing* also serves to highlight the open-ended nature of any process of convergence in either policy content or policy outcomes. And it does so principally by identifying a series of potential points of mediation, the recognition of each of which makes it less likely that common pressures will translate simply or directly into convergent outcomes.

Each step in the five-stage sequence can, then, be seen as a potential point of mediation.

Mediation point 1: differential exposure to common challenges

Even where common external pressures (such as those associated with heightened economic interdependence) and common challenges (such as those associated with an ageing population) can be identified, different welfare states are exposed to them to different degrees and in different ways. Thus, put simply, some economies are more open than others, whilst some face more of a demographic time bomb than others. Clearly the more diverse such patterns of exposure are, the less likely it is that these will lead ultimately to policy convergence.

Mediation point 2: differential framing of common challenges

Even where welfare states are similarly exposed to common challenges, the processes of cognitive filtering in and through which such challenges are identified, understood and responded to may vary considerably, reflecting the prevalence of different policy paradigms, traditions and policy-making styles. Again, the more diverse the nature of such traditions, paradigms and styles, the less likely we are to see policy convergence in response even to common challenges to which welfare states are similarly exposed.

Mediation point 3: domestic political mediations in the process of implementation

Even where elite political actors may share common cognitive templates and policy paradigms to reach very similar assessments of the policy responses desirable in the face of a given set of common challenges, the policy-making process may serve to militate against the realisation of such policy goals as a series of domestic political mediations steer outcomes in particular ways. Domestic political sensitivities and sensitivities as well as the internal politics of holding together a coalition government may, for instance, lead the process of policy development in rather different directions in different polities even where the policy has a common inspiration.

Mediation point 4: the adoption of different legitimatory strategies

Even where ostensibly similar policies are adopted and implemented in ostensibly similar ways in response to common understandings of a common challenge they may well be legitimated in very different ways, as policy-makers adjust their legitimatory discourse to the specificities of domestic political culture and traditions. Thus, welfare retrenchment in Europe has been justified by reference to the economic imperatives of competitiveness in an era of globalisation, by reference to the desirability of meeting the Maastrict Convergence Criteria or as desirable in its own terms and not as the necessary price to pay for the attainment of some other end (Hay and Rosamond 2002).

Mediation point 5: the differential impact of similar policies in different polities

Finally, even very similar policies implemented in very similar ways may produce divergent outcomes in different institutional and cultural contexts (see, for instance, Dolowitz 2001).

With each additional mediation point identified, the likelihood of common pressures (such as are typically associated with globalisation), driving processes of convergence even in institutionally similar political and economic systems (the liberal and co-ordinated economies of the varieties of capitalism literature, for instance) recedes. Policy-making, even in response to common external challenges and commonly perceived imperatives, is a highly complex and differentiated process characterised by a succession of case-specific mediations. This makes the type of blanket convergence or co-convergence widely anticipated in response to globalisation, demographic change and, even, European integration rather unlikely. And that of course suggests the value of an inductive and empirical rather than a deductive and theoretical approach to the question of convergence. As this suggests, it is to the evidence that we must turn if we are to establish whether welfare states in Europe can meaningfully be said to have converged.

The real worlds of welfare convergence, divergence and continued diversity

With no a priori theoretical rationale for anticipating either convergence or divergence amongst welfare regimes and clusters, the turn to the empirical evidence is a logical next step if we are to discern the developmental trajectories of European welfare states. Indeed, even if we had powerful theoretical reasons to expect convergence it would be important to test such an expectation against the empirical evidence (as in Hall and Gingerich 2009; and for a critique Kenworthy 2009). But we do need to be careful here. For there is a danger that we simply invest too much in the capacity of the empirical evidence to adjudicate between contending claims about convergence, divergence and continuing diversity. As we noted when discussing the limits of statistical tests of convergence, much of the literature is concerned with unavoidably subjective and qualitative aspects of welfare reform that simply do not avail themselves readily of such testing. Sigma, beta and gamma convergence tests do not mean a great deal when we are attempting to ascertain whether there has been a convergence in the ideas influencing access to child care provision, for instance. The point is that we are unlikely to be able to find discriminating and exacting data on each dimension of welfare reform in which we may be interested.

But this is no manifesto of despair. A couple of observations suggest that there is still quite a lot to be learned from this more inductive and empirical approach – just as there is quite a lot at stake in the potential findings of such research. First, it is of course likely to prove most difficult to establish definitively the direction of dispersion (convergence, divergence or continued diversity) where we are dealing with ideas – those influencing policy and/or those used to legitimate policy content. And, particularly when it comes to the ideas influencing policy, this is arguably one of the areas in which we are most likely to see (if perhaps not to be able to measure) convergence. But, as we have already argued, convergence in the ideas influencing policy is no guarantee whatsoever of convergence in policy content or policy outcomes. After all, neoliberal ideas which inform reforms that are implemented more enthusiastically in already liberal or residual welfare states will produce divergence not convergence in outcomes (Hay 2004b; see also Esping-Andersen 2002; Korpi and Palme 2003). Moreover, and rather more significantly, in the theories which predict convergence (whether simple or compound) it is invariably *policy outcomes* not the process leading to those outcomes nor the ideas influencing policy that is selected for. Thus, in the neo-classical view, in order to prevent capital flight it is not just necessary to 'talk neoliberal'; what is required is to translate such talk into a set of fiscal incentives sufficient to dissuade capital from exercising such 'exit' power as it possesses. As this suggests, ideational convergence is not nearly enough to confirm the neo-classical version of the convergence thesis – so we should not be overly concerned that this is likely to be one of the more difficult aspects of potential convergence to confirm empirically. Needless to say, it is far easier to gauge and to test empirically the kind of output measures that are likely to prove more discriminating when it comes to evaluating contending convergence theses.

It is such output measures that largely form the focus of analysis in the following survey of the evidence. But which output measures should we examine? Here, again, we find considerable controversy within the existing specialist literature. Conventionally, patterns of welfare reform have been gauged simply in terms of measures of aggregate welfare spending, invariably expressed as a proportion of gross domestic product (GDP). But in recent years this has come to be challenged by a number of authors advancing a version of the argument developed in Chapter 4. Their point is a simple one, but a crucial one nonetheless. Such measures, they suggest, fail to take account of changes in *demand* or *need* for welfare, with the effect that stable or rising aggregate welfare spending is typically assumed to show welfare resilience in the face of pressures for retrenchment (as in Pierson 2001) when in fact it may show nothing more than steeply rising demand or even just falling GDP (Montanari 2001; Korpi 2003; Korpi and Palme 2003; Castles 2004: 92). As Walter Korpi points out, 'a reliance on the conventional welfare state effort indicator may make an unemployment crisis appear as an actual increase in welfare state effort' (2003: 593).

In fact, this is merely the tip of the proverbial iceberg – and if it were just a matter of looking out for domestic spikes in levels of unemployment there would be no major problem here. But a problem there remains. For aggregate welfare effort may rise (as a percentage of GDP) for one of three reasons – because welfare states have become more generous, because the demands placed upon them (say, from an ageing population) have grown or, indeed, because, GDP has fallen whilst commitments have remained constant. Moreover, and more significantly, different welfare states are likely to be exposed to demand-inflationary factors (like population ageing, other forms of demographic change and unemployment crises) to different degrees and their rates of output growth (GDP) are also likely to vary. This makes it difficult to infer very much at all, certainly about welfare generosity, from any exhibited convergence in aggregate welfare effort – which might simply be an artefact of differential exposure to demographic change or any other demand-side factor or, indeed, the uneven fallout from the global financial crisis. As we saw in some detail in Chapter 4, demands on the welfare state have grown very significantly in recent decades. Consequently, the potential distortion that arises from assuming that welfare effort is a simple proxy for welfare generosity is greater than it has perhaps ever been.

This might suggest the value of simply ignoring aggregate trends in welfare effort, to look instead at more direct measures of welfare generosity. This is the approach typically adopted by the so-called 'power resources' school (see, for instance, Korpi 2003; Korpi and Palme 2003; Montanari 2001; Montanari *et al.* 2007). From this perspective the welfare state is understood, in the terms of T. H. Marshall, as a contract between the state and its citizens, providing the latter with social citizenship rights in return for the various duties and obligations they owe to the state. As such, measuring the welfare state entails capturing the social citizenship rights that it confers upon citizens – and this is gauged not by looking at aggregate welfare expenditure but at the entitlement of citizens to benefits and the level of income that those benefits replace (Montanari 2001: 472; see also Esping-Andersen 1990; Korpi 1989). As Ingalill Montanari and her colleagues suggest, 'the extent to which individual citizens are guaranteed protection by social insurance cannot easily be disclosed by total social expenditure figures', for the latter 'may depend on variations in the denominator, i.e., the GDP, and on variations in unemployment or the business cycle, as well as on demographic factors' (2007: 303). By contrast, evidence of a loss of entitlement or of reduced income replacement ratios *is* evidence of welfare retrenchment, regardless of the trend in the aggregate level of welfare spending.

There is undoubtedly much to commend in this. It is vital, if we are to assess the degree and unevenness of European welfare retrenchment that we give due attention to welfare entitlements in this way. But we are reluctant to abandon altogether a focus on aggregate welfare spending. There are two principal reasons for this. First, as the power resources school is often the first to concede (see, for instance, Korpi and Palme 2003: 443), the process of accessing and standardising this kind of data is immensely complex and time-consuming, with the effect that writing in 2011 we have access only to reliable European data up to and including 2000. At a time of considerable political economic turbulence with potentially profound consequences for the welfare state, this is major methodological limitation. Second, rightly or wrongly, when the existing literature predicts welfare convergence it is not anticipating convergence in income replacement ratios or entitlements, but convergence in aggregate welfare effort. Consequently, if we are to evaluate that literature empirically, we cannot afford to concentrate solely on indices of welfare generosity – however much more intuitively useful we may find them to be.

In the following discussion, then, we consider both welfare generosity and welfare effort. It is to the data on the latter that we turn first.

Aggregate welfare effort: convergence to 'type'?

A variety of more or less complex metrics can be used to examine aggregate trends in European welfare regimes since the 1960s. The first of these that we examine is time-series data, which in fact goes back as far as the early 1950s, on public social transfers – here, specifically, social security benefits and grants expressed as a share of GDP. The data comes from the online dataset accompanying Robert J. Franzese's important and empirically exhaustive *Macroeconomic Policies of the Developed Democracies* (2002; data available from www-personal. umich.edu/~franzese). To extend the analysis beyond the mid- 1990s, we have updated the original dataset with calculations supported by data from the 2009 update of the OECD's Social Expenditure Database (www.oecd.org/els/social/expenditure).

The results are presented in Figure 6.2. As well as the raw data for a number of European welfare states, we also show (on the right hand axis) a measure of dispersion – here Pearson's coefficient of variation (calculated simply by dividing the standard deviation by the mean).

The trends revealed by this graph are interesting in a number of respects. First, and perhaps least surprisingly, the graph shows a sustained and pretty consistent rise in social transfer payments for all the country cases considered from the 1950s to the present day – with the mean having risen by a factor of 2.5 in the last half century. No less unexpected is that the rate of growth has slowed somewhat in recent years, with the mean doubling between 1955 and 1980, but rising by less than a third in the period 1980 to 2005. As we shall see, the early 1980s are widely identified in the specialist literature on welfare state convergence as something of a point of inflection – marking the transition from what the 'power resources' school would see as the era of welfare state expansion to that of welfare state regress or retrenchment (see especially Korpi 2003: 597–8; Korpi and Palme 2003: 431–4;

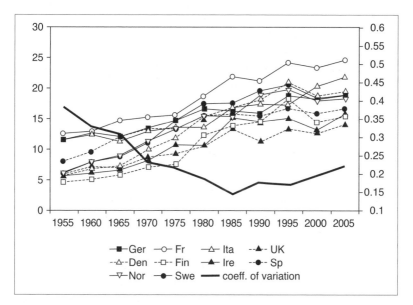

Sources: Calculated from Robert J. Franzese (2002); OECD *Social Expenditure Database*.

FIGURE 6.2 *Public social transfers (social security benefits and grants) as a share of GDP, 1955–2005*

Montanari *et al.* 2007: 295–6, 304–06, 309). To be fair, there is no evidence of retrenchment here – but, as discussed above, this kind of aggregate data is not the best place to go looking for such an effect. But what is interesting is that the data do offer some support for the idea that the early 1980s mark a point of transition between different phases of European welfare state development – a theme to which we will return presently. That support comes in two forms. First, as the best-fit trend lines for the periods 1955–80 and 1980–2005 (shown in bold in the graph) suggest, the rate of growth of aggregate social transfers is much reduced in the period after 1980. Second, and arguably more significant still, the trend in the coefficient of variation reverses at around the same point. There is quite a pronounced reduction in dispersion – in other words, convergence – from the 1950s until the mid-1980s and a subsequent increase in dispersion – in other words, divergence – thereafter, albeit at a lesser rate.

Of course, we need to be careful not to infer too much from trends in a single aggregate index of welfare effort, especially given the caveats about such data discussed above. But these findings are far from unprecedented (for similar observations drawn from the analysis of rather different data, see Bonoli *et al.* 2000; Brady *et al.* 2005; Castles 2004; Montanari *et al.* 2007; Starke *et al.* 2008). More to the point, they clearly confound the expectations of both the simple and dual convergence theses and they do so by looking at precisely the kind of data that these approaches would tend to see as discriminating.

The simplest interpretation of the data is of beta-(or 'catch-up') convergence whilst the welfare state is still in a phase of development and consolidation (in the 1950s, 1960s and 1970s), as later developers (welfare state laggards) start to close the gap on their earlier developing neighbours, followed by divergence, as the pressures and challenges on European welfare states mount in the wake of the crisis of the late 1970s. What they certainly do not suggest is that such pressures and challenges have driven, or are driving, a process of simple or compound convergence as welfare states gravitate towards Anglo-liberal welfare residualism or consolidate around liberal and co-ordinated market economy exemplars.

A final look at the aggregate data for individual welfare states completes the first part of this survey of the empirical evidence. This is presented in Figure 6.3 and looks in more detail at the most recent trends. It, too, draws on the 2009 update of the OECD social expenditure data series, this time looking not just at social security benefits and transfers, but all social transfers including public pension provision.

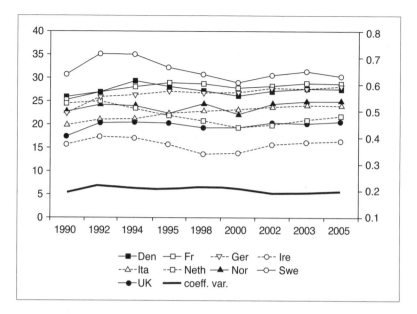

Note: Coefficient of variation plotted on the right-hand axis.
Source: Calculated from OECD *Social Expenditure Database*.

FIGURE 6.3   *Public social transfers (including pensions), 1990–2005
(% of GDP)*

Here, again, the story is one of continued diversity rather than convergence – as the trendless fluctuation in the coefficient of variation shows. Yet there is certainly evidence here of welfare states having reached some kind of plateau in terms, at least, of the aggregate value of the social transfers for which they are responsible. When this is set along-side the data, which we reviewed in Chapter 4, of a rapidly ageing population, it powerfully suggests that the welfare regress and retrenchment identified by the power resources school has been underway since at least the early 1990s and quite conceivably for some time prior to that. Yet what is perhaps most striking of all about this data is how stable and consistent levels of social transfers have been since the 1990s – with the separate traces in the graph very rarely crossing over one another and with absolutely no evidence whatsoever of convergence.

Having examined in some detail trends in aggregate expenditure at the level of individual welfare states, it is now useful to consider the same data for welfare state clusters. Here, we start from (and explore the value of using) the regime-clusters that draw inspiration form Esping-Andersen's hugely influential analysis of the advanced welfare

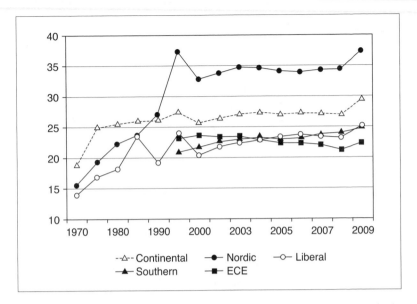

Notes: Social spending – the sum of 'social benefits in kind' and 'social transfers other than in kind' (% of GDP); Continental – Belgium, Germany, Luxembourg, the Netherlands, Austria; Nordic – Denmark, Finland, Sweden; Liberal – UK, Ireland; Southern – Greece, Spain, Italy, Cyprus, Malta, Portugal; ECE – Czech Republic, Estonia, Latvia, Lithuania, Poland, Slovenia, Slovak Republic.

Source: Calculated from European Commission (2010).

FIGURE 6.4   *Total social spending by welfare regime cluster (% of GDP), 1970–2007*

states (1990). This differentiates between the social democratic or, as here, *Nordic* regime, the Conservative, Christian democratic or, as here, *Continental* regime and the *Liberal* regime. Following our analysis in Chapter 2 – and as is now common (and, perhaps, accepted by Esping-Andersen himself, see 1999, 2002) – we add, the southern European regime (*Southern*) and, so as not to risk overlooking the potential specificity of the former state socialist east–central European (*ECE*) states, we also treat them as a separate cluster. The data is displayed in Figure 6.4, for the period 1970–2009, though the lack of time-series data preceding 1995 for some of the southern European and practically all of the east–central European cases lead us to show these data series only for the period 1995–2009. The reader should also be aware that there is a much smaller number of missing data points for some of the individual welfare states in the Nordic and Continental clusters before 1995 – consequently this data (which we do show) should be treated with some caution.

Such caveats notwithstanding, what the data strongly suggest is that it is only relatively recently that the distinctiveness of the Nordic (or social democratic) regime cluster has emerged. Since this is the most generous in terms of welfare provision and, as a consequence, that typically seen to be most exposed by virtue of globalisation, this is a particularly important observation. For it clearly stands in some tension with the predictions of the existing literature, particularly the neo-classical variant of the convergence thesis. For, far from being associated with pervasive welfare residualism and downward convergence, it would seem, the period of (supposedly) most intensive globalisation has seen the emergence and consolidation of the most generous welfare states the world has ever known. Moreover, as the most recent data show, the Nordic welfare regimes, certainly if gauged in terms of aggregate expenditure, are growing once again – no doubt largely because of the steep rise in unemployment associated with the onset of the global financial crisis.

Indeed, the striking thing about Figure 6.4 is, once again, just how little evidence of convergence it provides. The recent development of European welfare states may not be a story of divergence, but it is most certainly not a story of convergence either. Once their relative positions became established in the early to mid-1990s, it seems, each welfare regime cluster has continued to develop along its own established trajectory – with the Liberal, Continental and Nordic regimes evolving almost in parallel. Of course, it might be objected that the Southern, east–central European and Liberal regime groupings are very closely bunched. That it undoubtedly true, but the data suggest that they are certainly no more closely bunched today than at any other point since the mid-1990s (when the data series begins), that the composition of their welfare spending remains very different and that they remain as far from the Continental and, especially, the Nordic regimes as they ever have. One would have to try very hard to present this as compelling evidence of convergence.

This is all very well as far as it goes, but there is one significant objection to the preceding analysis. For it rests on the assumption that the five-fold welfare state classificatory schema that we have used continues to be a valid one. It could, for instance be the case that, although mean levels of aggregate welfare spending for each regime have failed to converge, this hides a widening dispersion amongst the welfare states within each regime group. In other words, the clusterings whose continued validity we have thus far simply assumed may have become increasingly anachronistic over time – as perhaps European welfare states have converged on liberal and co-ordinated market economy exemplars. In fact, there is nothing in the evidence that we have reviewed thus far to suggest that any kind of process like this is underway – and it almost certainly impossible to reconcile the evidence we have examined with such a view. But that is no reason to dispense with an obvious check that can be carried out on the augmented Esping-Andersen style welfare state clusters we have used.

That test is somewhat cumbersome and time consuming, but it is not a difficult one to perform. It requires calculating and plotting over time the coefficients of variation for the constituent members of each (assumed or potential) regime cluster. If the coefficient of variation for any one regime shows a pronounced upward trend, especially where that is accompanied by a convergence of its mean with that of another group, it is likely that the regime cluster is, indeed, spurious.

Figure 6.5 presents the results of precisely such an exercise. It shows, for each regime cluster considered separately, the total level of social spending (as a share of GDP) of each state and the overall regime cluster mean (plotted on the left hand axis) as well as the coefficient of variation (plotted on the right hand axis).

What it reveals is both reassuring and intriguing in equal measure. It is reassuring, certainly for those wedded in any way to the use of the Esping-Andersen clusters (in its original or augmented form), since no group fails the test at least with respect to aggregate welfare spending data. In fact, in only one case is there a statistically significant trend in the coefficient of variation over time. That case is the southern European cluster and the trend is downwards rather than upwards. In other words, there is evidence that southern Europe is becoming ever more tightly clustered, at least with respect to aggregate welfare spending.

More significantly, there is no evidence of the disintegration of distinct European welfare regime clusters. Indeed, since 2000, the coefficient of variation for each regime cluster has fallen with the sole exception of the east–central European welfare states (though even they have seen some convergence since 2005).

In short, European welfare states exhibit at least as much clustering today as they did in 1995 – there is no evidence of exposure to common pressures or challenges driving a process of welfare reform at the expense of European welfare regime diversity.

Scaling for demand: the real worlds of welfare retrenchment

This is already a very significant finding. But it is important not to be carried away by it. For, as we have noted throughout, aggregate expenditure data is not the best way to look at patterns of convergence and/or divergence, since such data does not control for variations in demand between welfare states and over time. In effect, thus far we have simply assumed that demand for welfare has been consistent over the period since the 1960s. Yet this we know not to be the case. It may well be, then, that if we control for increased need we will find that European welfare states have become less not more generous over time in real terms. In short, increases in welfare spending may have failed to keep pace with increases in welfare need. Indeed, scaling for variations in demand in this way may even serve to rehabilitate the convergence thesis. It is important, then, to re-evaluate the convergence and co-convergence theses in the light of this possibility.

What makes that task all the more urgent is that none of the considerable amount of evidence that we have thus far reviewed – all of it based on aggregate welfare spending data – gives any hint as to the widely identified process of welfare regress and retrenchment found by authors working on more disaggregated data. As this suggests, such data can provide, at best, only part of the picture. Consequently, it is to data on welfare entitlements and generosity that we must now turn if we are to complete our review of the available evidence and to build a more adequate perspective on European welfare trajectories.

Yet whilst aggregate data on welfare expenditure is not at all difficult to find, the same cannot be said for data on welfare entitlements and generosity. This, as already noted, is exceptionally tricky and time consuming to assemble, especially if that data is to be comparable between cases. Thankfully much of that work has been performed for us, at least for eighteen advanced welfare states, by the *Social Citizenship Indicator Programme* (SCIP), directed by Walter Korpi and Joakin Palme at the Swedish Institute for Social Research, Stockholm University (data available from www.dspace.it.su.se/dspace/handle/10102/7). The most recent update of this immensely valuable resource is for the year 2000, giving us data on entitlements and benefit levels (expressed as income replacement ratios) from the 1930s to 2000 at roughly five-year intervals. It is to the analysis of this data that we turn first.

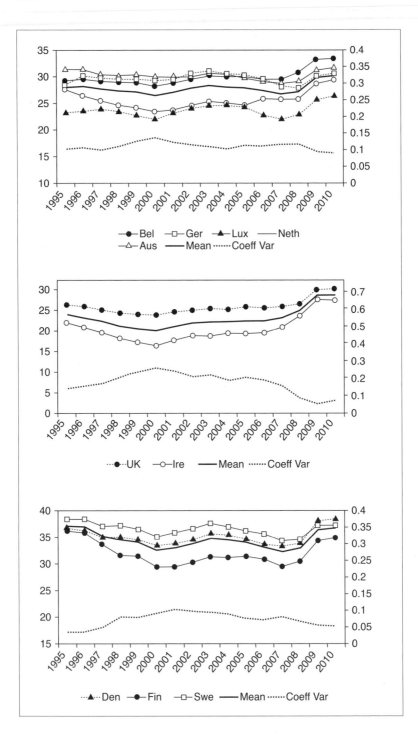

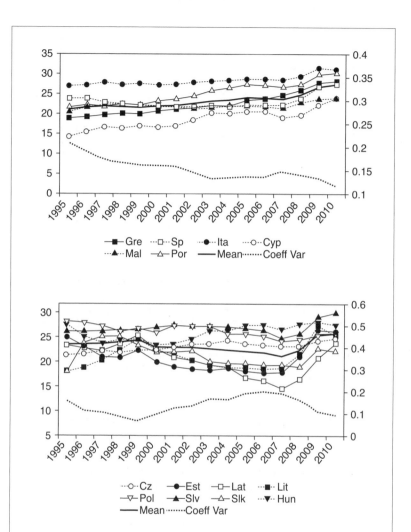

Source: Calculated from European Commission (2010).

FIGURE 6.5   *Dispersion of total social spending (% of GDP) by regime cluster*

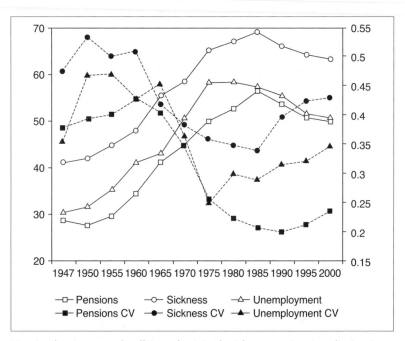

Note: Aarithmetic means and coefficients of variation for eighteen countries – Australia, Austria, Belgium, Canada, Denmark, France, Germany, Ireland, Italy, Japan, Netherlands, New Zealand, Norway, Sweden, Switzerland, UK and US.

Source: Calculated from the SCIP database www.dspace.it.su.se/dspace/handle/10102/7.

FIGURE 6.6   *Net replacement ratios for social insurance programmes,*
1947–2000

Figure 6.6 shows, for the post-war period (1947–2000), mean levels of pensions, unemployment benefits and sickness insurance (expressed as the proportion of the net wage of industrial workers) for the eighteen economies within the dataset (twelve of them European). It also shows (against the scale on the right hand axis), the coefficients of variation for the eighteen country cases with respect to each aspect of social insurance.

The data paint a very interesting picture, which largely confirms the findings of Montanari (2001) and Korpi and Palme (2003) based on analyses of earlier releases of the same dataset. Once again, as in the analysis of aggregate welfare effort – but here far more decisively – the late 1970s and early 1980s emerge as a point of transition between different phases of welfare state development – as growth and consolidation clearly give way to regress and retrenchment. Thus, throughout the post-war period benefit levels rise consistently until the late 1970s. From this point onwards, and at least initially in the context of escalating welfare costs as unemployment levels rise, benefits start to be scaled back – as, first unemployment benefits are cut, to be followed by later reductions in sickness insurance and pensions. Yet although it dates from the economic crises of the late 1970s, the process has continued unabated until at least 2000 (the final point for which we have this kind of data).

This in itself is very interesting, confirming some of our earlier suspicions that a continued upward trend in aggregate welfare spending might be masking a pervasive, if more subterranean, process of welfare retrenchment. But, for the purposes of this chapter, more significant still is what the data suggest about the relative dispersion of the advanced welfare states at different points in time – in short, about welfare convergence and divergence. Here, again, our findings reinforce those generated from an analysis of the aggregate spending data (particularly those arising from the analysis of Figure 6.2 above). They suggest both convergence and divergence, but at different points in time. The period of welfare state expansion and consolidation seems to be clearly associated with a convergence in net benefit replacement ratios, with the coefficients of variation for each aspect of social insurance falling consistently (and in a statistically significant way) for as long as generosity increases. This would appear to be a story of beta-convergence or catch-up, with later developing welfare states increasing the generosity of the benefits at a faster rate than those offered by their already well-established neighbours. Yet convergence gives way to divergence as soon as the generosity of benefits starts to fall, with the coefficients of variation for each aspect of social insurance now increasing (again, in a statistically significant way).

A closer look at the data for three of the country cases shows what is happening (see Figure 6.7).

This graph plots levels of unemployment benefit as net income replacement ratios for the UK, Sweden and Belgium in the post-war period. It suggests very clearly that the divergence picked up in the increase in the coefficient of variation in the previous figure from the late 1970s is a product of the already most residual (or Liberal) welfare states cutting their benefits earliest and hardest with the more generous Nordic and Continental welfare states cutting later and in a far less aggressive manner. This, of course, is a very powerful empirical refutation of the convergence thesis – which would predict precisely the opposite. The proliferation of common pressures and challenges that we tend to associate with the period from 1980 onwards, it would seem, have served not to undermine but in fact to reinforce and ever to

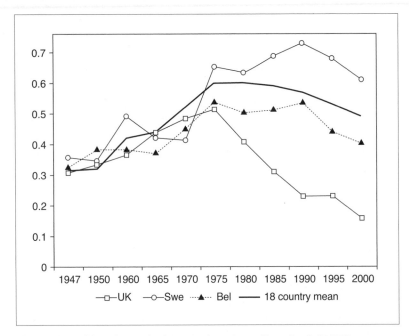

Source: Calculated from the SCIP database www.dspace.it.su.se/dspace/handle/10102/7.

FIGURE 6.7   *Divergence in retrenchment: unemployment benefits as income replacement ratios, 1947–2000*

re-establish the distinctiveness of European welfare states which had been converging in terms of generosity.

That impression is merely reinforced by one final pair of graphs. Figure 6.8 shows regime cluster means (in the first graph) and coefficients of variation (in the second), again for unemployment benefits as net income replacement ratios, for the European welfare states in the SCIP database. The limited country coverage prevents us from calculating similar plots for the southern European or east–central European clusters.

The evidence certainly suggests that, to date at least, it is the Nordic welfare states that have proved best able to sustain their (already high) levels of welfare generosity. This is the exact opposite of the convergence thesis' prediction. The Liberal welfare states, by contrast, would seem to have had most difficulty in defending welfare generosity. The Continental regimes fall somewhere in between. Retrenchment is clear in each case, but it has been very unevenly distributed, reinforcing rather than diminishing existing diversity in welfare regime clusters.

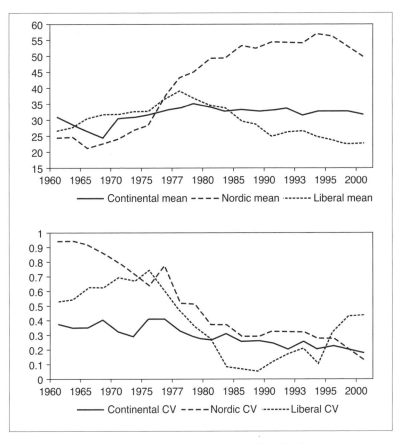

Source: Calculated from the SCIP database www.dspace.it.su.se/dspace/handle/10102/7.

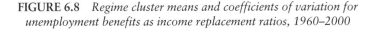

FIGURE 6.8   *Regime cluster means and coefficients of variation for unemployment benefits as income replacement ratios, 1960–2000*

Indeed, and as the coefficients of variation in the second graph show very clearly, the only convergence that this data shows in intra-cluster convergence – arguably even a convergence to *type*. Rather than generating convergence on liberal-resdiualism, in other words, this increasingly tight clustering may have forged some increasingly distinctive groups, perhaps even rescuing a version of Esping-Andersen's concept of types from its critics. Be that as it may, it would seem that, in response to common pressures and challenges, European welfare states have settled into ever more distinctive yet also ever more tightly knit regime clusters.

Conclusion

We have covered a great deal of important and much-trodden terrain in the political economy of European welfare capitalism in the preceding chapter. As we have seen the concept of convergence features extremely prominently in the existing literature. Yet it is typically invoked in the most casual and imprecise of ways to refer not to convergence at all, but to movement in a common direction (as in the term 'neoliberal convergence'). We have argued, instead, for a clear, consistent and explicit use of the term to refer (and only to refer) to the reduced dispersion of a number of cases (here welfare regimes) with respect to a specific variable (such as the aggregate level of welfare expenditure or the generosity of a given set of benefits). Understood in this way, the identification of a common trajectory of change (such as neoliberalisation or retrenchment) is neither a sufficient nor even a necessary condition of convergence.

We have argued, too, for a more detailed unpacking of the complex process by which potentially common pressures might impact upon different welfare regimes and be identified and responded to by policy-makers to produce convergent or, indeed, divergent outcomes. In so doing, we suggested the need to differentiate between a variety of forms of convergence (such as input convergence, policy convergence and outcome convergence) and to see the relationship between them as contingent rather than given. In a similar vein, we argued for the importance of recognising the various institutional mechanisms in and through which potentially common pressures (such as financial liberalisation or, more generally, globalisation) are translated into potentially convergent outcomes. Building on existing institutionalist scholarship, we noted that with each and every point of mediation identified, the likelihood of common pressures producing convergent outcomes recedes, using this to suggest that the question of convergence amongst European welfare regimes cannot be resolved theoretically and must be approached empirically (see also Hay 2004b).

To provide such an empirical assessment was the task we set ourselves in the second half of the chapter. In this we showed that, whether we look at aggregate indices of welfare effort or more differentiated assessments of welfare generosity, there is strong and clear evidence of *convergence* amongst European welfare regimes in the period until 1985 or thereabouts and equally clear evidence of *divergence* subsequently. This is in almost direct conflict with the expectations of the globalisation thesis and it is not much more easily reconciled with the influential 'varieties of capitalism' perspective (Hall and Soskice 2001a). Yet it is, we suggest, both intuitively plausible and credibly explicable, especially when it is noted that 1985 is the point at which, in terms of the generosity of welfare benefits, European welfare states move from expansion to retrenchment. In other words, we find *convergence in the period of welfare state expansion and divergence in retrenchment.* The former convergence we attribute largely to 'catch up' effects; the latter divergence to the more enthusiastic conversion to neoliberalism in welfare regimes that were already more liberal or residual in character. Thus, whilst almost all European welfare states have partaken in some way in the process of retrenchment, such retrenchment has been implemented at different paces in different regime clusters to produce, to date at least, divergent not convergent outcomes. Yet, intriguingly, the overall divergence between cases has been simultaneous with the growing convergence within specific regime clusters – as within-cluster dispersion has reduced and clustering has become stronger. Retrenchment has, in effect, produced reversion to cluster 'type'.

In the final chapter, we ask whether such trends are likely to be reinforced or undermined by the global financial crisis and the continent-wide turn to austerity that it has prompted.

Chapter 7

European Welfare Capitalism in Hard Times

If there a single core theme that has run throughout this volume it is the centrality of political economy – the attempt to capture the interaction between political and economic factors – to our understanding of welfare trajectories in Europe, as elsewhere. And if there is a central theme that has run through the wider literature on welfare reform in recent years it is surely the extent of the time-lag effects involved in translating political economic change into substantive welfare outcomes (see especially Korpi 2003; Pierson 1994, 1996, 2001, 2004).

Taken together these two insights present something of a problem when it comes to gauging the likely trajectory of European welfare reform in the years ahead – a core part of our task in this concluding chapter. For it is difficult not to see the times through which we are currently living as almost unprecedentedly challenging for the European political economy, mired, as to some extent it still is, in the longest and deepest recession since the advent of the modern welfare state. Indeed, core European institutions and the eurozone itself (certainly in its current form) may yet prove to be casualties of the crisis. It is, in other words, difficult not to see such challenges as central to European welfare trajectories in the years ahead. Yet, as students of the new institutionalism, we are also acutely aware that the consequences of such challenges for European welfare trajectories may well take many years to become clear. In effect, we know that something potentially crucial for the future of European welfare capitalism is afoot, but we still have relatively little substantively to go on in assessing its likely implications.

That makes much of what follows in this concluding chapter necessarily prospective. In it we seek to establish the significance of the financial crisis that has engulfed the world economy since 2007 for European welfare regimes, considering the extent to which a global financial crisis might be seen to prompt a crisis of the European tradition of welfare capitalism and the public institutions with which it is so intimately linked. In the process, we revisit many of the themes of previous chapters in the light of the global financial crisis, reassessing in particular the fine balance between the competitiveness-enhancing and competitiveness-corrosive effects of welfare expenditure and re-evaluating arguments for European welfare convergence, divergence or continued diversity in the light of the differential turn to austerity which the crisis has prompted. We suggest that European welfare trajectories remain more politically contingent, even in the wake of the global financial crisis, than is typically assumed. But, on the basis of the limited available evidence to date, we nonetheless anticipate the continued diversity or even further divergence of European welfare regime clusters as the effects of the differential exposure to the crisis and the turn to austerity in response to the crisis serve to reinforce existing welfare reform trajectories. If all European welfare states face hard times, some undoubtedly face harder times than others.

The argument of the chapter is developed in three core sections. In the first of these we seek to describe and explain the origins of the crisis. We point in particular to the significance of oil price rises in puncturing the low inflation–low interest rate equilibrium that had persisted since the early 1990s. Such benign conditions, we argue, were conducive to the development of a variety of asset price bubbles on which the distinctive 'Anglo-liberal' growth model had been built. Higher interest rates burst these bubbles, profoundly destabilising the Anglo-liberal growth model, with catastrophic consequences for those economies reliant on such a growth model directly or, indeed, indirectly, through financial or trade interdependence. As this suggests, the crisis was prompted by a combination of internal (or endogenous) and external (or exogenous) factors – and different European economies were exposed to these (and hence to the crisis) in different ways. In the second section, we seek to describe and map such patterns of exposure. Here we distinguish between three sources of crisis dynamics: (i) those associated with the direct bursting of asset price bubbles and the exhaustion of what we term 'Anglo-liberal growth' (an endogenous factor); (ii) those relating to contagion arising from financial interdependence (a first exogenous factor); and (iii) those relating to contagion arising from trade interdependence (a second exogenous factor). We consider the differential exposure of European economies to each, distinguishing in the process between the 'first-wave' economies (whose exposure was largely endogenous and typically the greatest), the 'second-wave' economies (whose exposure was initially financial) and the 'third-wave' economies (whose exposure has been principally through trade interdependence). In the final section of the chapter we proceed to map this analysis of the crises unfolding in three waves onto the European welfare regimes clusters identified in the preceding chapter. This mapping is by no means simple, but what we tend to find is that Liberal welfare regimes and a variety of southern and east–central European cases were most directly implicated in the crisis and hence most acutely exposed to its effects. In contrast, the exposure of the Continental and Nordic welfare regime clusters has been more attenuated, principally indirect and much more a product of contagion effects (associated with financial and trade interdependence). In the conclusion we reflect on the implications of such differential exposure to the crisis for European welfare diversity in the years ahead – in the new climate of region-wide austerity that is the most immediate legacy of the crisis.

The global financial crisis: an exogenous shock or an endogenous pathology?

Yet if we are to establish any of this, it is to the details of the global financial crisis itself that we must first turn. For if we are to gauge the potential implications of the crisis for the future of the welfare state in Europe we must first establish its nature as a crisis and the exposure of European economies to it. Above all, it is important to consider whether the welfare state might be seen to be implicated directly in the crisis itself or whether it is more accurate to see the welfare state as an indirect (perhaps even an innocent) casualty of the broader political and economic damage the crisis has wreaked (see also *Social Policy and Administration*, 2011). It is important to get this right. For whether we see the crisis as the product of an exogenous (external) shock or of an endogenous (internal) pathology is likely to have major implications for our assessment of the continued viability, resilience and sustainability in the years ahead of the welfare institutions to which European societies have become accustomed.

That, however, is no simple task – and opinions on a series of key issues, not least the appropriate response to the crisis, still remain divided. Nonetheless, with the benefit of a little hindsight a perhaps surprisingly highly conserved account of the unfolding and transmission of the crisis is now beginning to emerge. It begins, typically and, from our perspective, correctly, with the US case – more particularly with the puncturing of the US housing bubble in late 2006 (Gamble

2009a: 19–20; Mason 2009: 84). This followed a steep rise in interest rates in response to the sliding value of the dollar on international markets, a build up of domestic inflationary pressures as the economy eventually recovered from the bursting of the dot.com bubble and 9/11 and, crucially, a sharp rise in oil prices. Of these factors it is the third, the tripling of the price of oil in three years, that we suggest is the most important (Hay 2011a; Taylor 2009). This was driven at least in part by economic fundamentals – specifically anxiety about the capacity of oil supply to keep pace with escalating demand from the US and from the rapidly developing BRIC economies (Brazil, Russia, India and, especially, China). But the basic price signal in the market for oil was reinforced significantly by speculative dynamics (on the speculative character of the process of price formation in oil markets see Davidson 2009; Kaufmann and Ullman 2009; Sornette, Woodward and Zhan 2009).

In an attempt both to defend the dollar and to control inflation the Federal Reserve raised US interest rates almost five-fold between mid-2004 and early 2006, precipitating a major crisis of affordability in the US housing market. Unremarkably, mortgage default rates rose steeply as the higher repayments associated with the dramatically increased cost of borrowing proved simply beyond the means of those who had been enticed into the housing market by years of stable and low interest rates and rapidly appreciating property values. Predictably, the highest default rates were in the so-called 'sub-prime' mortgage market, which had risen from less that 5 per cent of mortgage lending in the US in 1994 to more than 20 per cent by 2006 (Martin 2011: 10). Such sub-prime mortgages had typically been offered to those who would not normally be considered creditworthy, who lacked a deposit (and were thus seeking a mortgage of close to 100 per cent of the value of the property) and who thus posed the greatest risk of mortgage default. To compensate lenders for this greater default risk, such loans were offered (often after a short honeymoon period at an attractive lending rate), at punitive rates of interest and with very high administration fees (payable to the initiator of the loan and added to the capital outstanding). Yet, however punitive their terms, in a rapidly rising housing market such loans did make sense – as a route into the (potentially lucrative) housing market for those who would not otherwise have one. In a rising housing market, sub-prime borrowers could expect to re-mortgage on far more favourable terms within a few years. For, even if they were only servicing the interest on their loan, with every day that passed the value of their property was rising and, crucially, the debt/equity ratio of their mortgage was falling. At some point this would drop below the sub-prime threshold, allowing them to re-mortgage on standard or 'prime' terms.

As this suggests, US mortgage lending was well configured to provide access to a rising housing market for those with low and middle incomes – and the additional demand for private property that this generated undoubtedly contributed to impressive house price inflation. But this seemingly virtuous cycle was only sustainable so long as interest rates remained low. The Fed's near quintupling of the base rate in a little under two years was almost bound to prove catastrophic. The majority of sub-prime mortgagees now had little or no chance of meeting their repayments and, as house prices started to fall precipitously, little incentive to attempt to do so. For, far from falling, the debt/equity ratios of their loans were now rising, trapping them seemingly indefinitely in the sub-prime snare. With no prospect of escape from the punitive terms of their loan, nor of holding onto their property in the absence of such an escape, their very strong incentive was to cease making any mortgage repayment and to cease doing so immediately.

Yet it would be wrong to see the unprecedented rise in interest (and hence mortgage lending) rates as posing a problem solely for sub-prime lenders. For if there had been powerful incentives for those at the fringes of the housing market to take on sub-prime loans whose repayment terms they could scarcely afford even when interest rates were at their lowest, the incentives for prime lenders to extend (indeed, to over-extend) themselves in the housing market were arguably greater still. Much of the US housing market was, then, cruelly exposed to any step-level increase in interest rates (Schwartz 2009).

A further factor merely compounded the high level of systemic risk building in the US residential and consumer economy in the run up to the crisis. For one of the principal ways in which US homeowners had come to use the rising property market to their advantage was to re-mortgage regularly. This, in effect, allowed them to release much of the equity accruing in their homes to fuel their wider consumption. Private debt was thus closely aligned, as we shall see in more detail presently, with demand in the wider economy. The effect was to make demand and hence growth highly – and increasingly – sensitive to interest rate variations. A near five-fold increase in the base rate was thus likely to precipitate not just a crash in the housing market, but a full scale US recession, with knock-on consequences for global demand.

This goes some way to explaining the wider significance of all of this for the world economy – and hence, at least indirectly, for European welfare capitalism. But it overlooks one key feature. For it was neither first nor principally through trade interdependence, but in fact through financial interdependence, that the crisis proved contagious. To see why we need to return to the US housing market and to ask ourselves how it could possibly be that high mortgage default rates amongst sub-prime lenders in the Midwest might threaten to precipitate a global depression?

The answer – mortgage securitisation – might seem neither immediately intuitive nor immediately illuminating. But it is, in fact, a key part of the crises transmission mechanism (Helleiner 2011). From the 1980s onwards in the US and a number of other Anglo-liberal economies, mortgage lenders were able, in effect, to sell on to domestic and international financial intermediaries the income streams associated with their lending (Langley 2006; Watson 2010). This they did, typically, by passing on their mortgage debt to investment banks who repackaged it in the form of mortgage-backed securities (MBSs). These in turn were sold to international investors keen to hold high-yielding assets denominated in dollars. In the process US mortgage risk was passed 'downstream', with the initiator of the loan invariably bearing none of the risk. Whilst the housing bubble continued to inflate such MBSs, particularly those associated with the sub-prime portion of the market (with the highest transaction fees and the least favourable lending terms), generated a very healthy return for investors. Consequently, demand for such assets soared, with the effect that mortgage brokers and initiators (whom, of course, bore none of the downstream risk) became less and less scrupulous in certifying as credit worthy potential mortgagees whilst their administration fees per transaction grew significantly. At the same time, hedge funds and investment banks started to respond to the growing international demand for mortgage-backed investment vehicles by issuing a range of financial derivatives, thereby effectively magnifying the exposure of the global economy to any systemic risk associated with the US housing market.

A complex mechanism was now in effect in place to ensure the global diffusion and transmission of any crash in the US housing market with an economy's exposure to the crisis being in almost direct proportion to the density of its financial interconnections with the US. As this suggests, when the crisis hit, its effects radiated outwards from its epicentre in the US financial sector, travelling down lines of financial interconnectedness to topple like dominos those banks and other financial institutions around the world exposed through downstream debt diversification to US mortgage default risk. The result, as we now know, has been an unprecedented wave of bank insolvencies around the world, prompting the largest ever bailout of the financial sector, and a deep and prolonged global recession.

Thus far we have presented a pretty conventional account of the unfolding and onward transmission of the crisis. This is very much the story of a crisis borne in the US that has proved globally – or at least, internationally – contagious (Krugman 2008; Rajan 2010; Roubini and Mihm 2010; and, for a useful review, Helleiner 2011). From the perspective of European welfare capitalism, it is also, of course, an account of the crisis as an external shock. After all, if the crisis had its origins in the US, it is difficult to see European welfare capitalism as implicated directly in it in any obvious way.

But things are in fact rather more complicated than this simple if conventional account implies – and in ways that challenge the idea that the crisis can be seen, simply and unambiguously, as an exogenously generated shock to the European political economy. A number of points might here be made.

First, the US was by no means the only economy to have experienced the inflation and puncturing of a housing bubble. As the data in Figure 7.1 show very clearly, relative to many European economies (and, indeed, even to the eurozone average), house price inflation in the US since 1998 has in fact been quite modest. Moreover, although the US housing market was the first to crash (in late 2006), the UK, Spain and, in particular, Ireland have all experienced rather sharper falls in house prices, from much higher initial peaks.

Such data indicate the (albeit differential) participation of European economies in the inflation and puncturing of a house price bubble – or, in other words, a strong endogenous element to the crisis. That is borne out by a further observation – that there is little in the account developed above of the puncturing of the US housing bubble that might not apply equally to a number of European cases. Indeed, if – as we have argued – the key factor in accounting for the crisis of affordability in the US housing market that developed between 2004 and 2006 is the sharp rise in interest rates associated with a three-fold increase in the price of oil, then this begins to look less like a specifically US crisis. For whether one paid for one's oil in dollars, euros or sterling, the price was rising with worryingly inflationary effects to which monetary policy authorities responded with interest rate rises.

This, again, is clear from the evidence. Figure 7.2 shows (on the right- hand axis) interest rate settings by the Federal Reserve, the Bank of England and the European Central Bank in the run up to the crisis

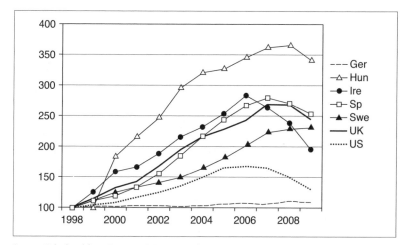

Source: Calculated from European Mortgage Federation (2010).

FIGURE 7.1 *Nominal house price inflation in Europe and the US (1998=100)*

and (on the left-hand axis) the price of oil. It might, at this point, be objected that oil prices continued to rise well beyond the point at which US (and, indeed, ECB and Bank of England) interest rates peaked. This is certainly true but, we would contend, is a simple reflection of the damage that such interest rate hikes had already done to the US, euro-zone and UK economies by the time they peaked (a point to which we return in more detail presently) and the fact that interest rate settings followed more closely oil futures prices than actual prices.

As this suggests, and certainly for those economies most exposed to the bursting of a housing bubble, this was as much an endogenous crisis of growth as it was for the US. Indeed, this is in turn suggestive of the crisis as one of a rather more prevalent growth model (the 'Anglo-liberal' growth model) present, albeit to different degrees and in subtly different variants, in a number of European cases (Hay 2011a, 2011c). To be clear, though such a growth model was undoubtedly present in the European liberal cases (the UK and Ireland), elements of it can also be detected in a number of southern and east–central European cases (such as Spain and Hungary, respectively). As this implies, there was certainly no simple one-to-one correlation between welfare regime cluster and growth model.

That, at least, is the argument we seek to develop through a more detailed examination of a number of these European cases. But before

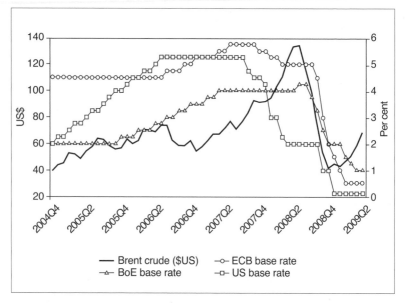

Source: US Energy Information Administration.

FIGURE 7.2   *Oil prices and interest rates*

turning to these directly, it is important first to deal with a potential objection to the depiction of this as an endogenous crisis, even for the US case.

That objection is a very simple one – and one rather familiar to political economists of the advanced industrial economies in the post-war period. It is that this can hardly be said to be a very endogenous crisis if it is precipitated by a tripling in the price of oil. For the determinants of the price of oil are surely external to the political economy of individual country cases? What makes this a familiar argument is that much the same point was made about the crisis of the mid to late 1970s – itself widely held to have been precipitated by an ostensibly similar quadrupling in the price of oil associated, this time, with the Arab–Israeli War (Zysman 1983; Gourevitch 1986; Hall 1986; Cairncross 1992: 182–7).

On the face of it, the objection would seem to be a sound one. For the crisis of the 1970s – or, indeed, that today – is exogenous insofar as it is seen to arise from factors beyond the parameters of our conventional understanding of the system in question. If the crisis of European welfare capitalism in the 1970s is seen as a knock-on effect of the Arab–Israeli conflict and the Arab–Israeli conflict is acknowledged to lie outside of the core of comparative European political economy, then it is surely right from such a perspective to see the crisis as the product of an exogenous shock Similarly, if today's crisis – a potential crisis of European welfare capitalism too – is seen as a knock-on effect of the tripling of the price of oil, then surely it too is rightly seen as the product of an exogenous shock? But things are not quite as simple as this suggests. For the crisis can be viewed differently – less as a discrete event precipitated by specific external or exogenous shocks and rather more as the longer-term product of a series of endogenous frailties and pathologies exposed by a change in the context. Such frailties might include the dependence of growth on asset-price bubbles, over-reliance on demand for exports generated in economies in turn dependent for their own growth on such bubbles, exposure through financial interdependence to the bursting of such bubbles, or the running of substantial budget deficits. In the end it is an analytical choice whether to emphasise the specific change in the external environment prompting the crisis or the incapacity of the domestic economy to deal with any such change. But the point is that we do not need to be nor become experts in the determinants of oil prices in order to see that, whether in the 1970s or today, the growth models of some European (and other) economies were likely to struggle to cope with an inflationary shock, whatever its specific source. That frailty is endogenous rather than exogenous.

If this is accepted then it has important implications. For if the incapacity of an economy's existing growth model to deal with an inflationary shock is seen as an endogenous factor, as we have argued it should be, then the balance between endogenous and exogenous factors in the present crisis varied between European cases – with potentially highly significant implications for their respective welfare trajectories in the years ahead. The crisis was, in short, more endogenous for some European economies than it was for others.

Endogenous and exogenous factors in the unfolding and transmission of the crisis

To see this, it is useful to differentiate between three rather different mechanisms through which potentially crisis-inducing effects were generated, one (largely) endogenous, two (largely) exogenous.

The first, and the sole endogenous mechanism, was the puncturing of a housing (and related asset-price) bubble reliant for its persistence on continued low interest rates and hence likely to be threatened by inflationary pressures (whether endogenously or exogenously generated). Economies might be seen to have been prone to a crisis induced in this way in proportion: (i) to the extent of the bubble in their housing market; and (ii) the extent to which their growth model rested on consumer demand generated through private debt typically secured against a rising property market. The Anglo-liberal economies and a number of the Baltic and east-central European states, as we shall see presently, were exposed to the crisis principally through this route – and were typically amongst the first to feel its effects.

The second, the first of two exogenous mechanisms for the transmission of the crisis, was through contagion borne of financial interdependence. In order to suffer from such an effect, economies did not need to have experienced any housing or other asset-price bubble, but simply to have (or have had) a system of financial regulation sufficiently liberal to allow banks (commercial or investment) and other financial intermediaries to hold securities, assets and derivatives which exposed them to US (or, indeed, wider Anglo-liberal) mortgage default risk. It was largely through this route that economies such as Germany, which had experienced virtually no increase in house prices since the 1990s, were exposed to the crisis. In general, economies were exposed to the fallout of the crisis in this way in proportion to the relative size of their banking sector, the extent of their financial interdependence and, in particular, the direct and indirect exposure of their financial institutions to US mortgage and housing-linked assets, securities and debt. As this suggests, a number of European economies already reeling from the implosion of their own asset-price bubbles and from the damage this was inflicting on their own banking sectors were also extremely vulnerable through such financial interdependence to crisis contagion via this route.

The third and final mechanism for the transmission of the crisis, or at least the effects to which it gave rise, was through trade interdependence. As the US economy slid into recession so, almost inevitably, did aggregate demand in the world economy for exported goods and services – both through the direct effects of reduced demand in the US economy and as credit conditions tightened around the world.

The effect, unremarkably, was a global recession and, with it, a pronounced decline in the volume of world trade, even gauged relative to world economic output. Around the world, cash-strapped consumers' shopping baskets shrank in size whilst the space taken in those baskets by imported luxury items relative to locally sourced staples also tended to fall.

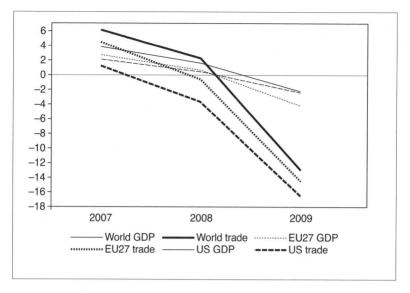

Source: Calculated from World Trade Organization (2010).

FIGURE 7.3 *The de-globalisation of trade in recession, 2007–09 (%
annual change at constant prices of GDP and trade volumes)*

The consequences of this are clearly seen in Figure 7.3, which shows
year-on-year changes in GDP and merchandise trade for the world
economy as whole and for the US and EU-27 economies separately.

What it demonstrates is that although world, US and EU economic
output all fell alarmingly between 2007 and 2009, trade volumes fell at
a far greater rate in each case. In other words, though economic output
was itself falling, the proportion of such economic output that was
traded was also falling. Or, put slightly differently, the world was
becoming less integrated in terms of trade for the first time since the
1930s.

Whether or not this decline in world trade volumes proves temporary it is has already exacted a high price from a number of the more
export-oriented European economies in particular – the extent of their
exposure to contagion effects of the crisis transmitted in this way being
in proportion both to their trade openness and their (initial) balance of
trade position. Though contagion through trade interdependence
proved a rather slower transmission mechanism, with a downturn in
world trade volumes only becoming evident from the second half of
2008, its effects have then been considerable.

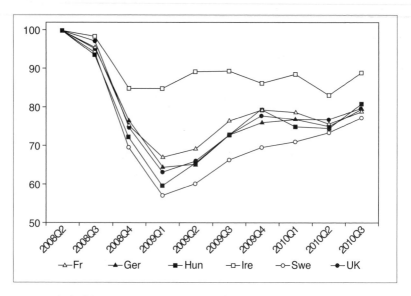

Note: Standardised data (2008Q2 = 100); raw data in $ billions, seasonally adjusted.

Source: Calculated from OECD (2011) *International Trade and Balance of Payments Dataset*, Paris: OECD (http://stats.oecd.org/index.aspx).

FIGURE 7.4   *The declining value of European exports*

The extent and uneven distribution of the damage inflicted on European economies by shrinking export markets is shown clearly in Figure 7.4.

This shows the volume of exports for a number of European economies with figures standardised at 100 for the second quarter of 2008. Such standardised data allow us better to compare trends between different country cases. For the most part, the data reveal a pattern that is remarkably highly conserved between European economies. Interestingly, it is Ireland that stands out as something of an exception to the general trend; the impressive improvement of its balance of trade position is clearly not simply a product of a haemorrhaging of demand for imports. Crucially (and encouragingly), Ireland's share of world export markets has held up rather well – certainly far better than for many of its European neighbours. Indeed, given the extent of the decline in world trade volumes described in Figure 7.3, Ireland has undoubtedly increased its share of world export markets during the crisis.

But despite this impressive performance, revenue from exports still fell by the equivalent of just over 6 per cent of GDP between 2008 and

2009. The point is, though, that this still compares very favourably with Ireland's nearest neighbours. In the UK exports fell by the equivalent of just under 10 per cent of GDP, in Germany by 17 per cent, in Sweden 22 by per cent and in Hungary by a whopping 38 per cent. This is worrying indeed. Yet perhaps more alarming still is that although export volumes have recovered quite significantly since their trough early in 2009, those that have stabilised would appear to be doing so considerably below their pre-crisis levels. That suggests a step-level reduction in European exports (matched, it should also be noted, by an equivalent reduction in European imports) equivalent to lost revenue of between 5 and 15 per cent of GDP. Given the link between such receipts and the revenue streams out of which the welfare state has typically been funded, especially in the smaller and more open export-oriented northern European economies, this is troubling indeed (see also Vis, van Kersbergen and Hylands 2011).

Such figures are already powerfully suggestive of a mechanism – transmitted through trade interdependence and, more specifically, through declining world trade volumes – linking the global financial crisis to a potential fiscal crisis of the welfare state. Yet, as we have argued, it is but one of three key mechanisms. If we are to identify and evaluate the contribution of the others, it is important that we return to the internal workings of the European growth models that the crisis exposed.

The bursting of the bubble and the transmission of the crisis

As we have seen, the housing bubble burst first in the US and it was the US economy that was the first to experience recession. This makes it tempting to see the diffusion and onward transmission of the crisis to Europe (and elsewhere) solely as a product of contagion. But, as we have been at pains to demonstrate, that does not make such an account – the conventional account – correct. The crisis, as we have argued, is perhaps best seen as one precipitated by the demise of a specific ('Anglo-liberal') growth model, a model certainly present in the US but also present in Europe – most obviously in the UK and Ireland, but also in some of the Baltic and east–central European states and in the Iberian Peninsula (albeit in somewhat different forms).

As this suggests, it is possible to differentiate between those European economies whose first experience of the crisis was endogenous – arising from an internal puncturing of their own model of growth – and those whose first (and, indeed, whose only) experience of the crisis was exogenous – a product of contagion effects radiating outwards from the US and other centres of Anglo-liberal growth.

One way of doing this empirically is to examine the timing of the onset of the crisis in different economies. If we do this, three waves of the unfolding crisis can be identified – the first pitching a number of economies into recession in the first two quarters of 2008; the second producing recession in the third quarter of 2008; and the third precipitating recession in the final quarter of 2008 or later. Each, we suggest, can be associated with a rather different transmission mechanisms with its own distinctive temporality.

The 'first wave'– the demise of Anglo-liberal growth

In the first wave, entering recession in the first half of 2008, we see those economies whose initial experience of the crisis was essentially endogenous – typically those with the most over-inflated housing bubbles and with models of growth most reliant upon demand sourced by consumer debt secured against the housing market. In terms of timing, the US, of course, belongs in this category. Yet as the data in Tables 7.1–7.3 show, in terms of the aggregate economic fundamentals it is in fact something of an outlier – with rather lower levels of house price inflation and rather more modest increases in both mortgage debt and overall household indebtedness in the decade prior to the onset of the financial crisis.

This in itself is intriguing. For it suggests that the US was amongst the first wave of countries to enter recession not so much because of the extent of its financial and broader economic imbalances, but because of the severity and timing of the Fed's recalibration of interest rates. In no other leading economy did interest rates move so early nor so swiftly in an upward direction – and no other leading economy experienced a five-fold increase in the base rate. It might also be noted that a number of US states (such as California, Massachusetts and Florida), if analysed separately, would look much more 'first wave' in character (Dymski 2010; Martin 2011).

But in terms of such aggregate data the other first-wave economies were certainly much more alike. Predictably, they included the UK and Ireland, Spain, Hungary and the Baltic States. These economies were characterised, in the period leading up the crisis, by high and steeply rising mortgage and general household debt and rapid house price

TABLE 7.1 *Ratio of residential mortgage debt (as % of GDP), 2007 to 2000*

First wave (recession in Q1 or Q2 2008)		Second wave (recession in Q3 2008)		Third wave (recession in Q4 2008 or later)	
Estonia	7.74	France	1.62	Austria	1.72
Hungary	9.14	Germany	0.89	Belgium	1.36
Ireland	2.38	Italy	2.01	Denmark	1.38
Latvia	19.8	Luxembourg	1.48	Finland	1.51
Lithuania	14.2	Netherlands	1.44	Norway	1.60
Spain	2.05	Portugal	1.49	Sweden	1.50
UK	1.74				
US	1.10				
Mean*	8.14	Mean	1.49	Mean	1.51
Std Dev*	6.89	St Dev	0.36	St Dev	0.14

* Excluding US.

Source: Calculated from European Mortgage Federation (2010).

TABLE 7.2 *Ratio of outstanding household debt (as % of disposable income), 2007 to 2000*

First wave (recession in Q1 or Q2 2008)		Second wave (recession in Q3 2008)		Third wave (recession in Q4 2008 or later)	
Estonia	4.80	France	1.28	Austria	1.14
Hungary	—	Germany	0.91	Belgium	1.19
Ireland	2.31	Italy	1.38	Denmark	1.30
Latvia	17.0	Luxembourg	—	Finland	1.48
Lithuania	10.4	Netherlands	1.56	Norway	—
Spain	1.91	Portugal	1.38	Sweden	1.36
UK	1.53				
US	1.32				
Mean*	6.33	Mean	1.30	Mean	1.29
Std Dev*	6.19	St Dev	0.24	St Dev	0.14

* Excluding US.

Source: Calculated from Eurostat Household Financial Assets and Liabilities Database.

TABLE 7.3 *Ratio of house prices, 2007 to 2000 (own currency, constant prices)*

First wave (recession in Q1 or Q2 2008)		Second wave (recession in Q3 2008)		Third wave (recession in Q4 2008 or later)	
Estonia	3.15	France	2.06	Austria	1.09
Hungary	1.95	Germany	1.04	Belgium	1.82
Ireland	1.65	Italy	1.22	Denmark	1.86
Latvia	—	Luxembourg	—	Finland	—
Lithuania	—	Netherlands	1.44	Norway	1.74
Spain	2.33	Portugal	1.12	Sweden	1.81
UK	2.04				
US	1.53				
Mean*	2.22	Mean	1.38	Mean	1.66
Std Dev*	0.57	St Dev	0.41	St Dev	0.32

* Excluding US.

Source: Calculated from European Mortgage Federation (2010).

appreciation. They also tended to witness amongst the highest European rates of growth (suggesting the presence of asset-price bubbles), tended to have banking sectors more reliant on wholesale funding (and hence more susceptible to the freezing of inter-bank lending which immediately followed the crisis) and to have larger current account deficits (for a more in-depth statistical treatment, see Claessens, Dell'Ariccia, Igan and Laeven 2010).

These economies would almost certainly have endured deep and damaging recessions even in the absence of contagion effects from the US. Yet this did not make them exempt from such effects. If anything, the systemic fragility of their growth models and the financial and broader economic imbalances that they exhibited made them even more exposed to the contagion effects now radiating outwards from the financial epicentre of the crisis. These economies, in effect, suffered in a three-fold way – first, through the immediate effects of the bursting of their own housing and consumer booms (and through the direct consequences for their own banking sectors arising from this); second, through the contagion affects associated with their financial exposure to US assets and particularly their reliance on international lines of credit; and, third, through their exposure to a downturn in global trade volumes.

Consider the UK, perhaps the most exposed of the first-wave economies to the effects of financial contagion by virtue of the sheer size and the distinctive character of its financial services sector and the reliance of its growth model on access to personal credit. The highly securitised nature of the US mortgage market and the international diffusion of such securities meant that any bursting of the US housing bubble was always going to result in significant losses for UK financial institutions. But this was compounded by a second factor – the freezing up of both international and domestic inter-bank lending that followed as financial institutions licked their wounds, counted their losses and re-scaled (downwards) their expectations as to whom they might profitably lend. The brutal reality was that, given its levels of consumer debt and the dependence of growth on access to more of the same, the UK economy was always going to be more exposed to such a credit crunch than almost any other leading economy. No less significantly, the size and significance of financial services to the economy left the government with little option other than to underwrite the entire sector with public funds. The total funds committed were estimated by the National Audit Office, in December 2009, at £850 billion – a major contributor to a looming public sector deficit. Yet the rationale for a bail out of the banking sector on this scale was clear – to insure depositors and, rather more significantly, to re-secure the supply of credit on which the growth of the consumer economy for over a decade had been predicated.

As this suggests, contagion borne of financial interdependence is responsible for much of the damage inflicted on the UK economy since 2007. But it is not responsible for it all – and, crucially, the UK and other 'first-wave' economies were already in recession before such effects started to take hold. To understand why we need only remind ourselves of the link, established earlier, between oil prices (increasingly reinforced by speculative dynamics), inflation and interest rates.

From the second quarter of 2006 all three rose in parallel – in the UK and in the eurozone. Interest rate rises in Europe were, of course, much less pronounced than they were in the US. Yet, unremarkably, the increases in mortgage repayments to which they gave rise combined with a reduction in disposable income associated with rising prices led to a squeeze on consumer demand and an increasingly sharp fall in the number of housing transactions – followed soon thereafter by a no less sharp and accelerating depreciation in house prices. Having grown at around 12 per cent per annum since 1992 residential property prices in the UK were, in the final quarter of 2008, falling at around 20 per cent per annum. In Ireland the figures were more staggering still – having risen at over 25 per cent per annum since 1992, house prices were, by the end of 2008, falling at close to 30 per cent per annum. This brought about a quite brutal transformation in personal fortunes. In late 2006 the average UK earner living in the average home was seeing a wealth effect associated with house price inflation equivalent to three quarters of their pre-tax annual average earnings (Watson 2010). In other words, were they to release all the equity in their home they could effectively double their spending power. The equivalent figure in Ireland was in fact higher still, around 120 per cent of pre-tax annual average earnings. Yet two years later, with property prices in freefall, annual house price deflation in the UK was equivalent to over 120 per cent of the pre-tax earnings of the average citizen (Hay 2009a: 471) and closer to 150 per cent in Ireland. Any residual equity was seeping away at an alarming rate.

The housing market was no longer a source of growth but an impediment to it – because the low inflation–low interest rate equilibrium upon which its rise had depended had been disrupted, reducing demand for property and cutting off at source the equity that had drip-fed consumption for a decade and a half. The result was a highly corrosive combination of falling house prices and equity depreciation which, in combination with high interest rates and high and rising commodity prices, led directly to falling demand and, in due course, to rising unemployment.

Things were arguably worse still in a number of states in east–central Europe and the Baltics. The reason for this was simple – a combination of high levels of personal debt compounded by the exchange rate risk associated with the high proportion of such debt denominated in foreign currencies. Consider the Hungarian case. Here, partly in anticipation of eventual eurozone membership and partly resuscitating an earlier practice of many of its predominantly Austrian-owned banks, a growing proportion of new Hungarian mortgage lending came to be denominated in euros and Swiss francs (Becker 2007; Bohle 2010). It is not at all difficult to see why foreign currency denominated loans might prove highly attractive to aspirant homeowners in Hungary and, indeed, in many other accession states preparing themselves for eurozone entry. As Dorothee Bohle puts it:

> The significance of foreign currency consumer credits and mortgage lending has to be seen against the background of the policy of the National Bank. Preparing for Eurozone entry, it pursued a policy of high interest rates to fight inflation and the growing fiscal deficit. This made borrowing in Hungarian forint almost prohibitive. The much lower interest rates of the Swiss Franc denominated credits and the ensuing house price rises, however, relieved middle class consumers from the impact of restrictive domestic monetary policy, and simultaneously extended available credits. (2010: 7)

Access to loans denominated in currencies other than their own thus served to fuel the consumer economy in the absence of a domestic low inflation–low interest rate equilibrium. This was the east–central European variant of the Anglo-liberal growth model. The irony, of course, was that eurozone entry was itself made more likely by virtue of the pursuit of a hawkish anti-inflationary policy, the inevitable effect of which was a growing interest rate differential between the forint, on the one hand, and the euro and the Swiss franc on the other. This served further to incentivise borrowing in foreign currencies, thereby exacerbating Hungary's exposure to exchange rate risk. Yet financial institutions were only happy to offer loans denominated in currencies other than the forint so long as it was credible to believe that eurozone entry was an inevitability – an index of which was the interest rate differential between the forint and the euro.

Such a model delivered consumer growth and house price inflation, even in an economy saddled by high levels of public debt and a lack of external competitiveness, until 2006. But the precarious state of the public finances and the rejection by the European Council of the government's first convergence programme in 2005 led it to adopt a much more severe austerity package from 2006. This combined a short-term attempt to tackle the budget deficit with a longer-term programme of structural reform of the public sector (Bohle and Greskovits 2009). Yet its effect was also to drive down real wages, growth and consumption. This merely reinforced the already considerable vulnerability to the global financial crisis arising from the foreign ownership of so much of Hungary's public debt and the associated exchange rate risk this posed. Predictably then, in autumn 2008, at the height of the credit crunch and with financial institutions around the world seeking to de-leverage, there was a sharp run on the forint. To the horror of those whose mortgage lending was denominated in Swiss francs the forint lost a third of its value in a little over a month. As in the UK and Ireland, private debt secured against property had switched from providing the impetus to growth to become an impediment to growth. The currency was ultimately stabilised by a three base point increase in interest rates by the Monetary Council of the Central Bank, the Magyar Nemzeti Bank, and by the negotiation of a 20 billion euro loan from the IMF, the World Bank and the EU – conditional on further and yet more punitive austerity (Hodson and Quaglia 2009).

Yet although Hungary was the first European economy to seek external assistance in the crisis, it was by no means alone in witnessing a catastrophic implosion of its 'transnationalised' variant of the Anglo-liberal growth model. Indeed, as Figure 7.5 makes clear, although Hungary saw the most rapid increase in foreign currency denominated lending amongst the states that joined in 2004, exchange rate risk was in fact significantly greater in the Baltic states.

The story of the Latvian case unfolds in a very similar way to that in Hungary – though if anything the inflation and puncturing of its housing bubble was even more pronounced. Between 2000 and 2006, Latvia was in fact the EU's fastest growing economy – with GDP growth per annum well over 8 per cent. This was driven by the very strong link between foreign-currency denominated lending, house price inflation and domestic consumption. This, however, brought inflation and with it rising interest rates – reinforcing both the incentive to borrow in foreign currencies and the resulting exchange rate risk. As in Hungary, the global financial crisis led to speculation against the lat, with the Bank of Latvia consuming nearly a fifth of the country's reserves in an ultimately unsuccessful attempt to protect the currency,

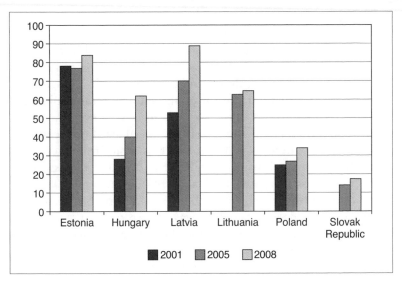

Source: Calculated from European Bank for Reconstruction and Development (2011)

FIGURE 7.5   *Proportion of outstanding household debt denominated in foreign currencies*

and with it indebted homeowners. National bankruptcy was only averted by a complex series of bail outs from the IMF, the EU, the World Bank and a number of bilateral creditors. These totalled some 5.8 billion euros – over 2,600 euros per Latvian citizen (Bohle 2010; Bohle and Greskovits 2009).

The 'second' and 'third' waves – contagion effects

As we have seen, the first wave of the crisis was largely associated with the puncturing of the housing and consumer bubbles that had emerged in a number of predominantly Anglo-liberal and east–central European economies and in the Baltic states. In the former cases this was principally a domestic story of the ending of the low inflation–low interest rate equilibria on which growth had been predicated in response to the inflationary shock of a three-fold increase in the price of oil. In the latter cases, things were a little more involved – since, in the absence of their own low inflation–low interest rate equilibria to draw upon, access to the comparatively cheap lending that might fuel a consumer and housing boom required access to credit markets denominated in other currencies. This 'transnationalisation' of the growth model (see also Bohle and Greskovits 2009) brought with it mounting exchange rate risk that was cruelly exposed by the credit crunch following the first phase of the crisis.

In this respect, the Baltic and east–central European economies, though already in recession before such effects took hold, were also amongst the worst casualties of the contagion effects borne of financial interdependence. Yet their exposure to such contagion effects – through exchange rate risk – was of a rather different kind to that of most leading European economies. For the Baltic and east–central European economies in fact had very little exposure to losses arising from US mortgage-backed securities. This was by far the most prevalent mechanism of financial contagion and was responsible for the initiation of a second wave of the crisis, engulfing economies, like Germany, that had seen virtually no increase in mortgage or total household debt nor any appreciable rise in house prices in the preceding decade. As the data in Tables 7.1–7.3 show, the second-wave economies were very different in the character of their housing and credit markets, with much more limited evidence of private debt secured against property acting as an agent of growth. Yet they were certainly no less exposed to financial contagion by virtue of this. Indeed, as for instance in the German case, one might plausibly argue the converse – with the absence of a domestic housing bubble contributing to the attractiveness for German banks of holding high yielding US mortgage backed securities. This meant that, when it came, the crisis in the US housing market proved rapidly contagious to the German banking sector – with IKB Deutsche Industriebank, for instance, being the first major European bank to be threatened because of its high levels of exposure to the US sub-prime market. The eventual bail out of the German banking sector by the government committed 480 billion euros of public funding and seems likely to end up costing the German state around 50 billion euros in non-recoupable losses.

The contagion effects of financial interdependence were, of course, transmitted very rapidly – with the bursting of the bubble in the US housing market leading almost immediately to a dramatic fall in the value of the income streams previously arising from mortgage securitisation (as default rates rose and mortgage repayments dried up). This in turn led to mortgage-backed securities being swiftly reclassified as 'toxic assets', to major losses for financial institutions around the world and, in the process, to a global credit crunch, with the effective suspension of inter-bank lending. But the contagion effects arising from the crisis were by no means limited to those transmitted through financial interdependence. The effects on trade, as noted above, have been no less significant – though there was undoubtedly more of a time lag between the onset of the crisis and the sharp deterioration in world trade volumes that would occur from the third quarter of 2008 (Chor and Manova 2011).

The contagion effects borne by trade interdependence, as well as deepening the recessions already underway in many first- and second-wave economies, initiated a third wave. This pushed over the brink into recession a number of northern European economies (such as the Nordic states) which had certainly experienced rapid house price inflation in recent years but without a pronounced increase in household indebtedness and whose banks were amongst the least exposed to the losses arising from US mortgage default risk and securitisation. Though they had, for a time, seemed largely immune to the crisis, they would now suffer considerably by virtue of their economic openness and, in particular, the dependence of their export-oriented growth models on international demand for high value-added goods. It was precisely such luxury product markets that were most hit by the overall reduction in world trade volumes, with Sweden suffering between the second quarter of 2008 and the first quarter of 2009 a loss in the value of her exports equivalent to 22 per cent of GDP. Though export volumes have recovered steadily since then, by the end of 2010, the value of Swedish exports was still lower (by some 10 per cent of GDP) than their pre-crisis level.

The consequences for the welfare state in Europe

Having sought to establish the nature of the crisis, the mechanisms of its transmission, and the degree of exposure of different European economies to it, we are now in a position to begin to assess its likely implications for the future of the welfare state in Europe. Yet, as should by now be clear, this is no simple task, involving the careful weighing up of a number of factors that pull in rather different directions. In what follows we seek, first, to identify those factors – drawing these out of the preceding analysis and reflecting on their potential implication for European welfare trajectories – before drawing them together to provide an overall assessment in a final, brief and necessarily tentative conclusion. Our aim in so doing is less to provide a series of bold and heroic predictions so much as to seek to identify the key factors likely to determine European welfare trajectories in the decades to come.

But before turning to these issues directly, it is perhaps useful first to describe our general approach to the crisis and to the implications of the crisis for the welfare state more specifically. The global financial crisis, we suggest, is perhaps best seen as a crisis of *growth* – arising from the disintegration of a number of the growth models that sustained the world economy throughout the so-called 'great moderation'. This may not seem especially controversial. But it is important to emphasise that it is in fact at some considerable odds with much of the political discourse of crisis that has emerged since 2007 (see also Hay 2011c). For, invariably, insofar as this has been appealed to in public discourse as a crisis, it has been appealed to as a *crisis of debt* (generally public debt) rather than as a *crisis of growth*. This may not seem especially significant; indeed, it might even seem like hair splitting. What makes it extremely significant, we would contend, is that the solution to a crisis of (public) debt is austerity – the rebalancing of public finances through some combination of cuts in spending and tax rises – whilst the solution to a crisis of growth is to identify and to make the transition towards an alternative growth model. It need hardly be pointed out that, to date at least, there is rather more evidence of the former than there is of the latter.

What is more, viewed through the lens of the 'debt crisis' discourse, the welfare state, as the largest single call on the public purse, stands between us and crisis resolution – and, as such, is almost bound to become the principle target of public austerity. Yet viewed, as it might be, through the lens of an alternative 'growth crisis' discourse, the welfare state might even be seen as part of the solution itself. As this suggests, the stakes for the welfare state of the terms in and through which we have come to define and thereby respond to the crisis could scarcely be higher (on the broader significance of crisis constructions, see Hay 1996, 2001, 2011c).

What this also suggests is the importance of assessing the potential sources of growth in the European economy and in the world economy more broadly in the years ahead if we are to gauge likely European welfare trajectories. It is for this reason that we turn first to trade.

World trade volumes – de-globalisation or re-globalisation?

It is clear from the preceding analysis that trade has been central to European growth throughout the 'great moderation', as it has in fact been during the entire post-war period. But, as we saw in Figure 7.4, the global financial crisis has led to a sharp reduction in global trade volumes at a time of falling world economic output. Crucially, it has also led to the world economy becoming less integrated in terms of trade (with the proportion of economic output being traded falling for the first time since the 1930s). This is alarming indeed, especially for the Nordic economies, whose capacity to develop and sustain the most generous and inclusive welfare states the world has ever known has typically been attributed to the success of an export-led model of growth – a reward to citizens, in effect, for the export success their (skilled) labour has wrought (Cameron 1978; Katzenstein 1985; Garrett 1998).

It is important to be clear about what is being said here. The problem is not the capacity of Europe's traditionally largest net exporters to continue to capture their share of world export markets – we have seen no evidence of this and, in the case of Ireland, for instance, some evidence to suggest that world market share has risen. But what we do see is unequivocal evidence that world export markets have contracted. Thus, even in the absence of the 1930s-style return to protectionism that many still fear, the value of the Nordic economies' export markets has shrunk by the equivalent of some 10 per cent of GDP, and it is by no means clear that this export shortfall is likely to prove a temporary phenomenon.

Yet this is not just a problem for the most export-oriented of European economies; it is arguably no less a problem for those European economies, like the UK for instance, whose Anglo-liberal growth model in effect compensated them for a significant and growing trade deficit. For, in the absence of a confidence in their capacity to resuscitate their old growth model, they have typically placed their faith in a 'rebalancing' of the domestic economy – in effect, in their capacity to discover or rediscover the secret of export-led growth. That is no simple task, especially at a time when it is by no means clear that global export volumes are set, any time soon, to return to pre-crisis levels.

Whether ultimately they do will depend on a great many factors – but perhaps most crucially the rate of growth of the US economy in the years ahead and the extent to which growth in China, in particular, translates into the increased purchasing power of China's citizens. We return to the prospects for the resumption of Anglo-liberal, and hence US, growth presently. But what is clear is that the US's nervousness about its own growth prospects in the years ahead has led it to place increasing pressure on China to allow the renminbi to appreciate against the dollar (see, for instance, Cohen 2012; Krugman 2009). The effect of any such exchange rate realignment would be an effective financial recalibration of the world economy, with the US' balance of trade deficit with China (and hence the rest of the world) reduced and with an equivalent reduction in its financial dependence on China. For Europe's beleaguered exporters there would be much to welcome in this, since any appreciation of the renminbi would be akin to a competitive devaluation of the euro and other European currencies in a potentially key export market.

Growth, output and taxation – a fiscal crisis of, or for, the welfare state?

This focus on trade perhaps already reminds of us the importance of the tax base to the funding of the welfare state – in the future just as now and in the past – and the significance of the crisis in such terms. From the perspective of the welfare state the crisis has manifest itself first and foremost as a severe constriction in the taxation base from which it is funded – though this should not lead us to overlook the increasing calls made on such limited public funds with the recapitalisation of the banking sector.

In this respect the crisis might well be argued to have precipitated a full-scale fiscal crisis of the welfare state – or, perhaps more accurately, a fiscal crisis *for* the welfare state (cf. Gough 2010). The distinction might seem narrowly academic, but it is important. For to suggest that this is a fiscal crisis *of* the welfare state would be to implicate the welfare state directly in the generation of the fiscal shortfall that now threatens it. To appeal to a fiscal crisis *for* the welfare state is to make no such assumption. Indeed, it is to suggest that the fiscal deficit which now threatens welfare state expenditure cannot be attributed to any dynamic internal to the welfare state itself. That, we would contend, is far more accurate.

The origins of such a fiscal crisis for the welfare state are, in fact, readily comprehensible and can be traced very clearly to the global financial crisis. They arise from the worsening of the condition of the public finances associated with: (i) the decline in fiscal revenue (the 'tax take') arising from the sharp downturn in economic output (GDP); (ii) the decline in fiscal revenue associated with (any) tax reductions designed to stimulate demand (temporary VAT reductions, stamp duty 'holidays' and the like); (iii) the costs of underwriting the banking sector with public funds; (iv) the costs associated with (any) sector-specific subsidies designed to support parts of the economy that were hit disproportionately (such as car scrappage schemes); and (v) the increased costs associated with meeting already sanctioned welfare needs as the number of those eligible for benefits rose as a consequence of the dislocating effects of the crisis.

Clearly the extent of the overall worsening in the public accounts varied considerably between economies, as did the relative share attributable to each of these elements. But, contrary to much of the public debate, by far the greatest contributory factor in each of the European cases was not the extent of the recapitalisation of the banking sector, but the simple reduction in the tax take arising from the sharp decline in taxable economic activity.

In the UK, for instance, had taxation revenue continued to grow at pre-crisis levels it would have exceeded the actual tax take by around £35 billion in 2008–09 and £92 billion in 2009–10. This equates to an 8 per cent reduction in taxation revenue arising directly from the crisis in 2008–09 and a 23 per cent reduction in 2009–10. The UK's budget deficit was around £49 billion in 2008–09 and £107 billion in 2009–10. In other words, approximately 70 per cent of the current account deficit in 2008–09 and 86 per cent in 2009–10 is attributable to lost taxation revenue (Hay 2011c).

Is it not, of course, difficult to see how such a profound destabilisation of the public finances might occur. For most of the state's outgoings are, in essence, the product of long-standing commitments – citizens, after all, have a right to receive those benefits, and to consume those public services for which they are eligible, regardless of the rate of growth of economic output. If the public finances are in modest balance before the onset of a crisis of this kind of magnitude, then they are most unlikely to remain in balance during and immediately following the crisis – since it is practically impossible for the state to reduce the size of its commitments proportionally to its loss in revenue as the crisis unfolds. But the point is that any failure to match reductions in the revenue stream with an equivalent and immediate rationing of welfare and other spending commitments will result in a growing current account deficit. A further factor merely compounds the problem. As growth turns negative, unemployment is bound to rise, albeit once again with some time-lag effect. The result, inevitably, is that, without any change in the eligibility criteria, the number of legitimate welfare claimants and total welfare expenditure both rise – with increased numbers of citizens claiming unemployment and associated benefits, a variety of means-tested payments and subsidies, and access to a range of public services for which they were previously ineligible.

TABLE 7.4   *Current account balance (as % of GDP), 2009*

First wave (recession in Q1 or Q2 2008)		Second wave (recession in Q3 2008)		Third wave (recession in Q4 2008 or later)	
Estonia	-1.7	France	-7.5	Austria	-3.4
Hungary	-4.0	Germany	-3.3	Belgium	-6.0
Ireland	-14.3	Italy	-5.3	Denmark	-2.7
Latvia	-9.0	Luxembourg	-0.7	Finland	-2.2
Lithuania	-8.9	Netherlands	-5.3	*(Norway*	*+13.0)*
Spain	-11.2	Portugal	-9.4	Sweden	-0.5
UK	-11.5				
Mean	-8.66	Mean	-5.25	Mean*	-2.96
Std Dev	4.41	St Dev	3.06	St Dev*	2.01

* Excluding Norway.
Source: Calculated from Eurostat Public Balance and General Government Debt data.

TABLE 7.5   *Rise in general government debt, 2006 to 2009 (% of GDP)*

First wave (recession in Q1 or Q2 2008)		Second wave (recession in Q3 2008)		Third wave (recession in Q4 2008 or later)	
Estonia	2.7	France	13.9	Austria	3.3
Hungary	12.7	Germany	5.5	Belgium	8.6
Ireland	39.1	Italy	9.3	Denmark	9.5
Latvia	25.4	Luxembourg	8.0	Finland	4.3
Lithuania	11.3	Netherlands	13.5	Norway	—
Spain	13.6	Portugal	12.1	Sweden	-3.4
UK	24.6				
Mean	18.49	Mean	10.38	Mean	4.46
Std Dev	12.03	St Dev	3.34	St Dev	5.14

Source: Calculated from Eurostat Public Balance and General Government Debt data.

Moreover, in the context of the current crisis, this all happens at a time when the stability and sustainability of the entire banking system is threatened as never before and as the state is called on to shore up and underwrite the entire sector with public funds. Put these three factors together and a sharp deterioration in the state of the public finances is effectively guaranteed. Tables 7.4 and 7.5 show, for the first-wave, second-wave and third-wave economies, the size of the resulting current account deficit in 2009 and the rise in general government debt over the period 2006–09.

Unsurprisingly, in the context of the analysis of this chapter, the deterioration in the condition of the public finances is dramatic in each case, but most severe in the first-wave economies. By contrast, the third-wave economies, whose principle exposure to the crisis was through the contagion effects arising from trade interdependence, have – to date – suffered the least. Yet this may well be attributable in part to the greater time-lag effects associated with trade interdependence as a mechanism of crisis transmission. If, for instance, it takes a decade for world trade volumes to return to pre-crisis levels, then it would clearly be wrong to gauge the severity of the impact of the crisis on different economies by simply comparing the rise in general government debt between 2006 and 2009.

Conclusion

This brings us to the crux of the matter. With such a profound destabilisation of the state of the public finances throughout Europe and with the welfare state invariably consuming at the onset of the crisis a higher proportion of state expenditure than ever before, it is not at all surprising that it should emerge as the prime target for budget cuts in the turn to austerity that has typically followed the crisis.

Yet, as the discussion of the preceding section already starts to suggest, certainly when combined with some of the broader themes of this volume, there may well be great dangers associated with an austerity-induced targeting of the welfare state.

First, there are clear macroeconomic advantages to running a budget deficit during and for some time after a profound economic crisis. As we discussed in some detail in Chapter 4, welfare state expenditure is, in effect, a natural macroeconomic stabiliser. Since a significant proportion of such expenditure is needs-related and since levels of need clearly vary across the business cycle, welfare spending tends to rise (whether as a percentage of GDP or in real terms) as the economy enters recession and to fall as it recovers. As this suggests, welfare expenditure is quite strongly counter-cyclical. But, as we also argued in Chapter 4, it is also counter-cyclical *in a very efficient way.* For it is the poorest in society who benefit the most from welfare benefits, certainly those such as unemployment benefit and means-tested income support that vary most in response to changing levels of need. Consequently, the potentially macroeconomically stabilising injection of demand into the economy that comes with the rise in welfare spending in a recession is strongly targeted on the poorest, the most needy and those most dislocated by the effects of the crisis. It restores, in effect, a proportion of the consumption potential of those whose capacity to spend (and hence whose potential contribution to aggregate demand in the economy) has been most depleted. Moreover, those in receipt of unemployment benefit and/or income support are also far more likely to spend what they receive in benefits than, say, a middle income consumer given a tax rebate. Accordingly, with perhaps one exception – the far more regressive policy of injecting demand into the economy by reducing VAT or other sales taxes – this is about the most efficient mechanism imaginable for stimulating demand within the economy. For so little of the state's demand stimulus is 'lost' in savings. Finally, those with the lowest levels of income tend also to consume a proportionately greater share of locally sourced staple goods relative to luxury, imported items. Thus, in contrast say to a VAT reduction, this is a most efficient mechanism for generating demand without effectively subsidising imports.

There is much to this broadly Keynesian argument. But, in the face of levels of general government debt in many European economies in excess of 50 per cent of GDP, there is little evidence of it tempering the perceived need for austerity and the associated downward recalibration of welfare commitments.

This makes a second argument all the more important. That argument builds from the observation, above, that the principal source of the public deficit that European economies now face is lost taxation revenue associated with reduced economic activity. The implication we draw from this is that the crisis is one of growth rather than of debt – or, perhaps, more precisely, that current levels of debt are a symptom, rather than the source, of a more deep-seated crisis of growth. That, in turn, suggests the potential dangers of austerity – a form of symptom amelioration, at best, rather than a form of crisis resolution.

The point, in a way, is a very simple one. The welfare state and the public sector more broadly undoubtedly contributes very significantly to economic output – both directly, in terms of the value of the goods and services it provides, and indirectly, in terms of the provision of a healthy, well-educated and appropriately skilled workforce, a public infrastructure and legal system that work, and in terms of the broader contribution to economic competitiveness discussed in detail in Chapter 4. If this is accepted, then austerity, understood in this context as the scaling back of the public sector, directly threatens the capacity to generate economic output. As such, it is only if the crisis is seen as one of debt and deficit alone, that austerity in the absence of growth can be seen as any kind of solution. For if the crisis is seen to have been precipitated by the exhaustion of a distinct growth model leading through contagion to a global crisis of growth then, almost by definition, reducing the capacity to generate economic output by reducing the size of the public sector can only compound the problem – threatening to throw the world economy back into recession and threatening to prompt a global depression.

Yet that is perhaps an overly bleak assessment. For although it might well apply to the Anglo-liberal economies and many of those Baltic and east–central European economies that grew so rapidly throughout the 'Great Moderation', it would be wrong to extrapolate from the exceptional experiences of these economies. Austerity, in most of the first-wave economies, is already firmly established and institutionalised – whether (as in the UK) through the product of a conscious political choice or (as in Hungary, Ireland and Latvia) through the stringent and binding terms of a bail out package. Either way, it seems, any meagre growth that temporarily returned as the deficit widened will be sorely tested by a wave of public sector retrenchment and redundancies with further serious knock-on consequences for the consumer economy and the housing market. What is more, if our analysis is correct, these economies have all lost a growth model and they have yet to discover another. The partial exception is Ireland that, as we have seen, grew throughout the 'great moderation' by combining elements of an Anglo-liberal growth model with a more traditional export-oriented growth strategy. It has witnessed amongst the most brutal of all recessions as the housing and construction bubble that it inflated burst spectacularly. But bolstered by the terms of its joint EU–IMF bail out it may yet manage to make the transition to a rather purer form of the northern European export-oriented growth model. For that to succeed, the transfusion of credit that it has received must be used not to reinflate the housing market but to reinforce the transformation.

Beyond the 'first-wave' economies, however, things do not look quite so bleak. In general terms, the depth of the recessions they have faced was not so pronounced. Such economies were exposed to the crisis not principally through the frailty of their own growth models, but through a series of contagion effects radiating outwards from the implosion of the Anglo-liberal growth model elsewhere. These revealed, in effect, how parasitic they had become on the demand generated by Anglo-liberal growth. This is perhaps the principal problem they face going forward – sustaining an export-led growth strategy in the absence of the contribution of Anglo-liberal consumer debt to world consumption. Most significantly, though, austerity is far less entrenched politically in these economies and it is rather more credible to think that they will be capable of rebalancing their public finances, albeit slowly, without a drastic reduction in the size of their public sectors.

If that is correct, then it generates a tentative prediction – of continued welfare regime divergence in Europe in the years ahead. The most generous welfare states the world has ever known – the Nordic and

Continental European welfare states – are here to stay and they are likely to retain their distinctiveness. But they are unlikely to remain as generous as they have been. For, as we have seen, the Europe-wide turn to public austerity has come at a time when even these economies were already engaged in cutting the generosity of welfare benefits and toughening eligibility criteria. That, as we have also seen, was a product to a considerable extent of an anticipated crisis of affordability associated, in particular, with an ageing population and rapidly rising health care costs. The inevitable conclusion is that, even in the Nordic countries, benefit levels and eligibility criteria will be toughened still further.

Yet, when compared with their liberal, east–central European and southern European counterparts, they will nonetheless look increasingly generous. This is most clearly evident if one looks at official government projections for public spending in the years ahead. These are shown in Figure 7.6.

Like all projections, of course, these need to be treated with some caution – all the more so since these indicate the aspirations of elected administrations for the years ahead and since, typically, the figures themselves are highly sensitive to the assumptions such administrations make about growth. But such caveats notwithstanding, such data undoubtedly give an indication of the extent to which planned deficit reduction will translate into cuts in public spending. And the picture they present is entirely in keeping with the analysis we have offered.

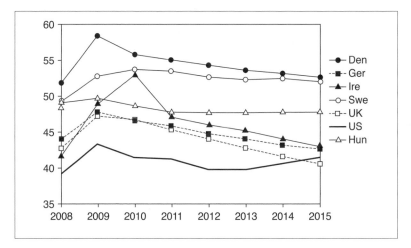

Source: Calculated from IMF World Economic Outlook Database (2011).

FIGURE 7.6 *Public spending projections, 2008–15*

Retrenchment and austerity, it would seem, are now very much the order of the day. But retrenchment implemented at different paces in different regimes through the differential imposition of austerity is likely to continue to produce divergent not convergent outcomes.

Bibliography

Aaron, Henry J. (1991) *Serious and Unstable Condition: Financing America's Health Care*. Washington: The Brookings Institute.

Ackerman, Bruce and Alstott, Anne (1999) *The Stakeholder Society*. New Haven, CT: Yale University Press.

Aglietta, Michel (1979) *A Theory of Capitalist Regulation*. London: New Left Books.

Alber, Jens (1995) 'A Framework for the Comparative Study of Social Services' *Journal of European Social Policy*, 5 (2), 131–49.

Alber, Jens (1996) 'Selectivity, Universalism, and the Politics of Welfare Retrenchment in Germany and the United States', paper for the 92nd Annual Meeting of the American Political Science Association, August, San Francisco.

Alber, Jens (1998) 'Recent Developments in Continental European Welfare States: Do Austria, Germany and the Netherlands prove to be birds of a feather?', paper for the 14th World Congress of Sociology, July, Montreal.

Allmendinger, J. (1989) 'Educational Systems and Labour Market Outcomes', *European Sociological Review*, 5 (3), 231–50.

Alter, Karen J. and Sophie Meunier-Aitsahalia (1994) 'Judicial Politics in the European Community: European Integration and the Pathbreaking *Cassis de Dijon* Decision', *Comparative Political Studies*, 24: 535–61.

Armstrong, Kenneth (2010) *Governing Social Inclusion: Europeanization through Policy Coordination*. Oxford: Oxford University Press.

Arts, W. I. L. and John Gelissen (2002) 'Three World of Welfare Capitalism or More? A State-Of-The-Art Report', *Journal of European Social Policy*, 12 (2), 137–58.

Ashton, David and Francis Green (1996) *Education, Training and the Global Economy*. London: Edward Elgar.

Assheton, Ralph (1944) Written Answers (Commons) National Finance 9 February, www.hansard.millbanksystems.com/written_answers/1944/feb/09/beveridge-report-sales.

Atkinson, Anthony B. (1995) *Incomes and the Welfare State: Essays on Britain and Europe*. Cambridge: Cambridge University Press.

Atkinson, Anthony B. (1999) *The Economic Consequences of Rolling Back the Welfare State*. Cambridge, MA: MIT Press.

Atkinson, Anthony B. and Gunnar V. Mogensen (eds) (1993) *Welfare and Work Incentives: A North European Perspective*. Oxford: Clarendon Press.

Avdagic, Sabena, Martin Rhodes and Jelle Visser (2005) 'The Emergence and Evolution of Social Pacts: A Provisional Framework for Comparative

Analysis', *European Governance Papers* (EUROGOV), No. N-05-01.
www.connex-network.org/eurogov/pdf/egp-newgov-N-05-01.pdf.

Badie, Bertrand and Pierre Birnbaum (1983) *The Sociology of the State*.
Chicago: University of Chicago Press.

Bacon, Robert and Walter Eltis (1976) *Britain's Economic Problem: Too Few Producers*. London: Macmillan.

Baldwin, Peter (1992) *The Politics of Social Solidarity: Class bases of European Welfare States 1875–1975*. Cambridge: Cambridge University Press.

Bank for International Settlements (2002) *Triennial Central Bank Survey of Foreign Exchange and Derivative Market Activity*. Basel, Switzerland.

Bank for International Settlements (2005) *Triennial Central Bank Survey of Foreign Exchange and Derivative Market Activity*. Basel, Switzerland.

Bank for International Settlements (2008) *Triennial Central Bank Survey of Foreign Exchange and Derivative Market Activity*. Basel, Switzerland.

Bank for International Settlements (2011) *Triennial Central Bank Survey of Foreign Exchange and Derivative Market Activity*. Basel, Switzerland.

Barr, Nicholas (1998) *The Economics of the Welfare State*. 3rd edn, Oxford: Oxford University Press.

Barr, Nicholas (2006) 'Pensions: Overview of the Issues', *Oxford Review of Economic Policy*, 22 (1), 1–14.

Barro, Robert (1991) 'Economic Growth in a Cross Section of Countries', *Quarterly Journal of Economics*, 106, 407–33.

Barro, Robert J. and Xavier Sala-i-Martin (1992) 'Convergence', *Journal of Political Economy*, 100 (2), 223–49.

Bayoumi, Tamim (1997) *Financial Integration and Real Activity*. Manchester: Manchester University Press.

Becker, Gary S. (1964) *Human Capital*. New York: National Bureau of Economic Research.

Becker, Joachim (2007) 'Dollarisation in Latin America and Euroisation in Eastern Europe: Parallels and Differences', in J. Becker and R. Weissenbacher (eds), *Dollarisation, Euroisation and Financial Instability*. Marburg: Metropolis.

Becker, Uwe (2000) 'Welfare State Development and Employment in the Netherlands', *Comparative perspective Journal of European Social Policy*, 10 (3), 219–39.

Bennett, Colin J. (1991) 'What is Policy Convergence and What Causes It?', *British Journal of Political Science*, 21, 215–33.

Berger, Suzanne and Robert Dore (eds) (1996) *National Diversity and Global Capitalism*. Ithaca, NY: Cornell University Press.

Bernanke, Ben (2004) 'The Great Moderation', Remarks at the meetings of the Eastern Economic Association, Washington DC, 20 February 2004 www.federalreserve.gov/BOARDDOCS/SPEECHES/2004/20040220/default.htm

Blanchard, Olivier J. (1986) 'The Wage Price Spiral', *Quarterly Journal of Economics*, 101 (3), 543–66.

Blyth, Mark (2002) *Great Transformations: Economic Ideas and Institutional Change in the 20th Century*. Cambridge: Cambridge University Press.

Bohle, Dorothee (2010) *East European Transformations and the Paradoxes of Transnationalism*. European University Institute Working Paper, SPS 2010/01.

Bohle, Dorothee and Béla Greskovits (2009) 'Poverty, Inequality and Democracy: East Central Europe's Quandary', *Journal of Democracy*, 20 (4), 50–63

Boix, Carles (1998) *Political Parties, Growth and Equality: Conservative and Social Democratic Economic Strategies in the World Economy*. Cambridge: Cambridge University Press.

Bonoli, G. (2005) 'The Politics of the New Social Policies: Providing Coverage Against New Social Risks in Mature Welfare States', *Policy and Politics*, 33 (3), 431–49.

Bonoli, Giuliano, Vic George and Peter Taylor-Gooby (2000) *European Welfare Futures: Towards a Theory of Retrenchment*. Cambridge: Polity.

Bosworth, Derek, Peter Dawkins and Thorsten Stromback (1996) *The Economics of the Labour Market*. Harlow: Longman.

Boyer, Robert (1990) *The Regulation School: An Introduction*. Chicago, IL: University of Chicago Press.

Brady, David, Jason Beckfield and Martin Seeleib-Kaiser (2005) 'Economic Globalisation and the Welfare State in Affluent Democracies, 1975–2001', *American Sociological Review*, 70 (6), 921–48.

Brailer, D. and R. Van Horn (1993) 'Health and the Welfare of US Business', *Harvard Business Review*, March/April, 125–32.

Briggs, Asa (1961) 'The Welfare State in Historical Perspective', *Archives of European Sociology*, II (2), 221–58.

Buchanen, James and Richard Wagner (1977) *Democracy in Deficit*. New York: Academic Press.

Buchanen, James and Richard Wagner (1978) *Fiscal Responsibility in Constitutional Democracy*. Boston: Martinus Nijhoff.

Bundesbank (1997) Deutsche Bundesbank Monthly Report, March 1997 www.bundesbank.de/download/volkswirtschaft/mba/1997/199703mba_art01_pubsecdb.pdf

Burley, Anne-Marie and Walter Mattli (1993) 'European Before the Court: A Political Theory of Legal Integration', *International Organization*, 47, 41–76.

Cafruny, Alan and Magnus Ryner (2003) *A Ruined Fortress? Neoliberal Hegemony and Transformation in Europe*. Lanham, MD: Rowman & Littlefield.

Cairncross, Sir Alec (1992) *The British Economy Since 1945*. Oxford, England: Blackwell.

Calmfors, Lars and John Driffill (1988) 'Bargaining Structure, Corporatism and Macroeconomic Performance', *Economic Policy*, 6, 13–61.

Cameron, David (1984) 'Social Democracy, Corporatism, Labour Quiescence and the Representation of Economic Interests in Advanced Capitalist

Society', in J. H. Goldthorpe (ed.), *Order and Conflict in Contemporary Capitalism*, Oxford: Oxford University Press.

Cameron, David R. (1978) 'The Expansion of the Public Economy: A Comparative Analysis', *American Political Science Review*, 72 (4), 1243–61.

Capoccia, G. and R. D. Kelemen (2007) 'The Study of Critical Junctures: Theory, Narrative and Counterfactuals', *Institutional Theory World Politics*, 59 (3), 341–69.

Carr, Edward, H. (1939) *The Thirty Years Crisis*. London: Macmillan.

Cass, David (1965) 'Optimal Growth in an Aggregate Model of Capital Accumulation', *Review of Economic Studies*, 32, July, 233–40.

Castles, Frances G. (2004) *The Future of the Welfare State*. Oxford: Oxford University Press.

Castles, Francis G. and Deborah Mitchell (1993) 'Worlds of Welfare and Families of Nations' in Francis G. Castles (ed.), *Families of Nations*. Aldershot: Dartmouth.

Cerami, Alfio (2005) 'Social Policy in Central and Eastern Europe. The Emergence of a New European Model of Solidarity?', paper presented at the Third Annual ESPAnet Conference 'Making Social Policy in the Postindustrial Age', 22–4 September, University of Fribourg, Switzerland.

Cerami, Alfio (2007) 'The Politics of Reforms in Bismarckian Welfare Systems: The Cases of Czech Republic, Hungary, Poland and Slovakia', paper presented at the conference 'Social Policy in Europe: Changing Paradigms in an Enlarging Europe?', ESPAnet Conference 20–22 September, Vienna University of Economics and Business Administration, Austria.

Cerny, Philip G. (1990) *The Changing Architecture of Politics*. London: Sage.

Cerny, Philip G. (1995) 'Globalisation and the Changing Logic of Collective Action', *International Organization*, 49 (4), 595-625.

Cerny, Philip G. (1997a) 'International Finance and the Erosion of Capitalist Diversity', in Crouch and Streeck (eds), *Political Economy of Modern Capitalism: Mapping Covergence and Diversity*. London: Sage.

Cerny, Philip G. (1997b) 'Paradoxes of the Competition State: The Dynamics of Political Globalisation', *Government and Opposition*, 49 (4), 595–625.

Chor, Davin and Kalina Manova (forthcoming) 'Off the Cliff and Back? Credit Conditions and International Trade During the Global Financial Crisis', *Journal of International Economics*; an earlier version is available at www.nber.org/papers/w16174.

Chwieroth, Jeffery (2010) 'How Do Crises Lead to Change?: Liberalizing Capital Controls in the Early Years of New Order Indonesia', *World Politics*, 62 (3), 496–527.

Citi, Manuele and Martin Rhodes (2007) 'New Modes of Governance in the EU: Common Objectives Versus National Preferences', European Governance Papers (EUROGOV) No. N-07-01 www.connex-network.org/eurogov/pdf/egp-newgov-N-07-01.pdf

Claessens, Stijn, Giovanni Dell'Ariccia, Deniz Igan and Luc Laeven (2010) 'Cross-Country Experiences and Policy Implications from the Global Financial Crisis', *Economy Policy*, 62, 267–93.

Clark, Gordon L. (1999) 'The Retreat of the State and the Rise of Pension Fund Capitalism', in Ron Martin (ed.), *Money and the Space Economy*. New York: Wiley.

Clayton, Richard and Jonas Pontusson (1998) 'Welfare-State Retrenchment Revisited: Entitlement Cuts, Public Sector Restructuring, and Inegalitarian Trends in Advanced Capitalist Societies', *World Politics*, 51 (1), 67–98.

Cohen, Benjamin J. (2012) 'The Yuan Tomorrow? Evaluating China's Currency Internationalisation Strategy', *New Political Economy*, 17 (3), forthcoming.

Coleman, William G. and Wyn P. Grant (1998) 'Policy Convergence and Policy Feedback: Agricultural Finance Policies in a Globalising Era', *European Journal of Political Research*, 34, 225–47.

Collins, Doreen (1975) *The European Communities: The Social Policy of the First Phase. Vol. 2, The European Economic Community 1958–72.* London: Martin Robertson.

Commission of the European Communities (1958) *First General Report on the Activities of the Community*, 1 Jan.–17 Sept.

Commission of the European Communities (1959) *Second General Report on the Activities of the Community*, 15 March.

Commission of the European Communities (1963) *Sixth General Report on the Activities of the Community*, June.

Commission of the European Communities (1989) *Community Charter of Fundamental Social Rights* Com (89) 471 final 2 October, Brussels: Commission of the European Communities.

Commission of the European Communities (1993a) *Growth, Competitiveness, Employment: The Challenges and Ways Forward into the 21st Century.* White Paper COM(93) 700.

Commission of the European Communities (1993b) *European Social Policy – Options for the Union.* Green Paper COM (93) 551.

Commission of the European Communities (1994) *European Social Policy – A Way Forward for the Union.* White Paper COM (94) 333.

Commission of the European Communities (2001) *European Governance.* White Paper COM (2001) 428.

Commission on Social Justice (1994) *Social Justice: Strategies for National Renewal.* London: Institute for Public Policy Research.

Cooke, W. N. and D. S. Noble (1998) 'Industrial Relations Systems and US Foreign Direct Investment Abroad', *British Journal of Industrial Relations*, 36 (4), 581–609.

Cox, Robert H. (1993) *The Dutch Welfare State: From Workers Insurance to Universal Entitlement.* Pittsburgh: Pittsburgh University Press.

Cox, Robert H. (2001) 'The Social Construction of an Imperative: Why Welfare Reformed Happened in Denmark and The Netherlands, But Not in Germany', *World Politics*, 53 (3): 463–98.

Cox, Robert H. (2004) 'The Path Dependence of an Idea: Why Scandinavia Welfare States Remain Distinct', *Social Policy and Administration*, 38 (2), 204–19.

Cram, Laura (1993) 'Calling the Tune Without Paying the Piper? Social Policy Regulation: The Role of the Commission in European Community Social Policy', *Policy and Politics,* 21 (2), 135–46.

Cram, Laura (1994) 'The European Commission as a Multi-Organisation: Social Policy and IT Policy', *Journal of European Public Policy,* 1 (2), 195–217.

Cram, Laura (1997) *The Politics of EU Policy-Making: Conceptual Lenses and the Integration Process.* London: Routledge

Crepaz, Markus M. L. and Nicole Crepaz (2004) 'Is Equality Good Medicine? Determinants of Life Expectancy in Industrialised Democracies', *Journal of Public Policy,* 24 (3), 275–98.

Crepaz, Markus M. L. and Ann W. Moser (2004) 'The Impact of Collective and Competitive Veto Points in Public Expenditure in the Global Age', *Comparative Political Studies,* 37 (3), 259–85.

Crouch, Colin and Henery Farrell (2004) 'Breaking the Path of Institutional Development Alternatives to the New Determinism', *Rationality and Society,* 5–43.

Crouch, Colin (2008) 'What Will Follow the Demise of Privatised Keynesianism?' *Political Quarterly,* 79 (4), 476–87.

Crozier, Michel, Samuel Huntingdon and Joji Watanuki (1975) *The Crisis of Democracy.* New York: New York University Press.

Davidson, Paul (2009) 'Crude Oil Prices: Market Fundamentals or Speculation?', *Challenge,* 51 (4), 110–18.

Deacon, Bob (2000) 'Social Policy in Eastern Europe: The Impact of Political Globalisation', *Journal of European Social Policy,* 10 (2), 146–61.

Deacon, Bob (ed.) (1992) *Social Policy, Social Justice and Citizenship in Eastern Europe.* Aldershot: Avebury.

De la Porte, Caroline and Philippe Pochet (2002) *Building Social Europe Through the Open Method of Coordination.* Brussels, Peter Lang.

Delors, Jacques (1992) *Our Europe.* London: Verso.

Dicken, Peter (2003) *Global Shift: Reshaping the Global Economic Map in the 21st Century,* 4th edn. London: Sage.

Dolowitz, David P. (2001) 'The British Child Support Agency: Did American Origins Bring Failure?', *Environment and Planning C: Government and Policy,* 19 (3), 373–89.

Donaghey, J. and P. Teague (2005) 'The Persistence of Social Pacts in Europe', *Industrial Relations Journal,* 36 (6), 478–93.

Doyal, Len and Ian Gough (1991) *A Theory of Human Need.* Basingstoke: Macmillan.

Drache, Daniel and Robert Boyer (eds) (1996) *States Against Markets: The Limits of Globalisation.* London: Routledge.

Drake, Helen (2000) *Jacques Delors: Perspectives on a European Leader.* London: Routledge.

Draxler, Juraj and Olaf Van Vliet (2010) 'Eurpean Social Model: No Convergence from the East', *Journal of European Integration,* 32 (1), 115–35.

Dunleavy, Patrick and Brendan O'Leary (1987) *Theories of the State*. London: Macmillan.

Dunning, J. H. (1988) 'The Eclectic Paradigm of International Production: An Update and Some Possible Extensions', *Journal of International Business Studies*, 19 (1), 1–32.

Dymski, Gary (2010) 'Why the Subprime Crisis is Different: A Minskyian Approach', *Cambridge Journal of Economics*, 34 (2), 239–55.

Dyson, Kenneth (1982) *The State Tradition in Western Europe: A Study of an Idea and an Institution*. Oxford: Blackwell.

Eccles, David (1949) House of Commons Debate on Budget Proposals and Economic Situation, 7 April, www.hansard.millbanksystems.com/commons/1949/apr/07/budget-proposals-and-economic-situation#S5CV0463P0_19490407_HOC_469

Edgerton, David (2006) *Warfare State: Britain 1920–70*. Cambridge: Cambridge University Press.

Eskildsen, Jacob K., Kai Kristensen and Anders H. Westlund (2004) 'Work Motivation and Job Satisfaction in the Nordic Countries', *Employee Relations*, 26 (2), 122–36.

Esping-Andersen, Gøsta (1985) *States Against Markets*. Princeton, NJ: Princeton University Press.

Esping-Andersen, Gøsta (1990) *The Three Worlds of Welfare Capitalism*. Cambridge: Polity.

Esping-Andersen, Gøsta (1994) 'The Welfare State and the Economy', in Neil J. Smelser and Richard Swedberg (eds), *The Handbook of Economic Sociology*. Princeton, NJ: Princeton University Press.

Esping-Andersen, Gøsta (1996a) 'After the Golden Age? Welfare State Dilemmas in a Global Economy?', in Gøsta Esping-Andersen (ed.), *Welfare States in Transition: National Adaptations in Global Economies*. London: Sage.

Esping-Andersen, Gøsta (1996b) 'Positive-Sum Solutions in a World of Trade-Offs', in Gøsta Esping-Andersen (ed.), *Welfare States in Transition: National Adaptations in Global Economies*. London: Sage.

Esping-Andersen, Gøsta (1996c) 'Welfare States Without Work: The Impasse of Labour Shedding and Familialism in Continental European Social Policy', in Gøsta Esping-Andersen (ed.), *Welfare States in Transition: National Adaptations in Global Economies*. London: Sage.

Esping-Andersen, Gøsta (1999) *Social Foundations of Postindustrial Economies*. Oxford: Oxford University Press.

Esping-Andersen, Gøsta (2000) 'Multi-dimensional Decommodification: A Reply to Graham Room', *Policy and Politics*, 28 (3), 535–9.

Esping-Andersen, Gøsta (2002) *Why We Need a New Welfare State*. Oxford: Oxford University Press.

Esping-Andersen, Gøsta (ed.) (1996) *The Welfare State in Transition*. London: Sage.

Esping-Andersen Gøsta and Korpi, Walter (1984) 'Social Policy as Class Politics in Postwar Capitalism: Scandinavia, Austria and Germany', in John

Goldthorpe (ed.), *Order and Conflict in Contemporary Capitalism.* Oxford: Oxford University Press.

European Bank for Reconstruction and Development (2011) *Transition Report 2010: Recovery and Reform.* London: EBRD.

European Commission (2006a) *European Union Foreign Direct Investment Yearbook 2006.* Luxembourg: EC/Eurostat.

European Commission (2006b) *European Economy: Public Finances in EMU 2006.* Brussels: DG Economic and Financial Affairs.

European Commission (2007) *European Economy, No. 3.* Brussels: Directorate-General for Economic and Financial Affairs.

European Commission (2010) *Statistical Annexe, European Economy.* Brussels: European Commission.

European Mortgage Federation (2010) *Hypostat 2009: A Review of Europe's Mortgage and Housing Markets.* Brussels: European Mortgage Federation.

Evans, Peter (1997) 'The Eclipse of the State? Reflections on Stateness in an Era of Globalization', *World Politics*, 50 (1), 62–87.

Evans, R. G., M. L. Barer and C. Hertzmann (1991) 'The 20 Year Experiment: Accounting for, Explaining and Evaluating Health Care Cost Containment in Canada and the United States', *Annual Review of Public Health*, 12, 481–518.

Faulks, Keith (2000) *Citizenship.* London: Routledge.

Feldmann, Magnus (2006) 'Emerging Varieties of Capitalism in Transition Countries: Industrial Relations and Wage Bargaining in Estonia and Slovenia', *Comparative Political Studies*, 39 (7), 829–54.

Fenger, H. J. M. (2007) 'Welfare regimes in Central and Eastern Europe: Incorporating Post-communist Countries in a Welfare Regime Typology', *Contemporary Issues and Ideas in Social Science*, August.

Ferge, Zsuzsa and Gábo Juhász (2004) 'Accession and Social Policy: The Case of Hungary', *Journal of European Social Policy*, 14 (3), 233–51.

Ferrera, Mauricio (1996) 'The "Southern Model" of Welfare in Social Europe', *Journal of European Social Policy*, 6 (1), 17–37.

Ferrera, Maurizio (1998) 'The Four "Social Europes": Between Universalism and Selectivity', in Martin Rhodes and Yves Mény (eds), *The Future of the European Welfare State: A New Social Contract?* Basingstoke: Macmillan.

Ferrera, Maurizio (2005) *The Boundaries of Welfare.* Oxford: Oxford University Press.

Ferrera, M., A. Hemerijck and M. Rhodes (2000) *'The Future of Social Europe: Recasting Work and Welfare in the New Economy'* Report for the Portuguese Presidency of the European Union. Oeiras, Celta Editora.

Fine, Ben (1998) 'The Triumph of Economics: Or, "Rationality" Can be Dangerous to Your Reasoning', in James G. Collier and Daniel Miller (eds), *Virtualism: A New Poltical Economy.* Oxford: Berg.

Finegold, David and Sockice, David (1988) 'The Failure of Training in Britain: Analysis and Prescription', *Oxford Review of Economic Policy*, 4 (3), 21–53.

Fisher, Sharon, John Gould and Tim Haughton (2007) 'Slovakia's Neoliberal Turn', *Europe-Asia Studies*, 59 (3): 977–98.

Fisher, Irving (1930) *The Theory of Interest*. Basingstoke: Macmillan.

Fisher, Irving (1935) *The Clash of Progress and Security*. Basingstoke: Macmillan.

Flora, Peter (ed.) (1986) *Growth to Limits: The Western European Welfare States since World War II. Vol. 1, Sweden, Norway, Finland, Denmark*. Berlin: de Gruyter.

Franco, Daniele and Teresa Munzi (1996) 'Public Pension Expenditure Prospects in the European Union: A Survey of National Projections', *European Economy: Aging and Pension Expenditures in the Western World*, Reports and Studies 3: 1–127. European Commission.

Frank, André Gunder and Barry Gills (eds) (1993) *The World System: Five Hundred Years or Five Thousand Years?* London: Routledge.

Frankel, Jeffrey A. (1997) *Regional Trading Blocs: In the World Economic System*. Washington, DC: Institute for International Economics.

Franzese, Robert J. (2002) *Macroeconomic Policies of the Developed Democracies*. Cambridge: Cambridge University Press

Fukuyama, Francis (1992) *The End of History and the Last Man*. London: Hamish Hamilton.

Gamble, Andrew (2009a) *The Spectre at the Feast*. Basingstoke: Palgrave Macmillan.

Gamble, Andrew (2009b) 'British Politics and the Financial Crisis', *British Politics*, 4 (4), 450–62.

Garrett, Geoffrey (1998) *Partisan Politics in the Global Economy*. Cambridge: Cambridge University Press.

Garrett, Geoffrey (1993) 'The Politics of Maastricht', *Economics and Politics*, 5 (2), 105–23.

Garrett, Geoffrey (1995) 'The Politics of Legal Integration in the European Union', *International Organization*, 49 (1), 171–81

Garrett, Geoffrey (1998) *Partisan Politics in the Global Economy*. Cambridge: Cambridge University Press.

Garrett, Geoffrey (2000) 'Shrinking States? Globalisation and National Autonomy', in N. Woods (ed.), *The Political Economy of Globalisation*. Basingstoke: Palgrave.

Gerschenkron, Alexander (1953) *Economic Backwardness in Historical Perspective*. New York: Frederick A. Praeger.

Gilder, George (1981) *Welfare and Poverty*. New York: Basic Books.

Gill, Stephen (1998) 'European Governance and New Constitutionalism: EMU and Alternatives to Disciplinary Neo-liberalism in Europe', *New Political Economy*, 3 (1), 5–26.

Glennerster, Howard (1997) *Paying for Welfare*, 3rd edn. Hemel Hempstead: Harvester Wheatsheaf.

Glennerster, Howard (2003) *Understanding the Finance of Welfare: What Welfare Costs and How to Pay For It*. Bristol: Policy Press.

Glennerster, Howard (2010) *Financing the United Kingdom's Welfare States*. 2020 Public Services Trust: London.

Goldthorpe, John H. (ed.) (1984) *Order and Conflict in Contemporary Capitalism*. Oxford: Clarendon Press.

Goodin, Robert (1985) 'Self-reliance versus the Welfare State', *Journal of Social Policy*, 14 (1) 25-47.

Goodin, Robert (1988) *Reasons for Welfare: the Political Theory of the Welfare State*. Princeton: Princeton University Press.

Goodin, Robert E., Bruce Headey Ruud Muffels and Henk-Jan Driven (1999) *The Real Worlds of Welfare Capitalism*. Cambridge: Cambridge University Press.

Gough, Ian (1979) *The Political Economy of the Welfare State*. London: Macmillan.

Gough, Ian (1996) 'Social Welfare and Competitiveness', *New Political Economy*, 1 (2), 209–32.

Gough, Ian (2000) *Global Capital, Human Needs and Social Policies*. Basingstoke: Palgrave.

Gough, Ian (2003) *Lists and Thresholds: Comparing the Doyal-Gough Theory of Human Needs with Nussbaum's Capabilities Approach*. WeD Working Paper No. 1 www.bath.ac.uk/soc–pol/welldev/research/workingpaperpdf/wed01.pdf.

Gough, Ian (2010) 'Economic Crisis, Climate Change and the Future of Welfare States', *Twenty-First Century Society*, 5 (1), 51–64.

Gough, Ian and J. Allister McGregor (eds) (2007) *Wellbeing in Developing Countries: From Theory to Research*. Cambridge: Cambridge University Press.

Gourevitch, Peter (1978) 'The Second Image Reversed: The International Sources of Domestic Politics' *International Organization*, 31: 881–912.

Gourevitch, Peter (1986) *Politics in Hard Times: Comparative Responses to International Economic Crises*. Ithaca, NY: Cornell University Press.

Gradstein, Mark and Moshe Justman (2002) 'Education, Social Cohesion and Economic Growth', *American Economic Review*, 92 (4), 1192–1204.

Grahl, John (2001) 'Globalized Finance: The Challenge to the Euro', *New Left Review*, 8 (March–April), 23–47.

Grahl, John and Paul Teague (2003) 'The Eurozone and Financial Integration: The Industrial Relations Issues', *Industrial Relations Journal*, 34 (5), 396–410.

Grandner, Margarete (1996) 'Conservative Social Politics in Austria, 1880–1890', *Austrian History Yearbook*, 27, 77–107.

Granger, Marie-Pierre (2005) 'The Future of Europe: Judicial Preferences and Interference', *Comparative European Politics*, 3 (2), 155–79.

Gray, John (1998) *False Dawn: The Delusions of Global Capitalism*. London: Granta.

Green-Pedersen, Christoffer (2004) 'The Dependent Variable Problem within the Study of Welfare State Retrenchment: Defining the Problem and

Looking for Solutions', *Journal of Comparative Policy Analysis*, 6 (1), 3–14.

Guillén, Ana M. and Bruno Palier (2004) 'Does Europe Matter? Accession to EU and Social Policy Developments in Recent and New Member States', *Journal of European Social Policy*, 14 (3), 203–9.

Habermas, Jürgen (1975) *Legitimation Crisis*. London: Heinemann.

Habermas, Jürgen (2001) 'Why Europe Needs a Constitution, *New Left Review*, 11 (September–October), 5–26.

Hacker, Jacob (2006) 'Policy Drift: The Hidden Politics of US Welfare Retrenchment', in Wolfgang Streeck and Kathleen Thelen (eds), *Beyond Continuity: Institutional Change in Advanced Political Economies*. Oxford: Oxford University Press.

Hagen, Kåre (1992) 'The Interaction of Welfare States and Labour Markets', in Jon Eivind Kolberg (ed.) *The Study of Welfare State Regimes*. Armonk, NY: M. E. Sharpe.

Hall, Peter A. (1986) *Governing the Economy: The Politics of State Intervention in Britain and France*. New York: Oxford University Press.

Hall, Peter A. (1993) 'Policy Paradigms, Social Learning and the State: The Case of Economic-Policy Making in Britain', *Comparative Politics*, 25 (2), 275–96.

Hall, Peter A. (2001) 'Organised Market Economies and Unemployment in Europe', in N. Bormeo (ed.), *Unemployment in the New Europe*. Cambridge: Cambridge University Press.

Hall, Peter A. and Robert J. Frazese (1998) 'Mixed Signals: Central Bank Independence, Coordinated Wage Bargaining and European Monetary Union', *International Organisation*, 52 (4), 502–35.

Hall, Peter A. and Daniel, W. Gingerich (2009) 'Varieties of Capitalism and Institutional Complementarities in the Political Economy: An Empirical Analysis', *British Journal of Political Science*, 39, 449–82.

Hall, Peter A. and David Soskice (eds) (2001a) *Varieties of Capitalism: The Institutional Foundations of Comparative Advantage*. Oxford: Oxford University Press.

Hall, Peter A. and David Soskice (2001b) 'An Introduction to Varieties of Capitalism', in P. Hall D. and Soskice (eds), *Varieties of Capitalism: The Institutional Foundations of Comparative Advantage*. Oxford: Oxford University Press.

Hall, Peter A. and Kathleen Thelen (2009) 'Institutional Change in Varieties of Capitalism', *Socio-Economic Review*, 7 (1), 7–34.

Hancké, Bob and Martin Rhodes (2005) 'EMU and Labor Market Institutions in Europe: The Rise and Fall of National Social Pacts', *Work and Occupations*, 32 (2), 196–228.

Hancké, Bob, Martin Rhodes and Mark Thatcher (2007) 'Beyond Varieties of Capitalism', in Hancké, Rhodes and Thatcher (eds), *Beyond Varieties of Capitalism: Conflict, Contradictions and Complementaries in the European Economy*. Oxford: Oxford University Press.

Harrington, Michael (1962) *The Other America*. New York: Macmillan.

Hárs, Agnes and András Kováts (2005) 'Hungary', in J. Niessen and Y. Schibel (eds), *Immigration as a Labour-Market Strategy: European and North American Perspectives*. Brussels: Migration Policy Group.

Harvey, David (2005) *A Brief History of Neoliberalism*. Oxford: Oxford University Press.

Hay, Colin (1996a) 'Narrating Crisis: The Discursive Construction of the Winter of Discontent', *Sociology*, 30 (2), 253–78.

Hay, Colin (1996b) *Re-Stating Social and Political Change*. Buckingham: Open University Press.

Hay, Colin (1997) 'Anticipating Accommodations, Accommodating Anticipations: The Appeasement of Capital in the Modernisation of the British Labour Party, 1987–1992', *Politics and Society*, 25 (2), 234–56.

Hay, Colin (1998) 'Globalisation, Welfare Retrenchment and the "Logic of No Alternative": Why Second-Best Won't Do', *Journal of Social Policy*, 27 (4), 525–32.

Hay, Colin (1999a) *The Political Economy of New Labour*. Manchester: Manchester University Press.

Hay, Colin (1999b) 'Crisis and the Structural Transformation of the State: Interrogating the Process of Change', *British Journal of Politics and International Relations*, 1 (3): 317–44.

Hay, Colin (2001) 'The "Crisis" of Keynesianism and the Rise of Neo-Liberalism in Britain: An Ideational Institutionalist Approach', in J. L. Campbell and O-K. Pedersen (eds), *The Rise of Neoliberalism and Institutional Analysis*. Princeton, NJ: Princeton University Press.

Hay, Colin (2004a) 'Re-Stating Politics, Re-Politicising the State', *Political Quarterly*, 75 (5), 38–50.

Hay, Colin (2004b) 'Common Trajectories, Variable Paces, Divergent Outcomes? Models of European Capitalism Under Conditions of Complex Economic Interdependence', *Review of International Political Economy*, 11 (2), 231–62.

Hay, Colin (2004c) 'Credibility, Competitiveness and the Business Cycle in Third Way Political Economy: A Critical Evaluation of Economic Policy in Britain Since 1997', *New Political Economy*, 9 (1), 39–57.

Hay, Colin (2005) 'Too Important to Leave to the Economists? The Political Economy of Welfare Retrenchment', *Social Policy and Society*, 4 (2), 1–9.

Hay, Colin (2006a) 'What's Globalisation Got to Do with It? Economic Interdependence and the Future of European Welfare States', *Government and Opposition*, 41 (1), 1–23.

Hay, Colin (2006b) 'Managing Economic Interdependence: The Political Economy of New Labour', in P. Dunleavy, R. Heffernan, P. Cowley and C. Hay (eds), *Developments in British Politics 8*. Basingstoke: Palgrave Macmillan.

Hay, Colin (2007a) *Why We Hate Politics*. Cambridge: Polity.

Hay, Colin (2007b) 'What Doesn't Kill You Can Only Make You Stronger: The

Doha Development Round, the Services Directive and the EU's Conception of Competitiveness', *Journal of Common Market Studies*, annual review.

Hay, Colin (2008) 'Globalisation's Impact on States', in J. Ravenhill (ed.), *Global Political Economy*, 2nd edn. Oxford: Oxford University Press.

Hay, Colin (2009a) 'Good Inflation, Bad Inflation: The Housing Boom, Economic Growth and the Disaggregation of Inflationary Preferences in the UK and Ireland', *British Journal of Politics and International Relations*, 11 (3), 461–78.

Hay, Colin (2009b) 'Globalisation', in M. Flinders, A. Gamble, C. Hay and M. Kenny (eds), *The Oxford Handbook of British Politics*. Oxford: Oxford University Press.

Hay, Colin (2010) 'Political Science in an Age of Acknowledged Interdependence', in C. Hay (ed.), *New Directions in Political Science: Responding to the Challenges of an Interdependent World*. Basingstoke: Palgrave Macmillan.

Hay, Colin (2011a) 'The 2010 Leonard Schapiro Lecture: Pathology without Crisis? The Strange Demise of the Anglo-Liberal Growth Model', *Government and Opposition*, 46 (1), 1–31.

Hay, Colin (2011b) 'The "Dangerous Obsession" of *Cost* Competitiveness ... And the Not So Dangerous Obsession of Competitiveness', *Cambridge Journal of Economics*, forthcoming.

Hay, Colin (2011c) 'Treating the Symptom not the Condition: Crisis Definition, Deficit Reduction and the Search for a New British Growth Model', *British Journal of Politics and International Relations*, forthcoming.

Hay, Colin and Ben Rosamondn (2002) 'Globalisation, European Integration and the Discursive Construction of Economic Imperatives', *Journal of European Public Policy*, 9 (2), 147–67.

Hay, Colin, Jari Matti RiihelÄinen, Nicola Jo-Ann Smith and Matthew Watson (2008) 'Ireland: The Outlier Inside', in K. Dyson (ed.), *The Euro at 10: Europeanisation, Power and Convergence*. Oxford: Oxford University Press.

Hay, Colin, Nicola Jo-Ann Smith and Matthew Watson (2006) 'Beyond Prospective Accountancy: Reassessing the Case for British Membership of the Single European Currency Comparatively', *British Journal of Politics and International Relations*, 8 (1), 101–21.

Heichel, Stephan, Jessica Pape and Joseph Sommerer (2005) 'Is there Convergence in Convergence Research? An Overview of Empirical Studies of Policy Convergence', *Journal of European Public Policy*, 12 (5), 817–40.

Heintzmann, Ralph and Brian Marson (2005) 'People, Service and Trust: Is There a Public Sector Value Chain?', *International Review of Administrative Sciences*, 71 (4), 549–75.

Held, David, Anthony McGrew, David Goldblatt and Jonathan Perraton (1999) *Global Transformations: Politics, Economics and Culture*. Cambridge: Polity.

240   *Bibliography*

Helleiner, Eric (2011) 'Understanding the 2007–2008 Global Financial Crisis: Lessons for Scholars of International Political Economy', *Annual Review of Political Science*, 14, 67–87.

Hennessy, Peter (1992) *Never Again: Britain 1945–51*. London: Penguin.

Hicks, Alex (1999) *Social Democracy and Welfare Capitalism*. Ithaca: Cornell University Press.

Hicks, Alex and Lane Kenworthy (2003) 'Varieties of Welfare Capitalism', *Socio-Economic Review*, 1 (1) 27–61.

Hill, Christopher and Michael Smith (2005) 'International Relations and the European Union: Themes and Issues' in Christopher Hill and Michael Smith (eds), *International Relations and the European Union*. Oxford: Oxford University Press.

Hinchingbrooke, Viscount Alexander (1949) House of Commons Debate on Budget Proposals and Economic Situation, 7 April, www.hansard.mill-banksystems.com/commons/1949/apr/07/budget-proposals-and-economic-situation#S5CV0463P0_19490407_HOC_413.

Hirst, Paul and Grahame Thompson (1996) *Globalisation in Question*, 1st edn. Cambridge: Polity.

Hirst, Paul and Grahame Thompson (1999) *Globalisation in Question*, 2nd edn. Cambridge: Polity.

Hirst, Paul and Grahame Thompson (2000) 'Globalisation in One Country? The Peculiarities of the British', *Economy and Society*, 29 (3), 335–56.

Hix, Simon (2006) 'Why the EU Needs (Left-Right) Politics? Policy Reform and Accountability are Impossible Without It', in S. Hix and S. Bartolini (eds), 'Politics: The Right or the Wrong Sort of Medicine for the EU?', *Notre Europe Policy Paper*, no. 19, pp. 1–28.

Hodson, Dermot and Lucia Quaglia (2009) 'European Perspectives on the Global Financial Crisis', *Journal of Common Market Studies*, 47 (5), 939–53.

Hollingsworth, J. Rogers and Wolfgang Streeck (1994) 'Countries and Sectors: Performance, Convergence and Competitiveness', in J. R. Hollingsworth, P. Schmitter and W. Streeck (eds), *Governing Capitalist Economies: Performance and Control of Economic Sectors*. Oxford: Oxford University Press.

Holloway, John (1981) *Social Policy Harmonisation in the European Community*. Farnborough: Gower.

Holzinger, Katharina and Christoph Knill, (2005) 'Causes and Conditions of Cross-National Policy Convergence', *Journal of European Public Policy*, 12 (5), 775–96.

Hoskyns, Catherine (1996) *Integrating Gender: Women, Law and Politics in the European Union*. London: Verso.

Howarth, David (2007) 'Internal Policies: Reinforcing the New Lisbon Message of Competitiveness and Innovation', *Journal of Common Market Studies*, 45, supplement, 89–106 www.europa.eu.int/growthandjobs/pdf/2004–1866–EN–complet.pdf.

Ikenberry, John (2001) *After Victory: Institutions, Strategic Restraint, and the Rebuilding of Order after Major Wars*. Princeton: Princeton University Press.

International Monetary Fund (2005) *Coordinated Portfolio Investment Survey*. Washington, DC: IMF.

International Organization of Migration (2006) *World Migration 2005: Costs and Benefits of International Migration*. London: IOM.

Iversen Torben (1999) *Contested Economic Institutions: The Politics of Macroeconomics and Wage Bargaining in Advanced Democracies*. Cambridge: Cambridge University Press.

Iversen Torben and Jonus Pontusson (2000) 'Comparative Political Economy: A Northern European Perspective', in T. Iversen, J. Pontusson and D. Soskice (eds), *Unions, Employers and Central Banks: Macroeconomic Coordination and Institutional Change in Social Market Economies*. Cambridge: Cambridge University Press.

Iversen, Torben, Jonus Pontusson and David Soskice (eds) (2000) *Unions, Employers and Central Banks: Macroeconomic Coordination and Institutional Change in Social Market Economies*. Cambridge: Cambridge University Press.

Jessop, Bob (1980) 'The Transformation of the State in Post-War Britain', in R. Scase (ed.), *The State in Western Europe*. New York: St Martin's Press.

Jessop, Bob (1994) 'Changing Forms and Functions of the State in an Era of Globalisation and Regionalisation', in Robert Delorme and Kurt Dopfer (eds), *The Political Economy of Diversity: Evolutionary Perspectives on Economic Order and Disorsder*. London: Edward Elgar.

Jessop, Bob. (2000) 'From the KWNS to the SWPR', in G. Lewis, S. Gewirtz and J. Clarke (eds), *Rethinking Social Policy*. London: Sage.

Jessop, Bob (2002) *The Future of the Capitalist State*. Cambridge: Polity.

Jones, Catherine (1993) 'The Pacific Challenge: Confucian Welfare States', in Catherine Jones (ed.), *New Perspectives on the Welfare State in Europe*. London: Routledge.

Jordan, Bill (1998) 'European Social Citizenship: Why a New Social Contract (Probably) Will Not Happen', in Martin Rhodes and Yves Mény (eds), *The Future of the European Welfare State: A New Social Contract?* Basingstoke: Macmillan.

Joskow, Paul L. and Roger G. Noll (1981) 'Regulation in Theory and Practice: An Overview', in Garry Fromm (ed.), *Studies in Public Regulation*. Cambridge, MA: MIT Press, pp. 1–78.

Kalecki, Michal (1943) 'Political Aspects of Full Employment', *The Political Quarterly*, 14, 322–30.

Kasza, Geoffrey (2002) 'The Illusion of Welfare "Regimes"', *Journal of Social Policy*, 31, 271–87.

Katzenstein, Peter J. (1985) *Small States in World Markets: Industrial Policy in Europe*. Ithaca, NY: Cornell University Press.

Kaufmann, R. K. and B. Ullman (2009) 'Oil Prices, Speculation and Fundamentals: Interpreting Causal Relations Among Spot and Futures Prices', *Energy Economics*, 31, 550–58.

Kenworthy, Lane (2009) 'Institutional Coherence and Macroeconomic Performance', in B. Hancké (ed.), *Debating Varieties of Capitalism*. Oxford: Oxford University Press.

Kerr, C. (1983) *The Future of Industrial Societies: Convergence or Continuing Diversity?* Cambridge, MA: Harvard University Press.

Kerr, C., J. T. Dunlap, F. H. Harbison and C. A. Myers (1960) *Industrialism and Industrial Man*. Cambridge, MA: Harvard University Press.

Kilbrandon (1973) *Report of the Royal Commission on the Constitution. Command 5460*. London: HMSO.

King, Anthony (1975) 'Overload: Problems of Governing in the 1970s', *Political Studies*, 23 (2–3), 284–96.

Kitschelt, Herbert, Peter Lange, Gary Marks and John D. Stephens (eds) (1999) *Continuity and Change in Contemporary Capitalism*. Cambridge: Cambridge University Press.

Kleinman Mark and David Piachaud (1993) 'European Social Policy: Conceptions and Choices', *Journal of European Social Policy*, 3 (1), 1–19.

Kloosterman, Robert (1994) 'Three Worlds of Welfare Capitalism? The Welfare State and the Post-industrial Trajectory in the Netherlands after 1980', *West European Politics*, 17 (4) 166–89.

Knill, Christoph (2005) 'Cross-National Policy Convergence: Concepts, Approaches and Explanatory Factors', *Journal of European Public Policy*, 12 (5), 764–74.

Kok, Wim (2004) *Facing the Challenge. The Lisbon Strategy for Growth and Employment*, Report from the High-Level Group chaired by Wim Kok. Luxembourg: Official Publications of the European Communities.

Korpi, Walter (1978) *The Working Class in Welfare Capitalism*. London: Routledge & Kegan Paul.

Korpi, Walter (1983) *The Democratic Class Struggle*. London: Routledge & Kegan Paul.

Korpi, Walter (1989) 'Power, Politics and State Autonomy in the Development of Social Citizenship', *American Sociological Review*, 54 (3), 309–28.

Korpi, Walter (2003) 'Welfare State Regress in Western Europe: Politics, Institutions, Globalisation and Europeanisation', *Annual Review of Sociology*, 29, 589–609.

Korpi, Walter (2003) 'Welfare State Regress in Western Europe: Politics, Institutions, Globalisation and Europeanisation', *Annual Review of Sociology*, 29, 589–609.

Korpi, Walter and Joakim Palme (2003) 'New Politics and Class Politics in the Context of Austerity and Globalisation: Welfare State Regress in 18 Countries, 1975–95', *American Political Science Review*, 97 (3), 425–46.

Krugman, Paul (1994) 'Competitiveness: A Dangerous Obsession', *Foreign Affairs*, March/April, 28–44, as reprinted in P. Krugman (1996) *Pop Internationalism*. Cambridge, MA: MIT Press.

Krugman, Paul (2008) *The Return of Depression Economics and the Crisis of 2008*. New York, Penguin.

Krugman, Paul (2009) 'Macroeconomic Effects of Chinese Mercantilism', *New York Times*, 31 December.

Kurzer, Paulette (1993) *Business and Banking*. Ithaca, NY: Cornell University Press.

Kynaston, David (2007) *Austerity Britain 1945–51*. London: Bloomsbury.

Langley, Paul (2006) 'Securitising Suburbia', *Competition and Change*, 10 (3), 283–99.

Leibfried, Stephan (1991) 'Towards a European Welfare State? On Integrating Poverty Regimes in the European Community', University of Breman Centre for Social Policy Working Paper 02/1991, www.zes.unibremen.de/homepages/stlf/arbeitspapierBeschreibung.php?ID=130&SPRACHE=de&USER=stlf.

Leibfried, Stephan (1992) 'Towards a European Welfare State? On Integrating Poverty Regimes into the European Community', in Zsuzsa Ferge and Jon Kolberg (eds), *Social Policy in a Changing Europe*. Boulder, Co: Westview.

Leibfried, Stephan (2005) 'Social Policy: Left to Courts and Markets?', in Helen Wallace, William Wallace and Mark Pollack (eds), *Policy-making in the European Union*. Oxford: Oxford University Press, pp. 243–78.

Leibfried, Stephan and Paul Pierson (1992), 'Prospects for Social Europe', *Politics and Society*, 20, 3: 333–66

Lendvai, Noémi (2004) 'The Weakest Link? EU Accession and Enlargement: Dialoguing EU and Post-Communist Social Policy', *Journal of European Social Policy*, 14 (3): 319–33.

Levitt, Theodore (1983) 'The Globalisation of Markets', *Harvard Business Review*, May–June, 92–102.

Levy, Jonah (2010) 'Welfare Retrenchment', in F. G. Castles, S. Leibfried, J. Lewis, H. Obinger and C. Pierson (eds), *The Oxford Handbook of the Welfare State*. Oxford: Oxford University Press.

Lewis, Jane (1992) 'Gender and the Development of Welfare Regimes', *Journal of European Social Policy*, 2 (3), 159–73.

Lindbom, Anders (1999) 'Dismantling the Social Democratic Welfare Model. Has the Swedish Welfare State Lost its Defining Characteristics?', paper for the ECPR, Joint Session of Workshops, 26–31 March, Mannheim.

Locke, Richard and Thomas Kochan (1995) 'The Transformation of Industrial Relations? A Cross-National Review of the Evidence', in Richard Locke, Thomas Kochan and Micheal Piore (eds), *Employment Relations in a Changing World*. Cambridge, MA: MIT Press.

Loriaux, Michael (1991) *France after Hegemony: International Change and Financial Reform*. Ithaca: Cornell University Press.

Lucas, Robert E. J. (1988) 'On the Mechanics of Economic Development', *Journal of Monetary Economics*, 22, (1), 3–42.

Lucas, Robert E. J. (2003) 'Macroeconomic Priorities', *American Economic Review*, 93 (1), 1–13.

MacDonald, Dwight (1963) 'Our Invisible Poor', *The New Yorker*, 19 January, www.newyorker.com/archive/1963/01/19/1963_01_19_082_TNY_CARDS_000075671?currentPage=all.

Maddison, Angus (1982) *The Phases of Capitalist Development*. Oxford: Oxford University Press.

Maddison, Angus (1991) *Dynamic Forces in Capitalist Development*. Oxford: Oxford University Press.

Majone, Giandomenico (1992) 'Market Integration and Regulation: Europe after 1992', *Metroeconomica*, 43, 131–56.

Majone, Giandomenico (1993) 'The European Community: Between Social Policy and Social Regulation', *Journal of Common Market Studies*, 31 (2), 153–69.

Majone, Giandomenico (1996) *Regulating Europe*. London: Routledge.

Majone, Giandomenico (1998) 'European Democratic Deficit: The Question of Standards', *European Law Journal*, 4, 5–28.

Majone, Giandomenico (2006) *Is the European Constitutional Settlement really Stable and Successful?* Notre Europe Etudes & Recherches, www.notre-europe.eu/uploads/tx_publication/Moravcsik–reponse–Majone–en_02.pdf.

Mares, Isabela (2010) 'Macroeconomic Outcomes', in F. G. Castles, S. Leibfried, J. Lewis, H. Obinger and C. Pierson (eds), *The Oxford Handbook of the Welfare State*. Oxford: Oxford University Press.

Marglin, Stephen and Schor, Juliet (eds) (1990) *The Golden Age of Capitalism: Reinterpreting the Postwar Experience*. Oxford: Oxford University Press.

Marquand, David (1994) 'Reinventing Federalism: Europe and the Left', *New Left Review*, 203, 17–26.

Marshall T. H. (1961) 'The Welfare State: A Sociological Interpretation' *European Journal of Sociology*. 2, 284–300.

Marshall T. H. (1963) 'The Welfare State: A Comparative Study', in T. H. Marshall (ed.), *Sociology at the Crossroads and other Essays*. London: Heinemann.

Marshall, T. H. (1992 [1950]) 'Citizenship and Social Class', in T. H. Marshall and Tom Bottomore (eds), *Citizenship and Social Class*. London: Pluto Press.

Martin, Andrew (1997) 'What Does Globalisation Have to Do With the Erosion of Welfare States? Sorting Out the Issues', *Arbeitspapier Nr. 1*. Bremen: Zentrum für Sozialpolitik, Universität Bremen.

Martin, Ron (2011) 'The Local Geographies of the Financial Crisis: From the Housing Bubble to Economic Recession and Beyond', *Journal of Economic Geography*, forthcoming.

Mason, Paul (2009) *Meltdown: The End of the Age of Greed*. London: Verso.

Mattli, Walter and Slaughter, Anne-Marie (1995) 'Law and Politics in the European: A Reply to Garrett', *International Organization*, 49 (1), 183–90.

McBride, Stephen and Russell A. Williams (2001) 'Globalisation, the Restructuring of Labour Markets and Policy Convergence', *Global Social Policy*, 1 (3), 281–309.

McCloskey, Deidre N. (1996) 'The Futility of Blackboard Economics', in *The Vices of Economists, The Virtues of the Bourgeoisie*. Amsterdam: Amsterdam University Press.

McKeown, Timothy J. (1999) 'The Global Economy, Post-Fordism and Trade Policy in Advanced Capitalist States', in Herbert Kitschelt, Peter Lange, Gary Marks, John D. Stephens (eds), *Continuity and Change in Contemporary Capitalism*. Cambridge: Cambridge University Press.

Milward, Alan (2000) *The European Rescue of the Nation-State*. London: Routledge.

Mishel, L. and J. Bernstein (1993) *The State of Working America, 1992–93*. Armonk, NY: M. E. Sharpe.

Mitchell, James (2006) 'Evolution and Devolution: Citizenship, Institutions and Public Policy', *Publius: The Journal of Federalism*, 36 (1), 153–68.

Montanari, Ingalill, Kenneth Nelson and Joakim Palme (2007) 'Convergence Pressures and Responses: Recent Social Insurance Development in Modern Welfare States', *Comparative Sociology*, 6 (3), 295–323.

Montanari, Ingalill (2001) 'Modernisation, Globalisation and the Welfare State: A Comparative Analysis of Old and New Convergence of Social Insurance Since 1930', *British Journal of Sociology*, 52 (3), 469–94.

Moran, Michael (1988) 'Crises of the Welfare State', *British Journal of Political Science*, 18, (3) 397–414.

Moran, Michael (2002) 'Understanding the Regulatory State', *British Journal of Political Science*, 32 (2) 391–413.

Moravcsik, Andrew (1995) 'Liberal Intergovernmentalism and Integration: A Rejoinder', *Journal of Common Market Studies*, 33 (4), 611–28.

Morgan, Kimberly (2001) 'Whose Hand Rocks the Cradle? The Politics of Childcare in Advanced Industrialized States', PhD, Princeton University.

Morgan, Kimberly (2003) 'The Politics of Mothers' Employment: France in Comparative Perspective', *World Politics*, 55 (2), 259–89.

Moses, Jonathan W. (1994) 'Abdication from National Policy Autonomy: What's Left to Leave?', *Politics and Society*, 22 (2), 125–38.

Moses, Jonathan W. (1995) 'The Fiscal Constraints on Social Democracy', *Nordic Journal of Political Economy*, 22 (1), 49–68.

Moses, Jonathan W. (1998) 'The Social Democratic Predicament and Global Economic Integration: A Capital Dilemma', in W. D. Coleman and G. R. D. Underhill (eds), *Regionalism and Global Economic Integration*. London: Routledge.

Nelson, Kenneth (2010) 'Social Assistance and Minimum Income Benefits in Old and New EU Democracies', *International Journal of Social Welfare*, 19 (4), 367–78.

Nickell, Stephen (1997) 'Unemployment and Labour Market Rigidities: Europe versus North America', *Journal of Economic Perspectives*, 11 (3), 55–74.

Nickell, Stephen, Nunziata, Lucia and Ochel, Wolfgang (2005) 'Unemployment in the OECD since the 1960s: What Do We Know?', *Economic Journal*, 115 (1), 1–27.

Notermans, Ton (2000) *Money, Markets and the State: Social Democratic Economic Policies since 1918*. Cambridge: Cambridge University Press.

Nussbaum, Martha C. (2000) *Women and Human Development: The Capabilities Approach*. Cambridge: Cambridge University Press.

O'Brien, Robert (1991) *Global Financial Integration: The End of Geography*. London: Pinter.

O'Connor, James (1973) *The Fiscal Crisis of the State*. New York: St Martin's Press.

O'Connor, Julia (1993) 'Gender, Class and Citizenship in the Comparative Study of Welfare State Regimes: Theoretical and Methodological Issues', *British Journal of Sociology*, 44 (3), 501–18.

O'Connor, Julia, Ann S. Orloff and Sheila Shaver (1999) *States, Markets, Families: Gender, Liberalism and Social Policy*. Cambridge: Cambridge University Press.

O'Rourke, Kevin H. and Jeffrey G. Williamson (1999) *Globalisation and History*. Cambridge, MA: MIT Press.

O'Rourke, Kevin H. and Jeffrey G. Williamson (2002) 'When Did Globalisation Begin?', *European Review of Economic History*, 6 (1), 23–50.

Obinger, Herbert and Uwe Wagschel (2010) 'Social Expenditure and Revenues', in F. G. Castles, S. Leibfried, J. Lewis, J. H. Obinger and C. Pierson (eds), *The Oxford Handbook of the Welfare State*. Oxford: Oxford University Press.

Obstfeld, Maurice and Kenneth Rogoff (1996) *Foundations of International Macroeconomics*. Cambridge, MA: MIT Press.

OECD (1994a) 'New Orientations for Social Policy', *Social Policy Studies*, No. 12. Paris: OECD.

OECD (1994b) *The OECD Jobs Study*. Paris: OECD.

OECD (2005) *International Investment Perspectives: 2005 edition*. Paris: OECD.

OECD (2006a) *International Investment Perspectives: 2006 edition*. Paris: OECD.

OECD (2006b) *Social Expenditure Database, SOCX*. Paris: OECD, www.oecd.org/els/social/expenditure.

OECD (2006c) 'Projecting OCED Health and Long-Term Care Expenditures: What Are the Main Drivers?', *Economics Department Working Paper*, No. 477, February. Paris: OCED.

OECD (2011) 'Is the European Welfare State Really More Expensive?: Indicators on Social Spending, 1980–2012; and a Manual to the OECD Social Expenditure Database (SOCX)', *OECD Social, Employment and Migration Working Papers, no. 124*. Paris: OECD.

Offe, Claus (1983) 'Competitive Party Democracy and the Keynesian Welfare State' in Stewart Clegg, Geoff Dow, Paul Boreham (eds), *The State, Class and Recession*. London: Croom Held.

Offe, Claus (1984) *The Contradictions of the Welfare State*. London: Hutchinson.

Ohmae, Kenichi (1990) *The Borderless World: Power and Strategy in the Interlinked Economy*. New York: Collins.

Ohmae, Kenichi (1996) *The End of the Nation State: The Rise of Regional Economies.* New York: Free Press.

Okun, Arthur M. (1975) *Equality and Efficiency: The Big Tradeoff.* Washington, DC: The Brookings Institute.

Orenstein, Mitchell A. and Martine R. Haas (2002) 'Globalization and the Development of Welfare States in Central and Eastern Europe', BCSIA Working Paper. John F. Kennedy School of Government, Harvard University (February).

Orloff, Ann S. (1993) 'Gender and the Social Rights of Citizenship: The Comparative Analysis of Gender Relations and Welfare States', *American Sociological Review*, 58 (3), 508–28.

Ormerod, Paul (1998) 'Unemployment and Social Exclusion: An Economic View', in Martin Rhodes and Yves Mény (eds), *The Future of the European Welfare State: A New Social Contract?* Basingstoke: Macmillan.

Oxley, H. and M. Macfarlan (1995) 'Health Care Reform: Controlling Spending and Increasing Efficiency', *OECD Economic Studies*, 24 (1), 7–55.

Palier, Bruno (2006) 'The Europeanisation of Welfare Reforms', paper delivered to the Inequality Summer Institute, Kennedy School of Government, Harvard University, www.hks.harvard.edu/inequality/Summer/Summer06/papers/Palier.pdf.

Parker, Barbara (1998) *Globalisation and Business Practice: Managing Across Boundaries.* London: Sage.

Parry, Richard (1986) 'United Kingdom' in Peter Flora (ed.) *Growth to Limits: The Western European Welfare States Since World War II. Vol. 2 Germany, United Kingdom, Ireland, Italy.* Berlin: de Gruyter.

Pascall, Gillian and Nick Manning (2000) 'Gender and Social Policy: Comparing Welfare States in Eastern Europe and the Soviet Union', *Journal of European Social Policy*, 10 (3), 240–66.

Pearce, Nick and Will Paxton (2005) 'Introduction' in Nick Pearce and Will Paxton (eds), *Social Justice: Building a Firer Britain.* London: Politicos and Institute for Public Policy Research.

Perraton, Johathan, David Goldblatt, David Held and Anthony McGrew (1997) 'The Globalisation of Economic Activity', *New Political Economy*, 2 (2), 257–78.

Persson, Torsten and Guido Tabellini (1994) 'Is Inequality Harmful for Growth?', *American Economic Review*, 84, 600–21.

Peltzman, Sam (1989) 'The Economic Theory of Regulation after a Decade of Deregulation', *Brookings Papers on Economic Activity: Microeconomics*, 1–41.

Petersen, Klaus and Jørn Henrik Petersen (2011) 'Confusion and Diffusion: Originas and Meanings of the Term "Welfare State" In Germany and Britain 1840–1940', paper delivered at the conference 'Crisis and Renewal: Welfare States, Democracy and Equality in Hard Times', Reykjavik 2–3 June.

Pettifor, Ann (2006) *The Coming Crisis of First World Debt.* Basingstoke: Palgrave Macmillan.

Pfaller, Alfred, Ian Gough and Gøran Therborn, (eds) (1991) *Can the Welfare State Compete? A Comparative Study of Five Advanced Capitalist Countries*. Basingstoke: Macmillan.

Phelps, Edmund S. (1967) 'Money-Wage Dynamics and Labour-Market Equilibrium', *Journal of Political Economy*, 76 (4), 678–711.

Pierson, Chris (1998) *Beyond the Welfare State?* Cambridge: Polity.

Pierson, Paul (1994) *Dismantling the Welfare State? Reagan, Thatcher and the Politics of Retrenchment*. Cambridge: Cambridge University Press.

Pierson, Paul (1996) 'The New Politics of the Welfare State', *World Politics*, 48 (2), 143–79.

Pierson, Paul (1998) 'Irresistible Forces, Immoveable Objects: Post-industrial Welfare States Confront Permanent Austerity', *Journal of European Public Policy*, 5 (4), 539–60.

Pierson, Paul (2004) *Politics in Time: History, Institutions and Social Analysis*. Princeton, NJ: Princeton University Press.

Pierson, Paul (ed.) (2001) *The New Politics of the Welfare State*. Oxford: Oxford University Press.

Polanyi, Karl (1944) *The Great Transformation*. Boston, MA: Beacon Press.

Pollin, Robert (1995) 'Financial Structures and Egalitarian Economic Policy', *New Left Review*, 214, 26–61.

Potsůček, Martin (2004) 'Accession and Social Policy: The Case of the Czech Republic', *Journal of European Social Policy*, 14 (3), 253–66.

Prabhakar, Rajiv (2009) 'Asset Inequality and the Crisis', *Renewal*, 17 (4), 75–80.

Prais, S. J. and K. Wagner (1987) 'Educating for Productivity: Comparisons of Japanese and English Schoolong and Vocational Preparation', *National Institute Economic Review*, 119, 40–56.

Presidency Conclusions (1993) Copenhagen European Council, 21–22 June.

Presidency Conclusions (1994) Essen European Council, 9 December.

Presidency Conclusions (1997) Luxembourg Extraordinary European Council on Employment, 20–21 November.

Presidency Conclusions (1998) Cardiff European Council, 15–16 June.

Presidency Conclusions (1999) Cologne European Council, 3–4 June.

Presidency Conclusions (2000) Lisbon Extraordinary European Council, 23–4 March.

President's Commission on Industrial Competitiveness (1985) *Global Competition: The New Reality*. Vol. 2. Washington, DC: US Government Printing Office.

Przeworski, Adam and Michael Wallerstein (1988) 'Structural Dependence of the State on Capital', *American Political Science Review*, 82 (1), 11–30.

Rajan, Raghuram G. (2010) *Fault Lines*. Princeton, NJ: Princeton University Press.

Ramsay, Frank P. (1928) 'A Mathematical Theory of Saving', *Economic Journal*, 38, December, 543–59.

Razin, A. and Sadka, E. (1991a) 'Efficient Investment Incentives in the Presence of Capital Flight', *Journal of International Economics*, 31 (1/2), 171–81.

Razin, A. and Sadka, E. (1991b) 'International Tax Competition and Gains from Tax Harmonisation', *Economic Letters*, 37 (1), 69–76.

Regan, Sue and Will Paxton (eds) (2001) *Asset-based Welfare: International Comparisons*. London: Institute for Public Policy Research.

Regini, Marino (2000) 'Between Deregulation and Social Pacts – The Responses of European Economies to Globalization', *Politics and Society*, 28 (1), 5–33.

Rhodes, Martin (1995) 'Subversive Liberalism: Market Integration, Globalisation and the European Welfare State', *Journal of European Public Policy*, 2 (2), 384–406.

Rhodes, Martin (1996) 'Globalisation and West European Welfare States: A Critical Review of Recent Debates', *Journal of European Social Policy*, 6 (4), 305–27.

Rhodes, Martin (1997) 'The Welfare State: Internal Challenges, External Constraints', in Martin Rhodes, Paul Heywood and Vincent Wright (eds), *Developments in West European Politics*. Basingstoke: Macmillan.

Rhodes, Martin (2001) 'The Political Economy of Social Pacts: Competitive Corporatism and European Welfare Reform', in Paul Pierson (ed.), *The New Politics of Welfare*. Oxford: Oxford University Press, pp. 165–94.

Rhodes, Martin (2002) 'Why EMU is (or may be) good for European Welfare States', in Kenneth Dyson (ed.) *European States and the Euro*. Oxford: Oxford University Press.

Rhodes, Martin and Bastiaan van Apeldoorn (1998) 'Capitalism Unbound? The Transformation of European Corporate Governance', *Journal of European Public Policy*, 5 (3), 406–27.

Ricardo, David (1817) *The Principles of Political Economy and Taxation*, 1996 edn. London: Prometheus Books.

Riley, Denise (1983) *War in the Nursery*. London: Virago.

Ringen, S. (1987) *The Possibility of Politics: A Study in the Political Economy of Welfare*. Oxford: Clarendon Press.

Robertson, D. (2007) 'Thick Constitutional Readings: When Classic Distinctions are Irrelevant', *Georgia Journal of International and Comparative Law*, 35, 277–331.

Rodríguez-Pose, Abdrés (2002) *The European Union: Economy, Society and Polity*. Oxford: Oxford University Press.

Rodrik, Dani (1997) *Has Globalisation Gone Too Far?* Washington, DC: Institute for International Economics.

Rødseth, Asbjörn (2000) *Open Economy Macroeconomics*. Cambridge: Cambridge University Press.

Rogoff, Kenneth (1996) 'The Purchasing Power Parity Puzzle', *Journal of Economic Literature*, 34, 647–68.

Rokkan, Stein, Peter Flora, Stein Kuhnle, and Derek Urwin (1999) *State Formation, Nation-Building and Mass Politics in Europe*. Oxford: Oxford University Press.

Romer, Paul M. (1990) 'Endogenous Technological Change', *Journal of Political Economy*, 98 (5), 71–102.

Room, Graham (2000) 'Commodification and Decommodification: A Developmental Critique', *Policy and Politics*, 28 (3), 331–51.

Rosamond, Ben (2002) 'Imagining the European Economy: Competitiveness and the Social Construction of "Europe" as an Economic Space', *New Political Economy*, 7 (2), 157–77.

Ross, George (1995) *Jacques Delors and European Integration*. Cambridge: Polity.

Roubini, Nouriel and Stephen Mihm (2010) *Crisis Economics*. New York: Penguin,

Ruffin, Roy J. (2002) 'David Ricardo's Discovery of Comparative Advantage', *History of Political Economy*, 34 (4), 727–48.

Ruggie, John (1982) 'International Regimes, Transactions and Change: Embedded Liberalism in the Postwar Economic Order', *International Organization*, 36, 379–415.

Sadurski, Wojciech (2002) 'Post-Communist Charters of Rights in Europe and the US Bill of Rights', *Journal of Law and Contemporary Problems*, 65 (2), 101–27.

Sajó, András (1996) 'How the Rule of Law Killed Hungarian Welfare Reform', *East European Constitutional Review*, 5 (1), 31–41.

Sala-i-Martin, Xavier X. (1996) 'The Classical Approach to Convergence Analysis', *Economic Journal*, 106 (July), 1019–36.

Salais, Robert (2003) 'Work and Welfare: Towards a Capability Approach', in Jonathan Zeitlin and David M. Trubek (eds), *Governing Work and Welfare in a New Economy*. Oxford: Oxford University Press.

Samuelson, Paul A. and Robert M. Solow (1960) 'Analytical Aspects of Anti-Inflation Policy', *American Economics Review*, 30 (2), 177–94.

Sapir, Andre (2006) 'Globalization and the Reform of European Social Models', *Journal of Common Market Studies*, 44 (2), 369–90.

Sapir, Andre *et al.* (2003) *An Agenda for a Growing Europe: Making the EU System Deliver*, report of an Independent High Level Group established at the initiative of the president of the European Commission (other members of the group: Philippe Aghion, Giuseppe Bertola, Martin Hellwig, Jean Pisani-Ferry, Dariusz Rosati, José Viñals and Helen Wallace), July, Brussels.

Saunders, Peter and Friederich Klau (1985) 'The Role of the Public Sector: Causes and Consequences of the Growth of Government', *OECD, Economic Studies*, 4.

Saville, John (1957/8) 'The Welfare State: An Historical Approach', *New Reasoner*, 3 (Winter), 5–25.

Scharpf, Fritz (1991) *Crisis and Choice in European Social Democracy*. Ithaca, NY: Cornell University Press.

Scharpf, Fritz (1999) *Governing in Europe: Effective and Democratic?* Oxford: Oxford University Press.

Scharpf, Fritz (2002) 'The Eurpean Social Model', *Journal of Common Market Studies*, 40 (4) 645–70.

Schwartz, Herman (2009) *Subprime Nation: American Power, Global Capital and the Housing Bubble*. Ithaca, NY: Cornell University Press.

Scruggs, Lyle and James Allan (2006) 'Welfare State Decommodification in 18 OECD Countries: A replication and Revision', *Journal of European Social Policy*, 16 (1), 55–72.

Scruggs, Lyle and James Allan (2008) 'Social Stratification and Welfare Regimes for the Twenty-first Century: Revisiting *The Three Worlds of Welfare Capitalism*', *World Politics*, 60 (4), 642–64.

Scruggs, Lyle and Jonas Pontusson (2008) 'New Dimensions of Welfare State Regimes in Advanced Democracies', paper presented to the American Political Science Association Annual Conference.

Seeliger, Robert (1996) 'Conceptualising and Researching Policy Convergence', *Policy Studies Journal*, 24 (2), 287–306.

Semmel, Bernard (1960) *Imperialism and Social Reform: English Social-imperial Thought 1895–1914*. London: George Allen & Unwin.

Sen, Amartya (1977) 'Rational Fools: A Critique of the Behavioural Foundations of Economic Theory', *Philosophy and Public Affairs*, 6 (4), 317–44.

Sen, Amartya (1985) *Commodities and Capabilities*. Oxford: Oxford University Press.

Shiller, Robert J. (2005) *Irrational Exuberance*, 2nd edn. Princeton, NJ: Princeton University Press.

Shonfield, Andrew (1969) *Modern Capitalism*. Oxford: Oxford University Press.

Silver, Harold and Pamela Silver (1991) *An Educational War on Poverty: American and British Policy-making 1960–1980*. Cambridge: Cambridge University Press.

Simmons, Beth A. (1999) 'The Internationalisation of Capital', in Herbert Kitschelt, Peter Lange, Gary Marks and John D. Stephens (eds), *Continuity and Change in Contemporary Capitalism*. Cambridge: Cambridge University Press.

Skocpol, Theda and Edwin Amenta (1988) 'States and Social Policies', *American Review of Sociology*, 12 (1), 131–57.

Smith, Adam (1976 [1776]) *An Inquiry into the Nature and Causes of the Wealth of Nations*. Oxford: Oxford University Press.

Snyder, Francis (1993) 'Soft Law and Institutional Practice in the European Community', *EUI Working Paper EUI LAW 1993/05*.

Social Policy and Adminstration (2011) 'Special Issue: The Times They Are Changing? Crisis and the Welfare State', *Social Policy and Adminsitration*, 45 (4).

Solow, Robert M. (1956) 'A Contribution to the Theory of Economic Growth', *Quarterly Journal of Economics*, 70 (1), 65–94.

Sornette, D., R. Woodward and W.-X. Zhan (2009) 'The 2006–2008 Oil Bubble: Evidence of Speculation and Prediction', *Physica A: Statistical Mechanics and its Application*, 388 (8), 1571–76.

Soskice, David (1990) 'Wage Determination: The Changing Role of Institutions in Advanced Industrialised Countries', *Oxford Review of Economic Policy*, 6, 36–61.

Soskice, David and Torben Iversen (1998) 'Multiple Wage-bargaining Systems in the Single European Currency Area', *Oxford Review of Economic Policy*, 14 (3), 110–24.

Starke, Peter, Herbert Obinger and Frances G. Castes (2008) 'Convergence Towards Where: In What Ways, If Any, Are Welfare States Becoming More Similar?', *Journal of European Public Policy*, 15 (7), 975–1000.

Stephens, John D. (1979) *The Transition from Capitalism to Socialism*. London: Macmillan Press.

Stephens, John D. (1996) 'The Scandinavian Welfare States: Achievements, Crisis and Prospects', in Gøsta Esping-Andersen (ed.), *Welfare States in Transition: National Adaptations in Global Economies*. London: Sage.

Stephens, John D. (2010) 'Social Rights of Citizenship', in F. G. Castles, S. Leibfried, J. Lewis, H. Obinger and C. Pierson (eds), *The Oxford Handbook of the Welfare State*. Oxford: Oxford University Press.

Stephens, John D., Evelyne Huber and Leonard Ray (1999) 'The Welfare State in Hard Times', in Herbert Kitschelt, Peter Lange, Gary Marks and John D. Stephens (eds), *Continuity and Change in Contemporary Capitalism*. Cambridge: Cambridge University Press.

Strange, Susan (1997) 'The Future of Global Capitalism: Or Will Divergence Persist Forever?', in C. Crouch and W. Streeck (eds), *Political Economy and Modern Capitalism*. London: Sage.

Streeck, Wolfgang (1995) 'From Market-making to State-building? Reflections on the Political Economy of European Social Policy', in S. Leibfried and P. Pierson (eds), *European Social Policy. Between Fragmentation and Integration*. Washington, DC: The Brookings Institution, 389–431.

Streeck, Wolfgang (1997) 'German Capitalism: Does it Exist? Can it Survive?', *New Political Economy*, 2 (2), 237–56.

Streek, Wolfgang and Kathleen Thelen (eds) (2005) *Beyond Continuity*. Oxford: Oxford University Press.

Summerfield, Penny (1988) 'Women, War and Social Change: Women in Britain in World War II', in A. Marwick (ed.), *Total War and Social Change*. London: Macmillan.

Swank, Duane (1998) 'Funding the Welfare State: Globalisation and the Taxation of Business in Advanced Market Economies', *Political Studies*, 46 (4), 671–92.

Swank, Duane (2001) 'Political Institutions and Welfare State Restructuring: The Impact of Institutions on Social Policy Change in Developed Democracies', in P. Pierson (ed.), *The New Politics of the Welfare State*. Oxford: Oxford University Press.

Swank, Duane (2002) *Global Capital, Political Institutions and Policy Change in Developed Welfare States*. Cambridge: Cambridge University Press.

Swenson, Peter A. (2002) *Capitalists Against Markets: The Making of Labour Markets and Welfare States in the United States and Sweden*. Oxford: Oxford University Press.

Tanzi, Vito and H. H. Zee (1997) 'Fiscal Policy and Long-Run Growth', *International Monetary Fund Staff Papers*, 44 (2), 179–209.

Tanzi, Vito and Ludger Schuknecht (1997) 'Reconsidering the Fiscal Role of Government: The International Perspective', *American Economic Review*, 87 (2), 164–68.

Tanzi, Vito and Ludger Schuknect (2000) *Public Spending in the 20th Century: A Global Perspective.* Cambridge: Cambridge University Press.

Taylor, John B. (2009) 'The Financial Crisis and the Policy Responses: An Empirical Analysis of What Went Wrong', National Bureau of Economic Research, Working Paper 14631, January.

Taylor-Gooby, Peter (1994) 'Ideology and Social Policy', *Journal of Sociology*, 30 (1) 71–82.

Taylor-Gooby, Peter (1999) 'Policy Change at a Time of Retrenchment: Recent Pension Reform in France, Germany, Italy and the UK', *Social Policy and Administration*, vol. 33, no. 1, pp. 1–19.

Taylor-Gooby, Peter (2002) 'The Silver Age of the Welfare State: perspectives on resilience', *Journal of Social Policy*, 31 (4), 597–621.

Teeple, Gary (1995) *Globalisation and the Decline of Social Reform.* Toronto: Garamond.

Temple, William (1941) *Citizen and Churchman.* London: Eyre & Spottiswoode.

Temple, William (1942) *Christianity and the Social Order.* London: Penguin

Therborn, Göran (1984 'The Prospects of Labour and the Transformation of Advanced Capitalism', *New Left Review*, 145.

Thurow, Lester (1994) *Head to Head.* New York: Nicholas Brealey.

Timmons, Jeffrey F. (2005) 'The Fiscal Contract: States, Taxes and Public Services', *World Politics*, 57 (4), 530–67.

Titmuss, Richard (1963) 'The Welfare State: Images and Realities', *Social Service Review*, 37 (1) 1–11.

Titmuss, Richard (1974) *Social Policy.* London: George Allen & Unwin.

Trägårdh, Lars (1997) 'Statist Individualism: On the Culturality of the Nordic Welfare State', in Bo Stråth and Øystein Sørensen (eds), *The Cultural Construction of Norden.* Oslo: Scandinavian University Press.

Traxler, F. and Woitech, B. (2000) 'Transnational Investment and National Labour Market Regimes: A Case of "Regime Shopping"?', *European Journal of Industrial Relations*, 6 (2), 141–59.

Ugur, Mehmet (ed.) (2001) *Open Economy Macroeconomics: A Reader.* London: Routledge.

UN Department of Economic and Social Affairs (2007) 'World Population Prospects: The 2006 Revision', New York: UN Population Division, www.esa.un.org/unpp.

United Nations (2003) 'Trends in Total Migrant Stock: The 2003 Revision', New York: United Nations.

Van Apeldoorn, Bastiaan (2002) *Transnational Capitalism and the Struggle over European Integration.* London Routledge.

Van der Veen, Romke, Willem, Trommel and de Vroom, Bert (1999) 'Institutional Change of Welfare States. Empirical Reality, Theoretical Obstacles', paper for the 11th SASE Conference, 8–11 July, Madison.

Van Kersbergen, Kees (1995) *Social Capitalism: A study of Christian Democracy and the Welfare State*. London: Routledge.

Van Kersbergen, Kees and Uwe Becker (1988) 'The Netherlands: A Passive Social Democratic Welfare State in a Christian Democratic Rulled Society', *Journal of Social Policy*, 17 (4), 477–99.

Vaughan-Whitehead, Daniel (2003) *EU Enlargement versus Social Europe: The Uncertain Future of the European Social Model*. Cheltenham: Edward Elgar.

Veit-Wilson, John (2000) 'States of Welfare: A Conceptual Challenge', *Social Policy and Administration*, 34 (1), 1–25.

Vis, Barbara, Kees van Kersbergen and Tom Hylands (2011) 'To What Extent did the Financial Crisis Intensify the Pressure on the Welfare State?', *Social Policy and Administration*, 45 (4), 338–53.

Wagener, Hans-Urgen (2002) 'The Welfare State in Transition Economics and Accession to the EU', *West European Politics*, 25 (2), 152–74.

Wanless, Derek (2004) 'The Wanless Report: Securing Good Health for the Whole Population'. London: HM Treasury.

Watson, Matthew (1997) 'The Changing Face of Macroeconomic Stabilisation: From Growth Through Indigenous Investment to Growth Through Inward Investment', in Jeffrey Stanyer and Gerry Stoker (eds), *Contemporary Political Studies 1997*, Vol. 2. Oxford: Blackwell/PSA.

Watson, Matthew (1999) 'Globalisation and British Political Development', in David Marsh, Jim Buller, Colin Hay, Jim Johnston, Peter Kerr, Stuart McAnulla and Matthew Watson (eds), *Postwar British Politics in Perspective*. Cambridge: Polity.

Watson, Matthew (2001a) 'International Capital Mobility in an Era of Globalisation: Adding a Political Dimension to the "Feldstein–Horioka Puzzle"', *Politics*, 21 (2), 81–92.

Watson, Matthew (2001b) 'Embedding the "New Economy" in Europe: A Study in the Institutional Specificities of Knowledge-Based Growth', *Economy and Society*, 30 (4), 504–23.

Watson, Matthew (2007) *The Political Economy of International Capital Mobility*. Basingstoke: Palgrave Macmillan.

Watson, Matthew (2009a) 'Headlong into the Polanyian Dilemma: The Impact of Middle-class Moral Panic on the British Government's Response to the Sub-prime Crisis', *British Journal of Politics and International Relations*, 11 (3), 422–37.

Watson, Matthew (2009b) 'Planning for a Future of Asset-Based Welfare? New Labour, Financialised Economic Agency and the Housing Market', *Planning Practice and Research*, 24 (1), 41–56.

Watson, Matthew (2010) 'House Price Keynesianism and the Contradictions of the Modern Investor Subject', *Housing Studies*, 25 (3), 413–26.

Watson, Matthew and Colin Hay (1998) 'In the Dedicated Pursuit of Dedicated Capital: Restoring an Indigenous Investment Ethic to British Capitalism', *New Political Economy*, 3, (3), 407–26.

Wedderburn, Dorothy (1965) 'Facts and Theories of the Welfare State', *Socialist Register*, 2, 127–46.

Weiler, Joseph (1982) 'The Community System: The Dual Character of Supranationalism', *Yearbook of European Law*, 1, 267–306.

Western, B. and K. Beckett (1998) 'The Free Market Myth: Penal Justice as an Institution of the US Labour Market', *Berliner Journal Für Soziologie*, 8 (2), 159–82.

Western, B. and K. Beckett (1999) 'How Unregulated is the US Labour Market? The Penal System as a Labour Market Institution', *American Journal of Sociology*, 104 (4), 1030–60.

Western, B., K. Beckett and D. Harding (1998) 'Penal Systems and the American Labour Market', *Actes de la Recherche en Sciences Sociales*, 124, 27–37.

Wickham-Jones, Mark (1995) 'Anticipating Social Democracy, Preempting Anticipations: Economic Policy-making in the British Labour Party, 1987–1992', *Politics and Society*, 23 (4), 65–94.

Widmaier, Wesely, Mark Blyth and Leonard Seabrooke (2007) 'Exogenous Shocks or Endogenous constructions? The Meanings of Wars and Crises', *International Studies Quarterly*, 51 (4): 747–59.

Wilensky, Harold L. (1975) *The Welfare State and Equality*. Berkeley, CA: The University of California Press.

Wilensky, Harold L. (1976) *The 'New Corporatism' Centralism and the Welfare State*. London: Sage.

Wilensky, Harold. L. (2002) *Rich Democracies: Political Economy, Public Policy and Performance*. Berkeley, CA: University of California Press.

Wilensky, Harold L. and Charles N. Lebeaux (1958) *Industrial Society and Social Welfare*. New York: The Free Press.

Wilkinson, R. (1996a) 'Health, Redistribution and Growth', in Andrew Glyn and David Miliband (eds), *Paying for Inequalities*. London: Institute for Public Policy Research.

Wilkinson, R. (1996b) *Unhealthy Societies: The Afflictions of Inequality*. London: Routledge.

Wincott, Daniel (1995) 'Institutional Interaction and European Integration: Towards an Everyday Critique of Liberal Intergovernmentalism', *Journal of Common Market Studies*, 33: 597–610.

Wincott, Daniel (2001a) 'Reassessing the Social Foundations of Welfare (State) Regimes', *New Political Economy*, 6 (3): 409–25.

Wincott, Daniel (2001b) 'Looking Forward or Harking Back? The Commission and the Reform of Governance in the European Union', *Journal of Common Market Studies*, 39 (5) 897–911.

Wincott, Daniel (2003) 'Beyond Social Regulation? New Instruments and/or a New Agenda at Lisbon', *Public Administration*, 81 (3) 533–83.

Wincott, Daniel (2006) 'European Political Development, Regulatory Governance, and the European Social Model: The Challenge of Substantive Legitimacy', *European Law Journal*, 12 (6) 743–63.

Wincott, Daniel (2011a) 'Ideas, Policy Change and the Welfare State' in Robert H. Cox and Daniel Bleland (eds), *Ideas and Politics in Social Science Research*. Oxford: Oxford University Press.

Wincott, Daniel (2011b) 'Images of Welfare in Law and Society: The British Welfare State in Comparative Perspective', *Journal of Law and Society*, 38 (3) 343–75.

Wincott, Daniel (forthcoming) 'The (Golden) Age of the Welfare State: Interrogating a Conventional Wisdom', *Public Administration*.

World Trade Organization (2010) 'International Trade Statistics', Geneva: WTO.

Zuckerman, Mortimer (1998) 'A Second American Century', *Foreign Affairs*, 77 (3), 18–31.

Zysman, John (1983) *Governments, Markets and Growth: Financial Systems and the Politics of Industrial Change*. Ithaca, NY: Cornell University Press.

Index

Igan, Deniz   210
Ikenberry, John   9
IMF (International Monetary Fund)
    28, 81, 82, 87, 145, 162, 213, 214
Import restrictions   83–4
Incarceration rates   127–8
Income replacement ratios   107
    see also Replacement ratios   107
Inflation   106–9
International Organisation of Migration
    78
International Social Security Association
    52–3
Investment   70, 72, 116–17, 119–20, 127
Ireland   35, 54, 100, 101–2, 103, 109,
    125, 131, 156, 161, 200, 206, 207,
    210, 213, 224
Italy   35, 50, 62, 88–9, 95, 109, 137,
    156, 158, 201
Iversen, Torben   166

Japan   85
Jessop, Bob   29–30, 106
Jones, Catherine   34
Jordan, Bill   106
Joskow, Paul L.   139
Juhasz, Gabo   145
Justman, Moshe   127

Katzenstein, Peter J.   218
Kaufmann, R. K.   197
Kenworthy, Lane   39, 41, 42, 48, 56,
    58, 175
Keynesian welfare state   106, 139
Keynesianism   12, 15, 26, 31, 32, 106,
    118, 124–5, 223
King, Anthony   11
Klau, Friederich   120
Kleinman, Mark   134
Kloosterman, Robert   34, 36
Knill, Christoph   165, 172
Knowledge-based economy   147, 149
Kok, Wim   150
Korpi, Walter   20, 22, 45, 176, 177,
    178, 179, 185, 188, 194
Kovats, Andras   90
Kristensen, Kai   119, 129
Krugman, Paul   200, 218
Kynaston, David   10

Labour
    cost of   118–119, 123
    supply of   120–1
Labour market
    flexibility   121, 127
    integration   77–8, 88
    regulation   49

Laeven, Luc   210
Langley, Paul   199
Larsson, Allan   155
Latvia   213–14, 224
Lebeaux, Charles N.   33
Leibfried, Stephan   34, 62, 131, 134, 138
Lendvai, Noémi   146
Levy, Jonah   99
Lewis, Jane   34, 48
Liberalism   54–5, 56–7, 58, 60
Lisbon agenda   96, 131, 134, 135, 145,
    146–7, 152, 161, 162, 163
Lloyd George, David   21
Loriaux, Michel   26
Lucas, Robert E.   126
Lucas, Robert   30
Luxembourg   157

Maastricht Treaty   151, 152, 153, 155,
    156, 157, 174
Macfarlan, M.   111
Majone, Giandomenico   30, 131, 132,
    134, 138, 139–41, 143, 144, 159,
    160
Manning, Nick   14
Manova, Kalina   216
Mares, Isabela   114
Marglin, Stephen   11
Market liberalisation   29, 144
Marshall, T. H.   17, 18, 20, 177
Marson, Brian   119
Martin, Andrew   106
Martin, Ron   197, 208
Masaryk, President Tomas   18
Mason, Paul   197
Mattli, Walter   141, 142
McBride, Stephen   166
McGregor, J. Allister   105
Means-testing   34, 35, 48, 52
Meunier-Aitsahalia, Sophie   142, 143
Migration   78, 88–90
Migration Policy Institute   89
Mihm, Stephen   200
Milward, Alan   133, 137
Mitchell, Deborah   34, 47
'Mitterrand Experiment'   26
Mogensen, Gunnar V.   118
Montanari, Ingalill   165, 170, 177–8,
    180, 188
Moran, Michael   140
Moravcsik, Andrew   143
Morgan, Kimberly   24, 48
Mortgage securitisation   199, 216
Moser, Ann W.   166
Munzi, Teresa   109

Natalism   48